We, the Mediated People

We, the Mediated People

Popular Constitution-Making in Contemporary South America

JOSHUA BRAVER

OXFORD
UNIVERSITY PRESS

OXFORD
UNIVERSITY PRESS

Oxford University Press is a department of the University of Oxford. It furthers the University's objective of excellence in research, scholarship, and education by publishing worldwide. Oxford is a registered trade mark of Oxford University Press in the UK and certain other countries.

Published in the United States of America by Oxford University Press
198 Madison Avenue, New York, NY 10016, United States of America.

© Joshua Braver 2023

Library of Congress Cataloging-in-Publication Data
Names: Braver, Joshua, author.
Title: We, the mediated people : popular constitution-making in contemporary South America / Joshua Braver.
Description: New York : Oxford University Press, [2023] | Includes index.
Identifiers: LCCN 2022008984 (print) | LCCN 2022008985 (ebook) |
ISBN 9780197650639 (hardback) | ISBN 9780197650653 (epub) |
ISBN 9780197650646 (updf) | ISBN 9780197650660 (online)
Subjects: LCSH: Constitutional conventions—South America. |
People (Constitutional law)—South America. | Constitutional history—Venezuela. | Constitutional history—Ecuador. | Constitutional history—Colombia. | Constitutional history—Bolivia.
Classification: LCC KH545 .B73 2023 (print) | LCC KH545 (ebook) |
DDC 342.802/9—dc23/eng/20220628
LC record available at https://lccn.loc.gov/2022008984
LC ebook record available at https://lccn.loc.gov/2022008985

DOI: 10.1093/oso/9780197650639.001.0001

1 3 5 7 9 8 6 4 2

Printed by Integrated Books International, United States of America

Note to Readers
This publication is designed to provide accurate and authoritative information in regard to the subject matter covered. It is based upon sources believed to be accurate and reliable and is intended to be current as of the time it was written. It is sold with the understanding that the publisher is not engaged in rendering legal, accounting, or other professional services. If legal advice or other expert assistance is required, the services of a competent professional person should be sought. Also, to confirm that the information has not been affected or changed by recent developments, traditional legal research techniques should be used, including checking primary sources where appropriate.

(Based on the Declaration of Principles jointly adopted by a Committee of the American Bar Association and a Committee of Publishers and Associations.)

You may order this or any other Oxford University Press publication
by visiting the Oxford University Press website at www.oup.com.

For Michael Braver who Instilled in me a Love of Learning

Contents

Contents

Introduction

"We, the People . . . do ordain and establish this Constitution . . ."[1] The U.S. Constitution, the oldest codified one in the world, was the first to invoke the people as the authors of a polity's highest law. It was far from the last; since 1789, "We, the People" has become the most common opening pronouncement of all constitutions, both for those in force today and for those that have been superseded.[2] If we use preambles as the measure, popular authorship has become the most important source of legitimacy for a constitution.[3] In every case, these opening words speak of and enact the final step in a long constitution-making process, a process that entails—or at least is imagined to entail—steps such as popular movements clamoring for change in the streets, presidents campaigning on promises of constitutional revolution, and the meeting of constitutional assemblies to draft a constitution.

The people are supreme during this rare and liminal space between the death of the old constitution and the birth of a new one. Normally, the constitution is the highest law and provides a binding framework within which normal lawmaking takes place. Under the authority of the constitution, representatives govern on a day-to-day basis, giving individuals the time and space to pursue their private endeavors, such as work and family life. The people may have acted in the past to create the constitution, but once it becomes valid, the people recede into the background.[4] They are a "sleeping sovereign."[5] But during a new round of constitution-making, the people awaken, and their rise unsettles the foundations of the legal system. If the

---

[1] U.S. Constitution, Preamble.

[2] Tom Ginsburg, Nick Foti, and Daniel Rockmore, "We the Peoples: The Global Origins of Constitutional Preambles," *George Washington International Law Review* 46 (2013), 119–21.

[3] Of course, many constitutions claim that they were authored by the people, but in practice they were imposed by elites or dictators. Additionally, Andrew Arato argues that the "round-table" or "post-sovereign" form of constitution making, a form that denies any role for the people but nonetheless claims democratic legitimacy, is spreading around the world. Andrew Arato, *Post Sovereign Constitution Making: Learning and Legitimacy* (Oxford: Oxford University Press, 2016), 75–107.

[4] Bruce Ackerman, *We the People: Foundations* (Cambridge, MA: Belknap Press of Harvard University Press, 1993); Richard Tuck, *The Sleeping Sovereign: The Invention of Modern Democracy* (Cambridge: Cambridge University Press, 2016).

[5] Tuck, *The Sleeping Sovereign*.

We, the Mediated People. Joshua Braver, Oxford University Press. © Joshua Braver 2023.
DOI: 10.1093/oso/9780197650639.003.0001

people can now act as a collective agent, the constitution has been demoted and is now subordinate. Its future lies in the people's hands, to be amended or shredded as they see fit.

Invoking this demotion, revolutionaries often claim, on behalf of the people, a right to circumvent the old constitution's amendment rule. To these rebels against the old constitution, the amendment rule is an illegitimate impediment on the people's right to found a new charter. They argue that the old amendment rule has no legitimacy because it is a relic and safeguard of the old regime, the very regime that revolutionaries seek to overturn.[6] The safeguarding method takes many forms. Some constitutions explicitly or implicitly forbid their wholesale replacement. Perhaps the best-known explicit limits are eternity clauses, which forbid the amending of certain key provisions of a constitution.[7] Even without eternity clauses, constitutions that make no provision for their own replacement and only accommodate amendments implicitly prohibit transformative constitutional change. This silent prohibition exists because the scope for constitutional amendments is often understood to be limited to relatively small changes.[8] Indeed, supreme and constitutional courts have proven themselves increasingly willing in recent decades to strike down far-reaching amendments to the constitution as "unconstitutional constitutional amendments."[9] Lastly, constitutional amendment procedures often limit the possibilities for change by empowering the legislature or other institutions of the old regime to draft revisions. Revolutionaries, for their part, prefer new, unsullied bodies like constitutional assemblies to draft a new constitution.[10] While their particular objections to the old constitution's method of change varies, it is common for revolutionaries to claim that the old constitution's amendment rule does not bind the "people" because the old constitution in most cases rests upon popular sovereignty for its own legitimacy.

---

[6] Jon Elster, "Constitutional Bootstrapping in Philadelphia and Paris," *Cardozo Law Review* 14 (1993), 549.

[7] Yaniv Roznai, *Unconstitutional Constitutional Amendments: The Limits of Amendment Powers* (Oxford: Oxford University Press, 2017), 15–39; Silvia Suteu, *Eternity Clauses in Democratic Constitutionalism* (New York: Oxford University Press, 2021).

[8] Since amendments are inappropriate vehicles for wholesale constitutional change, Richard Alberts calls these radical restructures "constitutional dismemberments." Richard Albert, *Constitutional Amendments: Making, Breaking, and Changing Constitutions*, 1st ed. (New York: Oxford University Press, 2019 76-96); Walter F. Murphy, *Constitutional Democracy: Creating and Maintaining a Just Political Order* (Baltimore: Johns Hopkins University Press, 2008); Carl Schmitt, *Constitutional Theory*, trans. Jeffrey Seitzer (Durham: Duke University Press, 2008).

[9] Roznai, *Unconstitutional Constitutional Amendments*.

[10] Elster, "Constitutional Bootstrapping in Philadelphia and Paris."

So far for revolutionaries, the old constitution has little or no role to play in the process of constitutional change. It is conceived primarily as an impediment to the people's will. But once we turn from the overthrow of the old constitution to the creation of a new one, the picture becomes significantly more complicated.

If the people's word is the highest law when creating a constitution, how do the people actually speak? There are a wide variety of ways of drafting and ratifying a constitution, and the choice of procedure has great consequences for the distribution of power over the creation of a new higher law. For example, depending on the electoral rule, a group might have more or fewer representatives in the constitutional assembly, which will affect the content of the new constitution. Understanding the stakes and seeking to maximize their own power, various groups will push for their own preferred set of rules, each claiming that its proposed procedures are the only ones that can truly capture the people's will. Normally, a constitution designates the procedures to create law, thereby settling conflicts of this sort. But in these extraordinary circumstances, the constitution's status is uncertain, and the legitimacy of the procedures it designates is contested. Whether to respect the existing constitution's amendment rule is one question. But even among those who agree that the existing amendment rule should be abandoned to allow for sweeping constitutional change, a series of difficult questions remain about whether and how existing law and institutions should structure the expression of the people's voice.

The questions that arise in these moments are the ones that this book examines: to what extent may political actors, in the name of the people, violate the old constitution to create a new one? What role do the legislature, the courts, and other institutions, whose authority derive from a dying constitution, have in the constitution-making process? How is the legitimacy of a people's project of constitutional renewal affected by either total disregard for or partial adherence to existing constitutional rules and limitations?

The answers to these questions have profound implications for our conception of the people. The more the existing constitution and its multiplicity of pluralistic institutions are respected, the more voice large political minorities within the country have during the process of constitutional change. Those who advocate for such inclusion can be understood as defending a pluralistic vision of the people. At the same time, adherence to the existing provisions of the constitution dampens the power of an insurgent majority to enact a true revolution. The battle lines in this conflict map onto starkly different visions of the people. Political actors in the contemporary world who confront the question of the role of existing institutions in constitution-making find themselves also providing an answer to the classic question of "Who are the People?"[11]

Contemporary populists in South America have a powerful answer to these questions: The people are a "lawless unity."[12] In other words, they are one homogenous segment of the population that must be completely un-bound by all law in order to be fully unleashed to overthrow its oppressors. The institutional implications of this view vary by context. In contempo-rary South America, the populist vision of a lawless people translates into empowering a president to set rules for electing a constitutional assembly and then giving that constitutional assembly all legal power including the right to purge all competing institutions. Populists claim that these extreme measures are necessary to defeat the intransigent enemy and enact a true rev-olution. Those seeking to defend liberal democracy against populism often respond by going to the opposite extreme by embracing legalism. They tend to argue that that the laws of constitutional amendment should be followed to the letter.

This book offers an alternative to the populist vision of the people and their relationship to law. It examines how and how not to violate law to con-struct an inclusive people. This inclusive people may realize their freedom to break with the past but still stave off the establishment of semi-authoritarian constitutions. I argue that through the "extraordinary adaptation" of old institutions, the people and their constitutional convention may include all parties. Rather than taking the route chosen by some populists of destroying old institutions and opening a legal void, in extraordinary adaptation, the revolutionary party gains office through democratic elections and then repurposes the old regime's institutions by bending, reinterpreting, and even breaking their rules. Extraordinary adaptation never creates a legal vacuum, and the old regime's institutions are not swept aside. This partial legal con-tinuity facilitates the participation of old parties that continue to hold some

---

[11] The literature on this question is very large, but some helpful explorations in political theory in-clude Jacques Derrida, "Declarations of Independence," *New Political Science* 7, no. 1 (June 1, 1986), 7–15; Bonnie Honig, "Between Decision and Deliberation: Political Paradox in Democratic Theory," *The American Political Science Review* 101, no. 1 (Feb. 1, 2007), 1–17; Edmund Sears Morgan, *Inventing the People: The Rise of Popular Sovereignty in England and America* (New York: Norton, 1989).

[12] As I discuss, the tradition of the idea of a lawless unity goes back to the French Revolution William Partlett, "The Dangers of Popular Constitution-Making," *Brooklyn Journal of International Law* 38 (2012), 193–238; Kim Lane Scheppele, "Autocratic Legalism," *The University of Chicago Law Review* 85, no. 2 (2018), 545–84.

power in the previous constitution's institutions. The adaptation must fulfill three principles: the revolutionary movement must (1) exhaust all other legal channels; (2) openly acknowledge the constitutional violations it undertakes and seek popular vindication; and (3) concede enough to the opposition so that it may begrudgingly acquiesce to the new constitution. Extraordinary adaptation will not achieve the revolution that radicals seek, but it may nonetheless create a significant and enduring rupture with the past.

I develop the theory of extraordinary adaptation inductively by examining all four instances of popular constitution-making in contemporary South America, the region with the highest number of freely and fairly elected constitutional assemblies within liberal democracies since the end of the Cold War.[13] I show how populist leaders in Venezuela and Ecuador established semi-authoritarian constitutions through lawless and exclusive constitution-making while Colombia and Bolivia managed to avoid the same fate by engaging in extraordinary adaptation. While the creation of constitutions in both Colombia and Bolivia are examples of extraordinary adaptation, only the latter country's process exemplifies the theory in full and difficult bloom because of its higher level of inclusion.

THE RADICAL AND LEGALIST CONSENSUS

Constitutional theory, whether it is praising or condemning populism, basically accepts populism's premise that the people are a "lawless unity." I coin and use the phrase "lawless unity" to capture the central premises of populism in the context of constitution-making. The term "lawless" describes the people's status as sovereign, as possessing all political power and thus cannot be checked or policed by other legally constituted bodies like legislatures or courts. I will often use the adjectives sovereign and lawless, in the sense of being unbound by law, interchangeably.[14] But the sovereignty or lawlessness

[13] Gabriel L. Negretto, "Constitution Making and Constitutionalism in Latin America: The Role of Procedural Rules," in *Comparative Constitutional Law in Latin America*, eds. Rosalind Dixon and Tom Ginsburg (Cheltenham, UK: Edward Elgar Publishing, 2017), 25–28.

[14] For my purposes, law is prospective and general, which is why many systems attempt to separate the creation and application of the law. Sovereignty then is antithetical to law because it concentrates all power in one place. It is often taken to be the expression of an individual or group's *will* at a particular moment rather than a standard that can endure through time. Carl Schmitt presents the most dramatic contrast between sovereignty and law in order to celebrate the former and ridicule the latter. Carl Schmitt, *Constitutional Theory*, 154–56; Carl Schmitt, *Legality and Legitimacy*, trans. Jeffrey Seitzer (Durham: Duke University Press, 2004). For a positive articulation of this idea of law,

of the people raises the problem of identifying the rules or procedures through which one could ascertain when and how the people speak.

Populists try to solve this problem by invoking the "unity" of the people.[15] Populists derive this unity by identifying one group as the true people, and the remainder of the population as enemies. For example, in response to criticisms of his creeping authoritarianism achieved through constitutional change, Turkish President Recep Tayyip Erdoğan retorted, "We are the People. Who are you?"[16] Everyone in Turkey knew the concrete groups to which Erdoğan was referring: devout and poor Muslim Turks, in contrast to the enemies like the Kurds and westernized, secular citizens often referred to as "white turks."[17] Like Erdoğan, right-wing populists in Hungary and Poland have transformed their constitutions in the name of a people defined by ethnicity and religion, in these cases a Christian culture in opposition to the cultures of Muslim migrants fleeing the Middle East.[18] In the late 1990s and early 2000s, left-wing populist presidents accomplished similar illegal and total constitutional transformations in Venezuela and Ecuador. But rather than relying on religious identity, these leftists claimed that they were acting on behalf of the poor and downtrodden. In all of these countries, populist presidents defined the people as one part of the population. And all of these presidents asserted a right, as the vessel of a unified people, to plunge the country into a legal abyss in order to defeat the enemy and inaugurate a new constitution.

Contemporary populist rhetoric resonates deeply with, and sometimes even draws upon, a near consensus in constitutional and political theory on the people's constituent power. Constituent power refers to the people's power to make a constitution. Strikingly, this consensus is shared by those who celebrate the idea of the people and by those who believe it is excessively

see Lon L. Fuller, *The Morality of Law*, Rev. ed. (New Haven, CT: Yale University Press, 1969); Jeremy Waldron, "Separation of Powers in Thought and Practice," *Boston College Law Review* 54 (2013), 433.

[15] Jan-Werner Müller, *What Is Populism?* (Philadelphia: University of Pennsylvania Press, 2016), 3.
[16] Müller, *What Is Populism?*, 3.
[17] Sedef Arat-Koç, "Culturalizing Politics, Hyper-Politicizing 'Culture': 'White' vs. 'Black Turks' and the Making of Authoritarian Populism in Turkey," *Dialectical Anthropology* 42, no. 4 (Dec. 1, 2018), 391–408.
[18] Reuters in Budapest, "Viktor Orbán: Our Duty Is to Protect Hungary's Christian Culture," *Guardian*, May 7, 2018, http://www.theguardian.com/world/2018/may/07/viktor-orban-hungary-preserve-christian-culture; Paul Blokker, "Populist Counter-Constitutionalism, Conservatism, and Legal Fundamentalism," *European Constitutional Law Review* 15, no. 3 (Sept. 2019), 519–43, Kim Lane Scheppele, "The Opportunism of Populists and the Defense of Constitutional Liberalism," *German Law Journal* 20, no. 3 (Apr. 2019), 314–31.

dangerous. I give each of these schools of thought a label to guide future discussion. The first are "radical" proponents of constituent power. They tend to be sympathetic to populism and are often constitutional or political theorists. I call them "radicals" because the term reflects their desire to enact a revolution. Radicals do not share a political ideology, but rather a desire for the popular overthrow of existing political and economic regimes. In the late eighteenth century, French revolutionary Emmanuel Sieyès invoked the people to destroy the noble order and replace it with a liberal democracy. Twentieth-century theorists Carl Schmitt and Antonio Negri both invoked the same actor as Sieyès, but to crush the very liberal regime Sieyès treasured. Yet Schmitt and Negri disagree on the regime that would ideally replace the liberal order: the former was a conservative authoritarian and the later favors anarchist democracy.[19]

Radicals disagree on the ideal type of government, but they agree on the need for and the means of revolution. Revolution's agent is the people and to act, the people must be unified. Without unity, it is impossible to attribute action to the people as they are merely, as Hobbes puts it, "a multitude, a number of men, each of whom has his own will and his own judgment about every proposal."[20] Law divides and fragments the people; it is a tool for the powerful to dominate the powerless, a means to imprison the people and empower their captors. The earliest radical proponents of constituent power, such as Thomas Hobbes and Emmanuel Sieyès, took aim at feudalism, but many today bear the same animosity toward liberal democracy. Its political and civil rights hide but do not mitigate the oppressive force of law. According to many radicals, liberalism's commitment to representative government and the separation of powers (in various forms) are meant to distance the people from the reins of power.[21] To be free, the people must step outside of all law and the mediating institutions characteristic of liberal constitutionalism. Thomas Hobbes, Jean-Jacques Rousseau, Emmanuel Sieyès, and Carl Schmitt all summarize the people's legal status in the same way: they

[19] Antonio Negri, *Insurgencies: Constituent power and the Modern State*, trans. Maurizia Boscagli (Minneapolis: University of Minnesota Press, 2009). On Schmitt's conservative authoritarianism, see William E. Scheuerman, *Carl Schmitt* (Lanham, MD: Rowman & Littlefield Publishers, 1999). For review of the literature on Schmitt's politics, Peter C. Caldwell, "Controversies over Carl Schmitt: A Review of Recent Literature," *The Journal of Modern History* 77, no. 2 (2005), 357–87.

[20] Thomas Hobbes, *Hobbes: On the Citizen*, eds. Richard Tuck and Michael Silverthorne (New York: Cambridge University Press, 1998), 75.

[21] The classic critique of liberal rights remains Karl Marx, "The Jewish Question," in *The Marx-Engels Reader*, ed. Robert C. Tucker, 2nd Rev. ed. (New York: W. W. Norton & Company, 1978).

are and must be in the "state of nature."[22] From this legal void, the component parts of the people can discover their fundamental homogeneity and, on that basis, install a new order. For radicals, the people are a lawless unity.

This vision of lawless unity undermines democracy. Law is not only a tool of oppression but also a coordinating device, a way to manage differences. Societies are diverse and splintered along the seemingly endless lines, such as class, religion, race, and sexuality. In a homogenous society, law would be unnecessary because everyone would already agree. The real world, however, is messy and pluralistic. Any claim to unity can only be made real through exclusion and through the suppression of difference. Claiming to embody the people in one site of representation becomes the method for squeezing out disagreement. Regardless of whether that site is the president, the general will, the sovereign of the Leviathan, the dictatorship of the proletariat or a constituent assembly, all these embodiments enable an entity to usurp power from the people while claiming to rule in their name. Unity justifies the centralization of power in a single site because no opposition is necessary when everyone agrees. In more concrete terms, the lawless unity of the people is a rationale for authoritarianism.

"Legalist" critics of the constituent power, working primarily in the field of comparative constitutional law, have exposed this authoritarian logic. Yet despite the differences between legalists and radicals concerning the dangers associated with the people, both groups agree on its definition as a lawless entity. "Legalists" are quick to embrace the radicals' definition of the people because doing so makes it easier to condemn the entire project of popular constitution-making. Their primary concern is the preservation of the rule of law and checks and balances. Through lengthy case studies, they show how constituent power imperils these values. To protect liberal democracy, they advise that constitutions be amended or remade in legal ways. Because of their emphasis on the rule of law, I call this group "legalists."[23]

---

[22] Thomas Hobbes, *Hobbes: On the Citizen*, eds. Richard Tuck and Michael Silverthorne (New York: Cambridge University Press, 1998), 69–74; Jean-Jacques Rousseau, *The Social Contract: And Other Later Political Writings* (New York: Cambridge University Press, 1996); Emmanuel Joseph Sieyès, "What Is the Third Estate?," in *Political Writings: Including the Debate between Sieyès and Tom Paine in 1791*, ed. Michael Sonenscher (Indianapolis: Hackett Publishing Co., 2003), 137–39; Carl Schmitt, *Constitutional Theory*, trans. Jeffrey Seitzer (Durham: Duke University Press Books, 2008), 128.

[23] I treat these three authors as the most emblematic legalists: Arato, *Post Sovereign Constitution Making*; David Landau, "Constitution-Making Gone Wrong," *Alabama Law Review* 64 (2012), 923; Partlett, "The Dangers of Popular Constitution-Making." In each country-specific chapter, I discuss the legalists who were significant in their own country's constitution-making episodes.

While legalists' misgivings about the radical and populist position are well-founded, their own solution is hardly more satisfactory than the radical one. Just as legalists are right about the dangers of the people, so too are radicals correct that legalists suppress the people's freedom to begin anew and in effect protect the entrenched inequalities that exist in many societies. Indeed, I deepen the radical critique of legalism by revisiting legalist case studies in post-Cold War South America to show how the status quo was unsustainable and how legislatures lacked the will and legitimacy necessary to change the constitution through legal amendment procedures. The people had to be invoked to break the gridlock over constitutional reform, to restore legitimacy to the political system and to resolve the state's political and constitutional crises. The legalist position is only tenable when the political and social background for a constitutional crisis is glossed over.

The debate between radicals and legalists has reached an impasse. Both have valid concerns, and each group launches trenchant critiques of the other. This book breaks through this intellectual paralysis by shifting the central question. For too long, theorists have focused on whether to embrace constituent power while avoiding the more fundamental question of how to define it, especially in relation to law. I turn away from radical proponents of constituent power, such as Hobbes and Schmitt, and toward Hannah Arendt in order to develop a new conception of the people's legal status called "extraordinary adaptation."[24] Arendt shares with radicals the concern that law inhibits the people, but also fears that its destruction threatens their plurality. In "extraordinary adaptation," law is simultaneously transcended to break with the past and drawn upon to ensure the inclusion of multiple actors. Even as many of the specific rules of the old institutions are bent, reinterpreted, or broken, those institutions are still "extraordinarily adapted" in principled

---

[24] Bruce Ackerman coined the term "Extraordinary Adaptation" to analyze the drafting and ratification of the U.S. Constitution. My account of these ideas relies and builds on his own. Bruce Ackerman, *We the People: Transformations, vol. 2* (Cambridge, MA: Harvard University Press, 2000), 11–13). However, our differences are significant, and I discuss them at length in Chapter Two. Briefly stated, Ackerman offers little guidance for how to handle the dangers for popular constitution-making. This absence may not be particularly significant in his work on the United States because they were not a significant danger at the Founding and Reconstruction, but such dangers are relevant to the countries Ackerman discusses in his comparative work and that are the subject of this book.

Furthermore, even though he draws extensively on Arendt, Ackerman does not address or embrace her idea that the people should be plural. Nor does he connect her idea of a plural people to the idea of extraordinary adaptation. For a compatible line of criticism and an understanding of Ackerman's work to which I am indebted, Andrew Arato, "Forms of Constitution Making and Theories of Democracy International Conference on Comparative Constitutional Law," *Cardozo Law Review* 17 (1995), 205–19.

ways to regulate the creation of the new constitution. The process may violate a law to realize a new beginning, but it does not plunge the country into a legal abyss. It may be illegal, but it is not lawless. A mediated, not lawless, people author the country's new highest law.

Extraordinary adaptation is the means for law to achieve a plural people, which is the normative lodestar of my project. Yet we do not yet have the resources to think about how the people can act in their plurality. As a result, the dominant conception of the people is one that takes some segment of the population as the true people, poised against the remainder, a detritus to be discarded. This mistaken view ignores that no one group is universal. The people are not a part, but the whole. The inclusive or plural concept of the people encompasses all citizens and gives them all input in the creation of a new constitution. What is developed in this book is an understanding of how the people can exercise authorship in the constitution-making process without losing their plurality.

In extraordinary adaptation, the bootstrapping of multiple institutions facilitates the creation of a plural people. The insurgent revolutionaries often claim the president as their own, as a vehicle for the people's will until a constituent assembly can be formed. Since the presidency is held by a single person, there is little representation of opposing viewpoints. By contrast, the entire purpose of the legislatures, state governments, and to some extent the courts is to represent the diversity of the entire country. Political groups that do not have the presidency may have majorities or at least significant representation in these other bodies and will push for a constitution-making process that gives some significant voice, such as having a proportional electoral rule for the constitutional assembly and protections for minorities once that assembly has been convened.

Extraordinary adaptation can include diverse parties because the rupture with the existing legal order is partial. In the radical's "true" revolution, the enemy is excluded so that the true people may totally break with the past. In the opposition's absence, the revolutionaries can avoid all compromise. But for extraordinary adaptation, the opposition—many of whom are political actors associated with the old regime— are not essentially antithetical to the revolution. The goal is not to destroy the forces of the old order, but to put them in their place. The opposition may negotiate, but it should realize the modest chips it brings to the table. It will be able to find a place in the new order, but that place will no longer be at the peak of power.

"True revolutionaries" will be disappointed by extraordinary adaptation. A plural people, constructed through the bending and twisting of old institutions, requires a redefinition of revolution so that it is no longer understood as a total upending of all spheres of social and political life. As I will show in the chapters on Bolivia and Colombia, this partial revolution may bring incredible political and social change, but elites often manage to stave off the more dramatic forms of economic redistribution for which radicals yearn. The price of incorporating one's enemies is the diminishment of the revolution's scale.

Most violations of the law by political actors are for illegitimate reasons of narrow self-interest. Yet there are sometimes compelling grounds for extralegal action. The theory of extraordinary adaptation proposes three principles to guide our judgments about when and how law may be legitimately violated in processes of constitutional change. Extraordinary adaptation cannot be reduced to a series of recommendations for how to draw up a constitution, however. It is not a recipe or a checklist. Principles, however, can provide a general framework for constitutional politics that will guide and constrain the process. The first principle is legal exhaustion or the failure of the legal system to enact a consensus about the need for far-reaching constitutional change. The second is popular approval of the violation of existing law to enact the change. The last is the inclusion of all parties in the process so that the opposition can begrudgingly acquiesce to the result. These principles—legal exhaustion, popular vindication, and inclusion—set out boundaries for how and when to violate the law in popular constitution-making. They give guidance to prevent extraordinary adaptation from degenerating into lawlessness or flimsy legal fig leaves for centralizations of power. In the chapters that follow, I use these principles to analyze each country's constitution process, carefully noting whether they adhere to or violate them.

I call my theory's form of adaptation "extraordinary" to distinguish it from its mundane counterparts. Political scientists Jacob Hacker, Paul Pierson, and Kathleen Thelen note that institutional adaptation is both "very common and very consequential."[25] They illustrate this with examples of "conversion" in which "political actors are able to redirect institutions or policies toward purposes beyond their original intent." For example, while the Sherman

---

[25] Jacob S. Hacker, Paul Pierson, and Kathleen Thelen, "Drift and Conversion: Hidden Faces of Institutional Change," in *Advances in Comparative-Historical Analysis* (Cambridge: Cambridge University Press, 2015).

Anti-Trust Act was originally intended to be wielded against corporations, years after its passage those same corporations successfully lobbied for it to be repurposed against unions. Conversion is ordinary and is orchestrated by interest groups and occurs "beyond the bright glare" of the public.[26] By contrast, constitution-making should be a rare, public, and collective act with high levels of mobilization and inclusiveness. It should not be mundane, but extraordinary.

To be sure, extraordinary adaptation is dangerous. Bending the law opens a Pandora's box of possible future violations of law. It calls into question the integrity of the legal system. An aspiring authoritarian leader might build on these openings to consolidate power. But the three principles offer robust protections. For example, the first principle of legal exhaustion ensures that extraordinary adaptation is reserved for rare circumstances. Most of the time, constitutional change should occur through normal channels of amendment or judicial interpretation. However, when the system is incapable of reforming itself and there is large-scale mobilization for change, extraordinary adaptation must be seriously considered. At that point, the revolution is necessary and inevitable, and the only question is its form.

With enough force, every tool can be misused, and extraordinary adaptation is no exception. If you slam a square peg into a round hole enough times, the surface will give. That jamming takes effort and time, however—time during which the opposition may rally and mobilize. Extraordinary adaptation is thus not a guarantee against semi-authoritarianism, but it offers significant resistance to the alternative of conjuring up a lawless people.

What is the difference between my theory and that of the radical proponents of constituent power on the issue of mediation? Many have criticized the radicals for positing the existence of the people as a fact without any need for explanation.[27] Indeed, radical theorist Carl Schmitt refers to the people as "a concrete political being" and a "will" with an "essentially existential character."[28] Beneath the surface, however, all radicals, even Schmitt, always mediate the people. What distinguishes extraordinary adaptation from the radical approach is the type of mediation. Post-Hobbesian radical theorists forge the people's unity through the friend-enemy distinction and through privileging one unified body as embodying a singular

---

[26] Ibid.
[27] See, e.g., Solongo Wandan, "Nothing out of the Ordinary: Constitution Making as Representative Politics," *Constellations* 22, no. 1 (Mar. 1, 2015), 44–55.
[28] Schmitt, *Constitutional Theory*, 125–26.

people.[29] Extraordinary adaptation mediates the people through the multiple institutions of the old constitution, which protects the people's plurality. At least in liberal democracies, a variety of institutions exist, each of which is able with its own voice to contest and check the others' claims to speak for the people. No one voice dominates. Even if these institutions have to bend or break some of their traditional rules, their preservation and multiplicity ensures that the people's heterogeneity is never lost. The mediation of law protects against the radicals' effort to destroy difference in order to establish a homogeneous people. We, the mediated people, are plural.

SOUTH AMERICA

I develop my theory of extraordinary adaptation inductively by analyzing all four instances of popular constitution-making within democracies in post-1989 South America. I use the term "popular" to denote the creation of constitutions in which the people's ostensible authorship had significant influence on the process, particularly in the invoking of constituent power to justify violating the law. This book is a comprehensive and in-depth analysis of all the region's efforts to establish, through constituent power, new constitutions in countries that had already transitioned to democracy.[30] The four South American cases I discuss are the 1991 Colombian, the 1999 Venezuelan, the 2008 Ecuadorian, and the 2009 Bolivian Constitutions.[31]

---

[29] Ibid., 239–42.

[30] My book is written in the vein of political theory and constituent power, which is the language of the participants themselves in South America. Others, however, have written about the region from different perspectives. In social science, Gabriel Negretto has written the most comprehensive analyses. Negretto, "Constitution Making and Constitutionalism in Latin America: The Role of Procedural Rules"; Gabriel L. Negretto, *Making Constitutions: Presidents, Parties, and Institutional Choice in Latin America* (Cambridge: Cambridge University Press, 2013). See also Renata Segura and Ana María Bejarano, "¡Ni Una Asamblea Más Sin Nosotros! Exclusion, Inclusion, and the Politics of Constitution-Making in the Andes," *Constellations* 11, no. 2 (2004), 217–36. David Landau has also written an article that classifies constitution-making in relationship to the constituent power. However, Landau casts doubt about the promise of debating constitution-making in the language of constituent power. Landau, David, "Constituent Power and Constitution Making in Latin America," in *Comparative Constitution Making*, eds. David Landau and Hanna Lerner (Cheltenham, U.K.: Edward Elgar Publishing, 2019), 587 (stating that efforts to "flesh out constituent power" is "both conceptually difficult and practically challenging at the level of enforcement.") Andrew Arato writes from a similar perspective to my own, and has compared Colombia and Venezuela. Arato, *Adventures of the Constituent Power*, 257–365.

[31] In addition to the four countries this book discusses, there are eight remaining countries in South America. None met the criteria of an example of (1) post-1989 constitution-making; (2) by the people invoking constituent power and (3) within a liberal democracy. Uruguay, Chile, Guyana, Suriname, and Brazil all created their constitutions before 1989. Chile is in the process of creating a

In this section, I discuss why these countries' experiences provide insights that can help in the development of a theory of constituent power. In the Conclusion to the book, I discuss the current and as of yet unfinished constitution-making process in Chile. There, leaders will likely avoid confronting the dilemmas of constituent power because the legal system did not block but rather instead facilitated change.

These South American countries' popular constitution-making processes starkly pose some of the richest and most difficult questions facing liberal

new constitution, but as I discuss in the Conclusion to this book, Chile does not meet the second criterion of invoking the constituent power because it has so far followed the legal path.

Brazil and Uruguay are also cases that require additional explanation. Brazil created its new constitution in 1988, right before the 1989 cutoff. However, it was created in an inclusive fashion that shared in the spirit of post-Cold War constitution-making, so even though it did not meet the 1989 criteria it seems to share in the underlying reason of setting the 1989 date. Even if we relax the date requirement, Brazil does not meet the other criterion of constitution-making by the people. The Brazilian Constitution was written in a transition from a military regime and the military's presence had substantial influence on the process. Juan J. Linz and Alfred Stepan, *Problems of Democratic Transition and Consolidation: Southern Europe, South America, and Post-Communist Europe* (Baltimore: Johns Hopkins University Press, 1996), 166–90.

The Uruguayan Constitution was ratified in 1967, far too early. However, it has been amended in 1989, 1994, 1996, and 2004. The 1996 amendments were so thorough that some consider it to be a new constitution. However, even if these amendments created a new constitution, the process was not understood as an act of constituent power and fittingly it followed the normal amendment procedure. David Altman et. al, "Constitutional Reforms and Political Turnover in Uruguay," Documento Online No. 2/11, 2011.

Once the 1989 cutoff is taken into account, that leaves remaining the constitutions of Paraguay, Peru, and Argentina. Like Brazil, the creation of 1992 Paraguayan Constitution did not occur within a liberal democracy, but rather was a part of a transition from authoritarian rule. In that environment, the armed forces continued to exert significant influence on the process. Marcial A. Riquelme and Jorge G. Riquelme, "Political Parties," in *The Transition to Democracy in Paraguay*, eds. Peter Lambert and Andrew Nickson (New York: Springer, 2016), 48.

The current Peruvian Constitution was ratified in 1993. It does not meet the criteria of constitution-making within a liberal democracy, but it is a close call because Peru had been a liberal democracy prior to 1992. Here, I follow David Landau who classifies "the regime starting point and context" of all countries that have created constitutions in Latin America since 1991. Landau classifies the four countries that are the subject of this book as democratic, but classifies Peru as a "competitive authoritarian regime seeking legitimacy." Landau, David, "Constituent Power and Constitution Making in Latin America," 570.

Why is Peru classified differently than Venezuela and Ecuador? All three countries were democratic, elected a populist president, became significantly more authoritarian, and had constituent assemblies. The difference is the role and timing of the constituent assembly. In Venezuela and Ecuador, the constituent assembly and constitution-making were the means of turning the regime semi-authoritarian. The elections to the assembly were free and fair and occurred within a liberal democracy. The constituent assembly then became a means to attack other institutions. By contrast, in Peru, then-president Alberto Fujimori used not the constituent assembly, but the army to purge Congress and the judiciary. The Constituent Assembly only occurred later and under significant international pressure. I thank David Landau for his help in thinking through this point. On the decline of Peruvian democracy under Fujimori and the role of international pressure, Philip Mauceri, "Return of the Caudillo: Autocratic Democracy in Peru," *Third World Quarterly* 18, no. 5 (Dec. 1, 1997), 901.

The 1994 Argentinian Constitution was created through an amendment procedure that was not understood to be an expression of constituent power. See David Landau, "Constituent Power and Constitution Making in Latin America," 570; Negretto, *Making Constitutions*.

democracies that seek to create new constitutions. The other most prominent recent examples of popular constitution-making are Turkey and Hungary.[32] But in these countries, executives directly dominated and manipulated the constitution-making process. Executives and parliaments rewrote the constitution.[33] By contrast, in the countries of this study, there were freely and fairly elected constitutional assemblies. Although presidents were influential, they were one step removed. This makes it much more difficult to discredit the South American cases as undemocratic usurpations. It forces us to delve deeper into the pathologies of majoritarian and lawless constitution-making. Why should the elected majority not just get its way?

I chose the year 1989 as the starting point for the period considered in this book because the fall of the Berlin Wall stands as a symbolic marker of the end of the Cold War and the shifting of the ground rules for constitution-making in a democratic direction. Wars tend to undermine democracy, and the Cold War was no exception. During that era, constitution-making by and for dictators or military juntas was common.[34] Both sides in the war had their own rationalizations. In South America, in particular, many on the left reasoned that democracy kept open too many avenues for capitalists to topple the government. Fidel Castro's success in capturing the state in Cuba presented an alternative model in which a small vanguard could seize the reins of government, centralize power, and radically transform society.[35] With the collapse of the Soviet Union, Castro-style insurgencies lost much of their appeal and international support.[36] After 1989, the norm of elections took hold in South America and constitutional changes had to be enacted

[32] Poland is often mentioned as an example of democratic decay alongside Hungary and Turkey, but I did not include it as it formally did not replace its constitution. That distinction is of little weight in many contexts, and scholars may reasonably disagree whether it is relevant for this book's concerns. On Poland, Wojciech Sadurski, *Poland's Constitutional Breakdown* (Oxford: Oxford University Press, 2019).

[33] On Hungary, Arato, *Post Sovereign Constitution Making*; Kim Lane Scheppele, "Autocratic Legalism Symposium: The Limits of Constitutionalism—A Global Perspective," *University of Chicago Law Review*, no. 2 (2018), 545–84. On Turkey, Asli U. Bali, "The Perils of Judicial Independence: Constitutional Transition and the Turkish Example," *Virginia Journal of International Law* 52 (2012), 235–320.

[34] Aníbal Pérez-Liñán, *Presidential Impeachment and the New Political Instability in Latin America*, Illustrated ed. (Cambridge: Cambridge University Press, 2010), 40–64. Ginsburg and Huq make a similar point by distinguishing between authoritarian collapse and democratic erosion. Tom Ginsburg and Aziz Z. Huq, *How to Save a Constitutional Democracy* (Chicago: University of Chicago Press, 2018), 35–49.

[35] On the influence of Cuba on armed revolution in Venezuela, for example, see George Ciccariello-Maher, *We Created Chávez: A People's History of the Venezuelan Revolution* (Durham: Duke University Press Books, 2013), 31.

[36] See Pérez-Liñán, *Presidential Impeachment and the New Political Instability in Latin America*, 35–49.

through the ballot rather than the bullet. As David Landau has written, "Modern [South] America is . . . probably the world's richest laboratory of constitution-making under democratic conditions."[37]

This book considers processes of constitution-making only in South American countries that were already liberal democracies because it is only in these settings that extraordinary adaptation is a live possibility. In a transition from authoritarianism to democracy, other methods may be more appropriate for creating a new constitution. The old regime must often be given concessions and guarantees of power under the new system in return for laying down their arms. Elite negotiations rather than popular revolution may be necessary to prevent a bloodbath.[38] But sometimes, a full-scale insurrection may be necessary to topple a dictatorship. As the conflict intensifies, the rebels will seek to delegitimize and destroy the old institutions, and amid the heightened hatred it may be difficult to meaningfully incorporate old elites and adapt their institutions. By contrast, in a democratic country with separated powers and fair elections, new political actors can gain entry into the old institutions and act within them to achieve radical constitutional change. Indeed, the new post-Cold War constitutions of the Andes emerged, in odd and unorthodox ways, through preexisting democratic institutions.

Sheer numbers are another reason to focus on South America. Comparatively speaking, constituent assemblies are especially prominent in this region.[39] These examples provide a rich basis for comparison because the countries share similar political and constitutional histories and cultures that date back to the wars of liberation from the Spanish Empire. Indeed, these countries were in dialogue with each other during their respective processes of constitution-making, often exchanging advisers and seeking to replicate the successes and avoid the failures of the others.[40]

[37] Landau, David, "Constituent Power and Constitution Making in Latin America," 567. Landau's article is about constitution-making since 1990 in Latin America, not just South America. However, I took the liberty to adapt the statement because since 1990, the Dominican Republic is the only country in Central America to have made a new constitution.

[38] There is an extensive literature on negotiated transitions rooted in the third wave of democratization in Eastern Europe and Latin America. See, for example, Linz and Stepan, *Problems of Democratic Transition and Consolidation*; Adam Przeworski, *Democracy and the Market: Political and Economic Reforms in Eastern Europe and Latin America* (Cambridge: Cambridge University Press, 1991). For a take on these transitions that is rooted in the political theory of the constituent power, Andrew Arato, *Civil Society, Constitution, and Legitimacy* (Lanham, MD: Rowman & Littlefield Publishers, 2000).

[39] Negretto, "Constitution Making and Constitutionalism in Latin America: The Role of Procedural Rules," 26; Jonathan Wheatley and Fernando Mendez, *Patterns of Constitutional Design: The Role of Citizens and Elites in Constitution-Making* (Burlington, VT: Routledge, 2013), 29.

[40] As I discuss in the conclusion, Hugo Chávez and his constitutional advisers were profoundly influenced by the making of the 1991 Colombian Constitution. They and Chávez traveled to Colombia to speak with the key actors in the making of the 1991 constitution there. Hugo Chavez,

Even more remarkably, in Colombia, Venezuela, Bolivia, and Ecuador, the constitution-making processes all share the same pattern. Each of the four countries suffered from profound crises of representation that led to demands for a new constitution. In each country, Congress was unable to amend the constitution because Congress itself lacked legitimacy; it was the problem that a new constitution was supposed to fix. The only actors with the legitimacy necessary to write a new constitution were elected constitutional assemblies. Partial and halting reforms had already opened up political space for new forces to gain a foothold in government. Presidents representing them won office and claimed mandates to convoke a constitutional assembly. But the constitutions lacked provisions for such a convocation. It would have been illegal. Still, the presidents proceeded with their plans, arguing that the people's status as the highest authority and the source of constitutional legitimacy granted the people the right to violate the old amendment method to create a new constitution.

But how would the people be constructed? Would they exist within the law through the "extraordinary adaptation" of preexisting institutions, or would they form outside law to completely break with the past? Here, the countries diverged. In the coming chapters, I examine the conflicts within and the differences between each country's legal construction of the people, such as the electoral and ratification rules used. These variations provide a lens to examine conflicting ideas of the relationship between the concepts of law, the people, and revolution.

Let us examine the variation across cases, starting with Venezuela and Ecuador. While this does not follow the chronological order of the creation of the four constitutions considered in this book, I discuss these two countries first to show the pitfalls of the dominant vision of constituent power as outside of all law and to demonstrate how such a vision facilitates authoritarianism. Like their radical predecessors, such as Emmanuel Sieyès, Karl Marx, Vladimir Lenin, and Carl Schmitt, Venezuelan and Ecuadorian radical theorists and actors forged the unity of the people by dividing the

Marta Harnecker, and Chesa Boudin, *Understanding the Venezuelan Revolution: Hugo Chavez Talks to Marta Harnecker* (New York: Monthly Review Press, 2005), 32; Ricardo Combellas, *El proceso constituyente: una historia personal* (Caracas: Mercadeo Global, 2010), 10.

Two Spanish lawyers, Roberto Viciano and Rubén Martínez Dalmau assisted in the Venezuelan process and traveled to Ecuador and Bolivia to help spread the basic ideas of the sovereign constituent assembly as part of "The New Latin American Constitutionalism." See Roberto Viciano Pastor and Rubén Martínez Dalmau, "El nuevo constitucionalismo latinoamericano: Fundamentos para una construcción doctrinal," *Revista general de derecho público comparado*, no. 9 (2011), 1–24.

population into friends and enemies and then imposing unity on the friends through top-down representation in which one site came to incarnate the people completely. More specifically, Venezuelan and Ecuadorian radicals posited the poor as the people and their enemy as the oligarchic political barons. Top-down representation would occur through an electoral mandate given to the constituent assembly that could then be all-powerful because it would be an exact miniature of the people. The Venezuelan Supreme Court valiantly fought against Chávez in favor of extraordinary adaptation but lost. The victory of radicals was easier in Ecuador. Unlike in Venezuela, there were no significant sites of resistance to the Ecuadorian radicals. The opposition failed to earn the votes necessary to have a significant influence in the Constituent Assembly. Hence, there was little potential for extraordinary adaptation. Law can act as a buffer, but it will give way under overwhelming electoral pressure.

The path not taken in Venezuela was in fact the one chosen in Colombia during the creation of its 1991 constitution. The Supreme Court and the president extraordinarily adapted the state of emergency doctrine to produce a liberal democratic constitution. I caution against over-idealizing Colombia's success, however, because the process was only partially inclusive due to the lack of representation for the peasants, a large and vulnerable group in Colombia. We see extraordinary adaptation's true test in Bolivia with the creation of its 2009 constitution. The process was fully inclusive. According to the party ideology of the *Movimiento al Socialismo* (MAS), the people were the poor and indigenous peasants and workers, and their enemy were the corrupt mestizos in the northeast of the country. They hoped to mimic Venezuela and have a sovereign constituent assembly that would incarnate the true people. Although the country veered toward civil war, ultimately extraordinary adaptation meaningfully included the opposition and tempered the authoritarian impulses of the new regime.

The goal of the comparisons across these cases is not to tease out causal relations. This is not an exercise in social science, but in democratic theory. Of course, causality is still relevant. I rely on and benefit from a growing social science literature of small-n studies and large-n regression analyses that shows how exclusionary and majoritarian forms of constitution-making lead to centralization of power and semi-authoritarian or authoritarian regimes.[41] However, in South America the political actors themselves do not

---

[41] Arato, *Post Sovereign Constitution Making*; Zachary Elkins, Tom Ginsburg, and James Melton, *The Endurance of National Constitutions* (Cambridge: Cambridge University Press, 2009); Todd

answer the foundational normative questions of constitution-making with statistics; they speak in the fiery rhetoric of democracy, constituent power, and the people. In the assembly debates, in judicial decisions, in newspaper interviews, and from their offices and podiums, political actors orate in the normative terms of democratic theory. To engage in the politics of constitution-making in the Andes, the speaker must invoke or defeat the idea of constituent power.[42]

This language of popular sovereignty defines the horizon in which political contestation often occurs in South America. These theories are weapons in which combatants legitimize their positions to themselves and to the larger public. For political actors, the reigning views on popular sovereignty define the range of options that they believe are legitimate, and affect the reception of the proposals in the public sphere. Drawing from an almost two-century tradition, the norm in South America is that the people must write their own constitution. This may entail violating the old constitution's amendment rule, but such a violation is justified because the constitution is the people's creation, implying that they are free to alter or remake it. Since the end of the Cold War, this process has been understood in the Andes to require elections for a constituent assembly that would draft a new constitution. This bare-bones consensus still leaves many controversies unsettled. What will the electoral rule be for the assembly? What will the approval rule be inside the constituent assembly? Can the assembly change the approval rule, and to what extent can it form its own rules? Is the assembly superior or inferior to the government and in what domains? These questions, I contend, are largely fought on a theoretical terrain in which the central question is whether the people are bound by law.

Although these questions remain open and are subject to contestation, this does not mean that the combatants arrive on the battlefield equally armed. The Andes's dominant tradition of a lawless constituent power has superior rhetorical firepower. The same tradition is dominant in political theory and

---

A. Eisenstadt, Carl A. LeVan, and Tofigh Maboudi, "When Talk Trumps Text: The Democratizing Effects of Deliberation during Constitution-Making, 1974–2011," *The American Political Science Review; Washington* 109, no. 3 (Aug. 2015), 592–612; Gabriel L. Negretto, "Democratic Constitution-Making Bodies: The Perils of a Partisan Convention," *International Journal of Constitutional Law* 16, no. 1 (May 12, 2018).

[42] Gerardo Pisarello, *Procesos constituyentes: Caminos para la ruptura democrática* (Trotta, 2013); Pedro Vega Garcia, *La Reforma Constitucional Y La Problemática Del Poder Constituyente* (Tecnos, 1985).

in articles on popular constitution-making. Indeed, the scholarship fuels the practice, as political actors draw on and cite this literature to develop their own ideas.[43] This tradition fits easily with the history of constitution-making in South America, where new constitutions were often created after sharp and large-scale ruptures with the legal order caused by coups and civil wars. The Cold War helped to further cement the tradition through international actors' support and acceptance of right- and left-wing dictatorships that seized power by force rather than earning it through elections.

The end of the Cold War dramatically changed the theoretical possibilities for constituent power. The desire for new constitutions did not coincide with large legal ruptures. There were attempts. In Venezuela, Hugo Chávez tried to carry out a military coup in 1992. That same year in Bolivia, Álvaro Garcia Línera, who would later become the vice president but at that time was a member of an indigenous-inspired guerilla movement, carried out an attack of industrial sabotage. Both efforts failed miserably because they were out of step with the times.[44] Both men emerged from jail as reformed democrats and years later won the highest offices of the land through normal and legal electoral channels. Through those offices, they launched constitutional revolutions. The new liberal and democratic context opened up the possibility for a new method of constitution-making. Since old institutions were still functioning, they could be used in novel and odd ways to regulate the new constitution's creation.

The context, in some ways, is similar to that of the eighteenth-century United States. The first occurrence of extraordinary adaptation was the creation of the U.S. Constitution. At stake in this book is whether the U.S. process should remain a source of inspiration or whether it should be discarded as an aberration. While the eighteenth-century United States benefited

---

[43] In Colombia, Venezuela, and Bolivia, the three most commonly discussed theorists of constituent power are Emmanuel Sieyès, Carl Schmitt, and Antonio Negri, including by the key constitutional advisers or members of the constitutional assembly. "Toni Negri in Venezuela," *Revolts Now*, Mar. 7, 2013, https://revoltsnow.wordpress.com/2013/03/07/toni-negri-in-venezuela-social ism-of-the-21st-century; Ricardo Combellas, *Poder Constituyente* (En Cambio, 2000) (extensively discussing Sieyès and Schmitt); Raúl Prada Alcoreza, *Horizontes de la Asamblea Constituyente* (La Paz: Ediciones Yachaywasi, 2006), 50 (discussing Negri). For a more extensive account of Schmitt's influence in Venezuela and worldwide, see Chapter Three. David Landau, a U.S. law professor who writes on South America and whom I call a legalist, has been widely read as well. See, for example ,Colombian author, Jorge González-Jácome, "I·CONnect—On Abusive Constitutionalism: Two Critical Impulses," accessed Mar. 10, 2017, http://www.iconnectblog.com/2015/06/on-abusive-constitutionalism-two-critical-impulses/.

[44] Chávez, *Understanding the Venezuelan Revolution*, 36–38; Raquel Gutiérrez Aguilar, *Rhythms of the Pachakuti: Indigenous Uprising and State Power in Bolivia*, trans. Stacey Alba D. Skar (Durham: Duke University Press, 2014), xi.

from preexisting democratic institutions, countries transitioning from dictatorships lack that luxury. For that reason, some have argued that the creation of the U.S. Constitution offers little guidance in the present. Yet constitutional democracy has been the dominant model of governance in post-Cold War South America, making extraordinary adaptation a real possibility and therefore making the early American experience again relevant for modern experiments with constitutional change. The region's revolutionaries were now ready to take advantage of this opening. In the democratic context that existed after the end of the Cold War, South American revolutionaries entered into electoral competition, hoping that victories at the ballot box would empower them to create new constitutions to enact radical change. The French revolutionary Marquis de Condorcet's words about the United States in the late eighteenth century could just as well have described the Andean countries in the late twentieth and early twenty-first centuries: "the challenge is not to transition to democracy, but to transition from a free constitution to an even freer one." The U.S. legacy is and should remain alive and well.[45]

In the four countries of this study, some political actors recognized the possibility for a new theory of constituent power, but they had few theoretical resources to draw upon. I speak here not of the "legalists" in each country who refused to countenance any illegality and denied the people's existence.[46] As I explain in more detail in Chapter One, under conditions of crisis, legalist pleas for strict adherence to the letter of the law fell on deaf ears: change had long been needed and the current system had proven itself unable to provide it. My sympathies lie neither with the radicals nor the legalists, but with a third group buffeted between them who struggled to redefine the idea of the people. They worked under enormous pressure and with little time. No doubt they thought the theory of constituent power was central, but their attention was often divided over a whole range of questions and crises. Under

---

[45] Of course, as I discuss in more detail in Chapter Three, the U.S. Constitution-making process was not fully inclusive because of the exclusion of many groups, including women and Black people.

[46] For Venezuela, see Allan R. Brewer-Carias, *Asamblea Constituyente y Proces Constituyente 1999. Coleccion Tratado de Derecho Constitucional, Tomo VI* (Caracas: Fundación Editorial Juridica Venezolana, 2014); Allan R. Brewer-Carías, *Dismantling Democracy in Venezuela: The Chávez Authoritarian Experiment* (New York: Cambridge University Press, 2010). For Bolivia, Jorge Lazarte, *Reforma del "experimento" constitucional en Bolivia: claves de un nuevo modelo estatal y societal de derecho (para abrir un debate que nunca hubo)*, 2015, and for Ecuador, Daniela Salazar, "My Power in the Constitution" (unpublished manuscript, July 3 2015). In Colombia, the most important legalist figure was minister of the interior, Humberto de La Calle, who served as a key liaison between the president and the assembly. See his speech to the assembly, National Constituent Assembly, Report of the Plenary Session of May 3, 1991.

these conditions, to expect them to have reformulated the relationship of law to the people would be unrealistic. Nonetheless, they tried. They searched and fumbled in the dark for new concepts and ideas and for novel ways to use existing ones. They offered striking insights and willed their way through contradictions. But without a clear formulation, their efforts were troubled from the start: they often conceded too much ground to their opponents, failed to realize the full range of options, and acted too late or on the wrong set of issues. They were theoretically outgunned by the proponents of sovereign or lawless constituent power.

The goal of this book is to complete the work that this third group of besieged political actors began. I draw upon political theory and on the actors, theorists, and experiences of contemporary South American constitution-making to develop a new theory of the relationship between law and the people. My hope is that the theory of extraordinary adaptation will supply new resources for the next round of battles over the meaning of popular authorship. With the addition of this theory to the existing arsenal, there may be a fairer fight between those who unify the people to centralize power and those who seek to pluralize them to protect their freedom.

PLAN OF THE BOOK

Chapter One lays out the debate between legalist opponents and radical proponents of constituent power. Despite their disagreement over whether it is wise or reckless to invoke constituent power, they agree on its definition of the people as a lawless unity. I argue that neither side's theories are capable of both preserving the people's freedom to break from the past and guarding against excessive centralization of power in revolutionary governments. This agreement has obscured our ability to develop an alternative conception of constituent power that engages with law in unconventional ways to construct a plural people.

In Chapter Two, I explain the theory and principles of extraordinary adaptation. I show how Carl Schmitt's extensive influence in the contemporary literature on constituent power has contributed to a definition of the people as antagonistic to and outside of law. Next, I engage with the theories of Hannah Arendt and Bruce Ackerman, whose works lay a strong but incomplete foundation for my own theory. Using each author to critique and supplement the other, I show that Arendt misses the necessity of illegality, and that Ackerman pays insufficient attention to the threats that popular constitution-making poses to democracy. I then develop in greater detail the three principles of extraordinary adaptation: legal exhaustion, popular vindication, and inclusion.

In the remaining chapters I discuss how two different visions of the people's relationship to law—lawless vs. extraordinary adaptation—played out in South America. Chapter Three illustrates the dangers of lawless constitution-making through the examples of Venezuela and Ecuador. Chapters Four and Five discuss two examples of extraordinary adaptation, but distinguish them on the basis of the degree to which each exhibits extraordinary adaptation's third principle of inclusion. Colombia, the subject of Chapter Four, exemplifies partially inclusive extraordinary adaptation as it included many, but not all of the important groups. I end in Chapter Five with extraordinary adaptation in full bloom in Bolivia, a completely inclusive process that pushed the method to its limits.

What may have seemed a peripheral problem in South America now threatens to engulf liberal democracies around the world. Citizens are convinced that the political system is rigged and are calling upon populist leaders to scrap it in favor of unmediated forms of governance. Extraordinary adaptation began in the United States before migrating centuries later to South America. With the current crisis of liberal constitutionalism, it may be time for it to return home to the United States and spread to Europe. Extraordinary adaptation provides hope that the yearning for revolution can be fulfilled without a descent into chaos or authoritarianism.

1

The Lawless Unity of the People

The Legalists and Radicals' Consensus

The people[1] are the ultimate source of the authority for a constitution. But who are the people? In scholarship analyzing cases of popular constitution-making, the emerging consensus is that the people are outside of, unconstrained by, and superior to all law and constituted institutions.[2] They wield a radical constituent power to completely overthrow the old institutions to usher in a new order. Both "radical" proponents and "legalist" critics of the constituent power, or the people's power to make a constitution, have inadvertently collaborated to enshrine this definition for it serves both of their

---

[1] I have chosen to treat the "people" as a plural noun for the sake of convenience. What's at stake in this project is whether this characterization is correct or whether the people *is* a singular unity.

[2] Joel I Colon-Rios, *Weak Constitutionalism: Democratic Legitimacy and the Question of Constituent Power* (London: Routledge, 2013); Renato Cristi, "Metaphysics of Constituent Power: Schmitt and the Genesis of Chile's 1980 Constitution," *Cardozo Law Review* 21 (2000), 1749; Paul Kahn, *Political Theology: Four New Chapters on the Concept of Sovereignty* (Columbia: Columbia University Press, 2011) (discussing the United States); David Landau, "Constitution-Making Gone Wrong," *Alabama Law Review* 64 (2013), 923 (discussing Venezuela, Bolivia, and Egypt); Jan Muller, "Carl Schmitt and the Constitution of Europe," *Cardozo Law Review* 21 (1999), 1777; William Partlett, "Constitution-Making by 'We the Majority' in Egypt," *The Brookings Institution*, accessed Jan. 4, 2015, http://www.brookings.edu/blogs/up-front/posts/2012/11/30-constitution-egypt-partlett; William Partlett, "Elite Threat to Constitutional Transitions," *Virginia Journal of International Law* 56, no. 2 (2016), 408 (discussing Belarus and Armenia); William Partlett, "Dangers of Popular Constitution-Making," *Brooklyn Journal of International Law* 38 (2012) (discussing Russia, Belarus, and Kazakhstan), 193; Richard Stacey, "Constituent Power and Carl Schmitt's Theory of Constitution in Kenya's Constitution-Making Process," *International Journal of Constitutional Law* 9, nos. 3–4 (Oct. 1, 2011), 587–614; Lars Vinx, "The Incoherence of Strong Popular Sovereignty," *International Journal of Constitutional Law* 11, no. 1 (Jan. 1, 2013). For an account of the creeping influence of this lawless definition of constituent power in the United States, see Andrew Arato, "Carl Schmitt and the Revival of the Doctrine of the Constituent Power in the United States," *Cardozo Law Review* 21 (2000 1999), 1739. One exception is Andrew Arato's analysis of constitution-making in Poland, Hungary, Bulgaria, and South Africa as examples of post-sovereign constitution-making. Andrew Arato, *Post Sovereign Constitution Making: Learning and Legitimacy* (Oxford: Oxford University Press, 2016); Andrew Arato, "Conventions, Constituent Assemblies, and Round Tables: Models, Principles and Elements of Democratic Constitution-Making," *Global Constitutionalism* 1, no. 1 (2012), 173–200. Andrew Arato's post-sovereign model is difficult to classify. It avoids the idea of the people, relying on inclusivity and transparency for legitimacy, but still holds that extraordinary moments are necessary for creating legitimacy for the new constitution. For an exploration of the "assumptions, anticipations, and aspirations" of constituent power, Zoran Oklopcic, *Beyond the People: Social Imaginary and Constituent Imagination* (Oxford: Oxford University Press, 2018)

We, the Mediated People. Joshua Braver, Oxford University Press. © Joshua Braver 2023.
DOI: 10.1093/oso/9780197650639.003.0002

purposes. For "radicals," often drawing on the work of Carl Schmitt, the constituent power is a means to destroy an old corrupt order, such as capitalism, in favor of a more radical alternative.[3] "Legalists" then sound the alarm and point to the authoritarian actions of radical actors as evidence that the constituent power is reckless and dangerous.[4] They call for strict adherence to the law in order to protect liberal democracy. Although they disagree about the potential of the constituent power, both sides agree on its definition. Their consensus buries the possibility of a constituent power that both recognizes the people's freedom and right to institute their own foundations, but also avoids the despotism and instability accompanying the invocation of an unlimited power.

In this chapter, I lay out the shortcomings of both the legalist and the radical positions of constituent power. First, I argue that legalism's conservatism and its call for the legal route to constitutional change fails to recognize the legitimacy deficit of ordinary institutions during crises of governance as well as the insurgent majority's legitimate desire for social and political change. Next, I show that while radicals seek the revolutionary change that legalists too easily dismiss, the radical solution of a lawless and unified people stifles diversity and too easily serves as the underpinning for chaos or tyranny. Neither legalists nor radicals possess the theoretical tools that would allow constitution-makers to, on the one hand, permit the illegalities that are necessary for constitutional change while still warding off the lawlessness that invites semi-authoritarian constitutions. Neither possesses the insights necessary for the creation of popular but democratic constitutions.

Putting "Legalism" in Perspective

The legalist critics of popular constitution-making are part of a long tradition of using law as a check on majority tyranny. In this tradition, the people and

---

[3] See Andreas Kalyvas, *Democracy and the Politics of the Extraordinary: Max Weber, Carl Schmitt, and Hannah Arendt* (Cambridge: Cambridge University Press, 2009); Antonio Negri, *Insurgencies: Constituent Power and the Modern State*, trans. Maurizia Boscagli (Minneapolis: University of Minnesota Press, 2009); Colón-Ríos, *Weak Constitutionalism: Democratic Legitimacy and the Question of Constituent Power*. For a similar radical construction of the people, but with a focus broader than the constitutional context, Ernesto Laclau, *On Populist Reason* (London: Verso, 2007).

[4] See Arato, "Conventions, Constituent Assemblies, and Round Tables"; David Landau, "Constitution-Making Gone Wrong," *Alabama Law Review* 64 (2013), 923; Partlett, "Dangers of Popular Constitution-Making," 193; Lars Vinx, "The Incoherence of Strong Popular Sovereignty," *International Journal of Constitutional Law* 11, no. 1 (Jan 1, 2013), 101–24.

law are two opposed forces. The latter can restrain the irrational passions and prejudices of the people in order to protect property, order, minorities, and the greater good. Much of this tradition has focused on protecting individual rights against their violation by executives or legislatures. .[5]

Today's legalists, in the context of popular constitution-making, see the constitutional assembly as the threat to the rule of law and have embraced the traditional legal supermajoritarian amendment method as the solution.[6] Legalist opponents of popular constitution-making call attention to the danger that "constitutional . . . replacement can be used by would-be autocrats to undermine democracy with relative ease."[7] One legalist, David Landau, has called this "abusive constitutionalism" and the term has come to stand for the central challenge facing the field of constitution-making. David Landau and fellow traveler William Partlett are particularly wary of the circumvention and violation of normal law through the use of constituent assemblies to create new constitutions that centralize power. Calling attention to this pernicious phenomenon has provided a valuable service to comparative constitutional law. Yet, although legalists have the right diagnosis, they are prescribing the wrong medicine. The abuses of popular constitution-making are cited to justify the near or complete discarding of the idea of constituent assemblies and of popular authorship itself so that these countries' fragile stability may be maintained.

In this section, I put legalism in perspective. Its solutions are unviable and needlessly conservative. Its cure is almost as problematic as the disease. I will primarily discuss post-Cold War South America since that is the focus of both this book and of the work of David Landau, who coined the term "abusive constitutionalism" and whose work is perhaps most widely cited to lay out the dangers of popular constitutionalism. I will also take note of several

---

[5] For example, seeRonald Dworkin, *Law's Empire* (Cambridge, MA: Belknap Press, 1986); Owen M. Fiss, "The Supreme Court, 1978 Term," *Harvard Law Review* 93, no. 1 (1979), 1–281.

[6] I thank Bryan Garsten for suggesting the term legalism. While there are important similarities, my and Judith Shklar's use of the term are distinct. Shklar's legalists fetishize law as an end in and of itself. It is "the ethical attitude that holds moral conduct to be a matter of rule following, and moral relationships to consist of duties and rights determined by rules." Judith N. Shklar, *Legalism: Law, Morals, and Political Trials,* Revised ed. (Cambridge, MA: Harvard University Press, 1986). By contrast, the legalists I discuss believe that law is a means to the ends of protecting checks and balances. Andrew Arato even accepts that legality in moments of constitution-making is a necessary fiction. Arato, *Civil Society, Constitution, and Legitimacy,* 167–99.

[7] David Landau, "Abusive Constitutionalism," *U.C. Davis Law Review* 47 (2013), 189–260. See also Rosalind Dixon and David Landau, *Abusive Constitutional Borrowing: Legal Globalization and the Subversion of Liberal Democracy* (Oxford, United Kingdom: Oxford University Press, 2021), 117–129.

cases of post-communist constitutional transitions spurred by the fall of the Soviet Union, as discussed in the work of William Partlett. I will also touch on the work of Andrew Arato. Like Landau and Partlett, Andrew Arato is against the idea of the people, but he departs from the other two authors in his pursuit of still attaining an extraordinary moment for constitution-making by virtue of elected constitutional assemblies limited to considering only specific topics. Although not the only legalists, their work is well representative of the school of thought.[8]

I have two main arguments. First, constituent assemblies were the only feasible means to resolve crises of representation and achieve sorely needed and long-pending constitutional change in the Andes. This is a result of citizens' near-complete loss of trust in their legislatures, and it reflects these countries' long tradition of constituent power, as embodied in elected constituent assemblies. Second, the movements for new constitutions were part of a broader movement to mobilize the disadvantaged in order to achieve more just societies. Landau devalues the goal of social and political change because of his aversion to conflict and his status quo bias. Rather than discarding or restraining the people, as Landau recommends, the goal should be to articulate a new vision that harnesses and channels them to avoid the dangers of despotism or breakdown.

Constituent Assemblies and Breaking Gridlock

In post-Cold War South America, constituent assemblies were necessary to break long-standing gridlock over constitutional reform. Colombia, Venezuela, and Bolivia all suffered from deep crises of governability and representation that created a consensus for the need for constitutional change. Could the old institutions carry it out? "Legalists" argue yes, and they place a particular emphasis on the legislature as the preferred agent for change.[9] Yet,

[8] Other works I would include in the legalist camp include Allan R. Brewer-Carias, *Asamblea Constituyente y Proces Constituyente 1999. Coleccion Tratado de Derecho Constitucional, Tomo VI* (Caracas: Fundación Editorial Juridica Venezolana, 2014); Allan R. Brewer-Carías, *Dismantling Democracy in Venezuela: The Chávez Authoritarian Experiment* (New York: Cambridge University Press, 2010); Jorge Lazarte, *Reforma del "experimento" constitucional en Bolivia: Claves de un nuevo modelo estatal y societal de derecho (para abrir un debate que nunca hubo)*, 2015; Daniela Salazar, "My Power in the Constitution" (unpublished manuscript, July 3, 2015). In Colombia, the most important legalist figure was presidential aide Humberto de La Calle. See his speech to the assembly, National Constituent Assembly, Report of the Plenary Session of May 3rd, 1991.

[9] William Partlett, "Elite Threat to Constitutional Transitions." David Landau places less stress than William Partlett on the advantages of Congress over constitutional assemblies Nonetheless,

in all three countries, Congress had repeatedly tried and failed to radically change the constitution through the amendment method. It failed because it lacked the necessary legitimacy to overcome the inevitable opposition that great change engenders. The Congresses were viewed as the corrupt tools of entrenched interests, whether it be the drug cartels in Colombia, oil barons in Venezuela, or the lords of the large landed estates in Bolivia. The Congresses were discredited actors; their popularity was at its nadir; Congress was the very problem that constitution-making would seek to fix.[10] The only actors with the legitimacy necessary to write new constitutions were elected constituent assemblies.

For "legalists," constituent assemblies are too dangerous because, through claims to embody the people, they can avoid all legal checks and controls on their power. What would David Landau or William Partlett replace the constituent power and assemblies with? In his article, "Abusive Constitutionalism," Landau slashes and burns through almost every possible solution to the very problem he raises. He ends on a near note of despair entitling his conclusion and almost accepting that the problems of popular constitution-making have set "An Impossible Agenda for Constitutional Theory?"[11]

Landau is on much stronger ground when he argues for achieving internal diversity within the constitution-making body, a solution that I endorse and discuss in more detail in the next chapter.[12] But Landau's suggestion is only a first step. To achieve diversity, the people's relationship to inclusion, law, and revolution must be retheorized. The populist presidents who seek majoritarian electoral rules have a principled argument, namely that empowering the majority is necessary to overthrow the old and "corrupt" regime and

---

Landau concludes that Congresses are preferable "because it may be easier for strongmen and other figures to control the timing of elections to extraordinary political assemblies than to ordinary legislatures because the timing of elections to the latter tends to be fixed. Landau, "Constitution-Making Gone Wrong," 967.

[10] For Venezuela, Miriam Kornblith, "Legitimacy and the Reform Agenda in Venezuela," in *Reinventing Legitimacy: Democracy and Political Change in Venezuela*, eds. Damarys J. Canache and Michael Kulisheck (Westport, CT: Praeger, 1998). For Bolivia, Carlos Romero Bonifaz, *El Proceso Constituyente Boliviano* (Santa Cruz: CEIJS, 2005), 155–237. On Colombia, Julieta Lemaitre Ripoll, *La Paz En Cuestión: La Guerra Y La Paz En La Asamblea Constituyente de 1991.* (Universidad de los Andes, 2014).

[11] Landau, "Abusive Constitutionalism," 259. In Landau's recent book with Rosalind Dixon, the co-authors express openness to several solutions for the dangers of constituent power, including the strategy of a "conceptual [re]-definition", a strategy I pursue in this book. Dixon and Landau, "Abusive Constitutional Borrowing," 199.

[12] Ibid., 973.

achieve a true revolution. Inclusion obstructs this change. From the point of view of insurgent majorities, minorities are oligarchs and counterrevolutionaries. Any attempt to diversify the constituent assembly to include these minorities must take on these arguments head-on. Some authors have taken steps in this direction by arguing that the constituent power is plural and must include everyone.[13] I agree, but this argument is insufficient to meet the threat of abusive constitutionalism. Since law helps to ensure inclusion, the redefinition must address the predominant argument that the constituent power is lawless. To address the tension between inclusion and new beginnings, we need a new theory of the relationship between law and the people.

William Partlett offers a different solution: drawing on examples from post-communist transition in Europe, the Caucasus, and central Asia, Partlett argues that parliaments are more deliberative and safer than the popular and irregular constitutional assemblies favored by constitutional theory.[14] Yet, there is a mismatch between Partlett's examples and the theory they are meant to disprove. In constitutional theory, such as in the work of Jon Elster or Joel Colón-Rios, extraordinary and elected constitutional assemblies are the most legitimate and deliberative way to draft a constitution. Partlett draws upon five different examples of popular constitution-making to disprove their theory, to show how popular participation destroyed deliberation and facilitated acts of abusive constitutionalism. But four of the examples have no constitutional assemblies at all.[15] In the fifth example of Russia, the Constituent Assembly was not elected, but appointed and was carefully controlled by the president.[16] These are examples of presidential and plebiscitarian constitution-making, not of the constituent assembly form that theorists of popular constitution-making support.

By contrast, freely elected constituent assemblies were the means to create five of the six new constitutions made after the end of the Cold War in South America.[17] In these cases, the record is mixed, with Venezuela and Ecuador excessively concentrating power in the executive while Bolivia and Colombia

---

[13] For these attempts to redefine the constituent power, see Colon-Rios, *Weak Constitutionalism*; Kim Lane Scheppele, "Unconstitutional Constituent Power," in Modern Constitutions (University of Pennsylvania Press, 2020), 154–206.

[14] William Partlett, "Elite Threat to Constitutional Transitions."

[15] Ibid., 433.

[16] Partlett, "Dangers of Popular Constitution-Making," 219.

[17] The exception is Peru in which President Fujimori led a coup against the Congress and the Judiciary but then had elections for a congress that would go on to both legislate and draft a new constitution.

produced constitutions that, by the region's standards, reasonably decentralize, check, and balance power.[18] This book attempts to bolster the conception of the people that justified the inclusive constitution-making process of the latter two countries.

Andrew Arato shares the legalists' desire for legal continuity, but unlike Landau or Partlett, he seeks to reconcile it with a constituent assembly to achieve transformative and democratic change. In Arato's "round-table" model, the legislature legally amends the constitution to provide rules for free elections to a constituent assembly. These election and other procedural rules are the result of a prior round-table meeting of all interested parties. The negotiations concern not only procedure for creating the constitution, but its substance as well. Before elections to the constitutional assembly, the round-table will grant to minorities, often those in power in the old regime, guarantees about the content of the new constitution to protect their interests.[19] The round-table model gives Arato the best of both worlds. On the one hand, continuity prevents violence and centralization, and, on the other hand, democratic legitimacy is achieved through the constitutional assembly.

I am sympathetic to Arato's model, but question its generalizability and its application to the Andes for three reasons. First, and this point is relevant to Partlett and Landau as well, legal amendment rules are not always a viable option. In Bolivia, Venezuela, and Colombia, the Congress tried to pass amendments to create legal constitutional assemblies, but the Congress lacked either the desire, will, legitimacy, or political capital necessary to achieve their goal. Furthermore, sometimes the amendment rule itself is too demanding. Think here of how the U.S. founding fathers violated the Articles of Confederation because it required the unanimity of all thirteen states for amendment, or as I discuss in 2005 Bolivia where the constitution required revolutionaries to wait at least four and a half years to legally initiate a process that was widely wanted.[20] Thus, unlike Arato, my model of extraordinary adaptation accepts that often illegality will be necessary to convene a constitutional assembly.

---

[18] For a ranking of executive, legislative, and judicial power in these and other countries, see Comparative Constitutions Project, "Constitution Rankings," available at http://comparativeconst itutionsproject.org/ccp-rankings/

[19] Arato, *Post Sovereign Constitution Making: Learning and Legitimacy.*

[20] See Akhil Reed Amar, *America's Constitution: A Biography* (New York: Random House Trade Paperbacks, 2006), 27.Pauline Maier, *Ratification: The People Debate the Constitution, 1787–1788* (New York: Simon & Schuster, 2011), 11, 28, 457–59.

Second, in Arato's model everyone is willing to negotiate in good faith due to a particular balance of power between opposing sides. The balance creates a stalemate in which the minority possesses the coercive apparatus of the state but lacks popular legitimacy. The majority has the opposite dilemma: it has the support of most citizens, and perhaps even the international community, but to achieve power by force it would have to face-off against a well-equipped army. Thus, it is in both parties' interests to negotiate a peaceful transition.[21] This was not the situation in post-Cold War Colombia, Venezuela, Ecuador, and Bolivia. Insurgent majorities had won the presidencies and many seats in Congress. Minorities could still obstruct their plans, but majorities had powerful tools to overcome their opposition. Thus, the majority had greater incentives to try and impose their majority will.

Third, Arato's model depends upon the majority party having a post-revolutionary consciousness. The origins of Arato's model lie in cases of constitution-making in Central and Eastern Europe, where the participants had suffered under the revolutionary ideology of the Soviet Union. Naturally, they would be more receptive to approaches geared to rejecting the pathologies of revolution. For that reason, participants and theorists refused to call 1989 a "normal" revolution. They experimented with a variety of names to try to capture the contradiction of a non-revolutionary revolution: it was a "velvet" revolution, a "refolution," a "gentle revolution," a "negative revolution," or a "self-limiting" one.[22] By contrast, in the Andes region, radicals invoked a revolution without qualifiers, and they connected it to its long history in Latin America and in the world. President Hugo Chávez, Rafael Correa, and Evo Morales allied themselves with Fidel Castro because they sought to continue the revolutionary tradition and reform it for the twenty-first century.

Recently, in response to revolutions in the Andes and in the Middle East, Arato has sought to show how the round-table model might fit a revolutionary situation.[23] But the push for a constituent assembly is a reflection of the long and robust tradition of constituent power in South America, especially in Venezuela, Bolivia, Colombia, and Ecuador. Constituent power is part of these countries' DNA. Even in the unlikely event that the academic

[21] Arato, "Conventions, Constituent Assemblies, and Round Tables," 195.

[22] Andrew Arato, Civil Society, Constitution, and Legitimacy (Lanham, MD: Rowman & Littlefield Publishers, 2000), 12, 81, 97.

[23] Andrew Arato, The Adventures of the Constituent Power: Beyond Revolutions? (Cambridge: Cambridge University Press, 2017)..

literature reached near-consensus that the constituent power was a pernicious idea, it would not end these countries' more than two-hundred-year
tradition embedded in countless treatises, speeches, and pamphlets.[24] The
centrality of constituent power is not open for debate there. The best intervention is not over whether constituent power is a good idea, but over
what constituent power consists in.[25] Once we realize that the constituent
assembly is the only viable option, we can turn from the legalist cataloging of
legal violations to formulating how to structure the process to avoid its worst
pathologies.

David Landau and William Partlett draw attention to the disasters of constituent assemblies. But these were not Colombia, Venezuela, or Bolivia's
first try. They were responses to years, even decades in Colombia's case, of
mounting frustration with the conventional reform paths. In all three, even
though there was a widespread consensus about the need for constitutional
change, Congress had been unable to achieve it. In 2002 Bolivia, the lower
house of Congress's passage of the "constitutional amendments for citizen
participation" spurred an indigenous and peasant march around the country
against the "neoliberal" amendments by "corrupt oligarchs." The Congress
tried to incorporate the protesters' demands, but ultimately squabbling over
other matters doomed the project.[26] In Venezuela, Congress failed in both
1992 and 1994 because of media opposition to the proposed regulations
and because of opposition to Congress's role in the process.[27] Lastly, the
Colombian Congress tried and failed to significantly amend the constitution five times, once each in 1977, 1979, 1983, 1986, and three times in
1988, before finally deciding to convene a constituent assembly in 1991.[28]

---

[24] See Gerardo Pisarello, *Procesos Constituyentes: Caminos para la Ruptura Democrática* (Trotta,
2013); Pedro Vega Garcia, *La Reforma Constitucional Y La Problemática Del Poder Constituyente*
(Tecnos, 1985).

[25] Critics do have an important role in discouraging the adoption of constituent power by some
countries who lack that tradition and also lack a tradition of liberal democracy. Without some
institutions of liberal democracy, the constituent power is far more dangerous. See Partlett, "Danger
of Constitution-Making," 202, 222.

[26] Carlos Romero Bonifaz, *El Proceso Constituyente* Boliviano, 155–237; Gustavo Rodríguez
Ostria, "Marco Histórico: La Larga Marcha a la Asamblea Constiuyente," in *Enciclopedia Histórica
Documental del Proceso Constituyente Boliviano*, ed. Juan Carlos Pinto Quintanilla, vol. 1 (Estado
Plurinacional de Bolivia: 2009), 108–23.

[27] Kornblith, "Legitimacy and the Reform Agenda in Venezuela," 13–15.

[28] In Colombia, there were seven failed attempts at constitutional reform. Five followed legalist formulas in which Congress was the key actor, but the first two attempts by Barco in 1988
tried to bypass Congress by disregarding the traditional amendment method in favor of referendums. John Dugas, *Explaining Democratic Reform in Colombia: The Origins of the 1991 Constitution*
(Bloomington: Indiana University Press, 1997), 267–303.

The previous attempts were defeated either by the courts or internal political division. Although written about Venezuela, Miriam Kornblith's words capture well the problem in all three countries, "The main political problem facing constitutional reform executed through Congress continued to be its extreme dependence on the intellectual, political and mobilizing capacity of the political parties, at a time when their legitimacy as leaders and representatives is seriously weakened and questioned." All three countries tried various method of legal amendment, and in all three it failed. New institutions, specifically constituent assemblies, were necessary to accomplish long-sought constitutional reform.

Popular Participation and Change

The argument for constituent power is not only a pragmatic one about breaking gridlocks but also a normative one. It is a powerful tool of inclusion and mobilization for the excluded to achieve significant change. David Landau fails to appreciate this because his argument suffers from a status quo bias. For Landau, if the status quo is stable, it should be preserved. As Landau states, his "conception of constitution-making views it as an essentially preservative rather than a transformative process."[29]

What would legalism preserve in the Andes? For hundreds of years, the underclass of the indigenous and workers have suffered immense stigma and discrimination. Inequalities of wealth in South America have long been among the worst in the entire world, fueling class prejudice. Adding insult upon injury, the 1990s saw the beginning of a decade of neoliberal policies and corruption that shredded the social safety net, eviscerated the workers' movement, and exacerbated long-standing inequality. The status quo was unjust. It was rightly changed, not preserved.

To disrupt the status quo, disorder is necessary, even desirable. Let's briefly focus on Bolivia to illuminate the role of disorder in achieving change. Before Evo Morales won the 2005 election by historic margins and became Bolivia's first indigenous president, the country had suffered five years of destabilizing protest. The blockades and marches drained the country's GDP and created many martyrs for the cause. This disorder was perhaps just as destabilizing as the constitution-making process that Landau condemns. But the actors

[29] Landau, "Constitution-Making Gone Wrong," 926.

were fully aware of the cost and were willing to pay it to pursue change. These moments of protest, nationally remembered as the "water and october wars" and consecrated in the preamble to the Bolivian Constitution are now among the proudest in Bolivian history because individuals sacrificed and suffered to achieve a more just future.[30] The constitutional process did not break a preexisting harmonious peace but was one more step in a long, disruptive, and agonizing process of the indigenous and peasant movements to retake their country.

Once we understand that tumult and change must go hand in hand, we can see that Landau's excessive concern for order has blinded him to the success of the Bolivian constitution-making process. For Landau, the example is a case of "constitution-making gone wrong" and "constitutional breakdown." But unlike his diagnosis in Venezuela, Landau does not conclude that it led to a more highly centralized constitutional order. Instead, he concludes that the new constitution "helped to unify the country and reduce regional tensions" and that "the process appears to have taught Morales and his supporters a considerable amount about governing."[31] Indeed, by the standards of the region and its own history, Bolivia has a fairly decentralized constitution with checks and balances.

Landau's problem, then, is not with the substance of the Bolivian Constitution, but with the unsightly process it took to get there. No one would call it pretty. The process was dangerous, agonizing, and even bloody. It demonstrates what activists all around the world already know: change requires sacrifice and is never achieved without conflict. In the Andes region, the idea of the people mobilized the excluded to retake their countries. It was a means of gaining dignity amidst poverty, of gaining agency amidst despair.

I agree with legalists that the idea of the people poses immense dangers and that addressing them should be a priority. We differ, however, on whether addressing these dangers entails abandoning the participatory ideals of constitution-making. I deny that this trade-off is necessary or even viable. Rather than give up on the idea of the people, I re-conceive it so that it breaks

---

[30] Several excellent books tell and in many ways glorify this story. Forrest Hylton and Adolfo Gilly, *Revolutionary Horizons: Past and Present in Bolivian Politics*, 1st ed. (London: Verso, 2007); Raquel Gutiérrez Aguilar, *Rhythms of the Pachakuti: Indigenous Uprising and State Power in Bolivia*, trans. Stacey Alba D. Skar (Durham: Duke University Press Books, 2014); Jeffery R. Webber, *Red October: Left-Indigenous Struggles in Modern Bolivia*, Repr. ed. (Chicago, IL: Historical Materialism, 2012).

[31] Landau, "Constitution-Making Gone Wrong," 958. Landau also seems to embrace aspects of the the Bolivian process as well: he concludes that the more proportional electoral system prevented the majority MAS from dominating the assembly. Ibid.

the gridlock over constitutional reform, so that it addresses the pent-up demand for popular processes to create a new constitution without degenerating into chaos or authoritarianism.

RADICAL PROPONENTS OF THE CONSTITUENT POWER

Radicals seek rapid and large-scale upheaval and transformation, but they differ widely in the new order they seek and the means by which to achieve it. Here, I explore one subset of radicals, the radical proponents of the constituent power or those who turn to the idea of a lawless and unified people to achieve their revolution. For this group of radicals, law is the old regime's means of domination. It is created by and privileges the oppressor and enslaves the people. The people must break the chains of law so that they can establish a new regime. But there is a problem: in a lawless vacuum, there is no method to identify who belongs to the people and when they have acted.

The radicals' solution—whether for supporters of a strong central state like Thomas Hobbes, Emmanuel Sieyès, and Carl Schmitt or for decentralizers like Karl Marx and Sheldon Wolin—is to conjure up a unified people. A unified people has agency so that it may, just like an individual, make decisions that are attributable to it. To be an agent, the people must be one. With unity, there is no need for law to recognize whose voice is authoritative. But the solution of unity raises new questions. How is this unity forged? How do diverse individuals split along the seemingly endless lines of interest and identities become one? How does the multitude become a people?

Drawing upon the work of Carl Schmitt, I argue that after Hobbes, theorists of the people usually forge popular unity by using the two categories of the friend-enemy relationship and top-down representation.[32] In the

[32] Thomas Hobbes and Emmanuel Sieyès are the originators of the dominant tradition in political thought about the antithetical relationship of the law and the people that runs through Jean-Jacques Rousseau, Alexis de Tocqueville, Karl Marx, Vladimir Lenin, and Sheldon Wolin. I do not want to oversimply the tradition, so some clarifications are in order. Not all members of the tradition are friends of the people: some, such as De Tocqueville, are anti-revolutionary and would like to bury the idea of the people as a singular agent capable of action. In Toqueville's case, he would replace it with decentralized spaces that never add up to a single people. See Bryan Garsten, "From Popular Sovereignty to Civil Society in Post-Revolutionary France," in *Popular Sovereignty in Historical Perspective*, eds. Richard Bourke and Quentin Skinner (Cambridge: Cambridge University Press, 2016). Most political theorists are irrelevant to the tradition as they are not theorists of the people as an active agent: some of them never discuss the issue at all, while others argue that the idea of the people is illusory. The ancients are not part of this tradition. Daniela Cammack, "The Dêmos in Dêmokratia," *The Classical Quarterly* 69, no. 1 (May 2019), 42–61. Of course, not all thinkers who wrote about the constituent power embraced it as a lawless unity. There are important exceptions

former, the theorist identifies an essential quality among a subset of the population as the basis for their unity and excludes from their body those who lack it. Next, in top-down representation the theorist identifies a singular site through which the people speak because it embodies them completely.

These two criteria are similar to those used in the large and sprawling literature on populism.[33] But my work has a shift in emphasis so that it focuses not only on politics but also on political theory. Populism scholars focus on how the language of populism helps political actors achieve their goals, most often executives seeking to centralize power or political and social movements on the streets seeking to mobilize their constituencies. I share this concern, but I also believe that these methods of forging popular unity are deeply embedded within a radical tradition of political theory. This "radical" tradition is responding, not only instrumentally to political events, but also to a set of genuine and deep theoretical issues these events raise, namely the problem of popular agency in moments of constitution-making. An effective response to radicals must address itself to the same set of problems.

While Schmitt's criteria are a useful starting-off point for analyzing the radical tradition, I also depart from him. Indeed, the project is an effort to discredit the entire radical project of which Schmitt is a culmination and perversion. But my differences also concern his overly stylized reading of the history of political thought. Schmitt coined the two categories of the friend-enemy relationship and top-down representation, the two categories through which I read much of the radical tradition of popular sovereignty. Yet, in the context of the people his analysis of the categories, in his treatise *Constitutional Theory*, are no longer than a few pages, and scholars have given them little attention.[34] In the relevant passage, Schmitt speaks

to tradition, such as John Locke, the Marquis de Condorcet, and James Madison, though Madison's thinking on the subject is underdeveloped. Nonetheless, my claim is a broad one: the dominant tradition in political theory understands the people as lawless and therefore as a revolutionary force. I call these thinkers "radicals" of the constituent power.

[33] For an overview of the literature on populism, Jane Mansbridge and Stephen Macedo, "Populism and Democratic Theory," *Annual Review of Law and Social Science* 15, no. 1 (2019), 59. For a discussion on populism in the constitutional context, Paul Blokker, "Populism as a Constitutional Project," *International Journal of Constitutional Law* 17, no. 2 (June 28, 2019), 536; Ming-Sung Kuo, "Against Instantaneous Democracy," *International Journal of Constitutional Law* 17, no. 2 (June 28, 2019), 554–75; Mark Tushnet and Bojan Bugaric, *Power to the People: Constitutionalism in the Age of Populism* (New York: Oxford University Press, 2021).

[34] Schmitt, of course, does write at great length about the friend-enemy relationship. Yet, this is in the context of defining the political, not as the basis for conceiving of the people. Aside from *Constitutional Theory*, his most relevant comments on the friend-enemy relationship in the context of the people are in the *Crisis of Parliamentary Democracy*, although there the explicit topic is democracy. I discuss *Crisis* in the below section on Schmitt.

about the categories as ontological truths and does not use them as a lens to understand other theorists of the people. Insofar as he engages with these theorists, his readings are often tendentious, flattening all previous theorists into holding a singular position whose full truth is only revealed in Schmitt's work. I deepen Schmitt's analysis by closely and carefully reading and showing the differences between Thomas Hobbes, Jean-Jacques Rousseau, Emmanuel Sieyès, Karl Marx, and Vladimir Lenin.

While all of these thinkers embrace the idea of the people as a lawless unity, they differ on the means and ends of that unity. Hobbes plants the seed of the tradition, but it is not yet fully developed in his work because he believes the people would achieve unity through rational and unanimous consent. Sieyès fully inaugurates the tradition by forging the unity of the people through positing a friend-enemy relationship between the Third Estate and the nobility and then claiming that through top-down representation, the Constitutional Assembly would embody the unity of the Third Estate. Later theorists varied the identity of the friend, enemy, and representer, but that basic framework remained the same from here on out for most political theorists of a revolutionary people. What differentiates Schmitt in this tradition is that he believes there is no fundamental truth as to who the friend, enemy, or representer are. Rather, he merely wants to identify whichever filler will, based on its widespread acceptance, best unify the people, and in his era that was ethnic nationalism.

While most theorists post-Hobbes rely on the same abstract categories to forge unity, they still differ on its ends. Hobbes and Sieyès were statists: the people's sovereignty could serve as the basis to legitimate and centralize all power in the modern state to instill domestic order and defeat external enemies. Radical democrats like Marx, Lenin, and Wolin sought to use a unified people for the exact opposite ends: to tear down the state to restore power to individuals and communities. Just as Hobbes and Sieyès would have predicted and desired, such unity strengthened rather than weakened the state. Radical democrats call upon the people to achieve freedom, but the substitute of unity re-enslaves them.

What is the relationship between these European theorists to the dilemmas of constitution-making in South America? South America participates and innovates within the same concept of constituent power, whose origins lie in debates in England and France that were then transmitted to South America in its wars of independence in the early nineteenth century. Today in the region, Sieyès, who coined the term constituent power, is still identified and cited as the central thinker of the concept.[35] Over the last two hundred years in the Andes, the idea of a lawless constituent power has been sanctified in countless speeches, pamphlets, and treatises.[36] To understand South American constitution-making, one must understand this common political vocabulary and its accompanying basic and inevitable dilemmas that appear whenever the people is invoked as an agent of revolution.

My contribution, however, goes beyond South America. The continent's experiences provide a stepping stone for rethinking the concept of constituent power writ large. South America is the continent where the idea of the Constituent Power remains the most influential. Even as the end of the Cold War and the failure of communism in the Soviet Union had left most Europeans disillusioned with the idea of revolution, the exact opposite has occurred in the Andes where it has flourished. South American theorists and actors draw upon a theoretical vocabulary, born from European experience, but refract it differently through new contexts. The same terms come to take on different meanings, and new ones are coined. South American ideas and experiences are the foundation for a new theory of constituent power.

Centralizers: Thomas Hobbes and Emanuel Sieyès

For Thomas Hobbes and Emanuel Sieyès, the people and centralization are inextricably intertwined. The feudal arrangements divided power among a dizzying array of guilds, families, and estates. As we'll see, for centralizers of the radical constituent power, this division was a source of chaos, weakness, and inefficiency. They concentrated power by placing it in one site: the people. The people's sovereignty could serve as the basis to legitimate the modern state. But how would this singular people be constructed within an order based on myriad and fixed social distinctions?

This question did not arise for adherents to the medieval or feudal order. For them, understanding the existence of the people was simple. The people were a concrete fact: they were the poor and the propertyless. They vied for power with the aristocrats and the monarchs. Each of these classes

---

[35] See, for example, the discussion of Sieyés in the Venezuelan Supreme Court opinion that permitted an extralegal referendum on whether to hold elections to a constituent assembly, Corte Suprema de Justicia [C.S.J.] [Supreme Court], Sala. Politico Administrativa enero 19, 1999, M.P. H. La Roche, revista del derecho PuBlico (Nos. 77–80, p. 56).

[36] Pisarello, *Procesos Constituyentes*, 10–55.

had a common interest and attributes. Each group laid a claim to rule, and theorists classified the regimes and outlined their character based on which socioeconomic group succeeded in this struggle. Each class's regime had its own vices that led to its regime's decay and destruction. Theorists of mixed government believed that they could solve this instability by having the different classes share power in one regime. A properly calibrated mixed regime would draw on the virtues and dampen the dangers of each class's particular form of rule.[37]

Hobbes lived within a mixed regime, the feudal order of seventeenth-century England, and in it he saw only chaos.[38] He listed mixed government as one of the "internal causes which tend to dissolve a commonwealth,"[39] writing that "if there had not first been an opinion received of the greatest part of *England*, that these powers were divided between the King, and the Lords, and the House of Commons, the people had never been divided and fallen into civil war."[40] The problem for the mixed regime and for polities in general was disagreement. Humans are quarrelsome; they disagree about the good life, about when danger is present, and how best to address it. Giving each group complete power over a different branch of government arms them for a battle over these different beliefs. In the mixed regime, each estate differs on fundamental issues, such as during the English civil war on "the liberty of Religion," and there was no one body to settle which view prevailed.[41] Without an ultimate arbiter, the system was subject to perpetual breakdown.

Hobbes sought to use a new conception of the people to give government a center, an ultimate authority whose word would be final. In this new order, the idea that "sovereign power can be divided [would be] a *seditious opinion*."[42] Whereas in the feudal regime, the people were a discrete part or class, the new people would include everyone.[43]

[37] McIlwain, *Constitutionalism*; Arihiro Fukuda, *Sovereignty and the Sword: Harrington, Hobbes, and Mixed Government in the English Civil Wars* (Oxford: Oxford University Press, 1997), 22–38. For ancient discussions of mixed government, Plato, *Republic*, ed. C.D.C. Reeve, trans. G.M.A. Grube, 2nd ed. (Indianapolis: Hackett Publishing Company, Inc., 1992); Aristotle, *Politics: Second Edition*, ed. Carnes Lord, 2nd ed. (Chicago: University Of Chicago Press, 2013); Polybius, *The Complete Histories of Polybius*, trans. W.R. Paton (Digireads.com, 2009).

[38] Arihiro Fukuda, *Sovereignty and the Sword*, 38–41.

[39] Thomas Hobbes, *Hobbes: On the Citizen*, eds. Richard Tuck and Michael Silverthorne (New York: Cambridge University Press, 1998).

[40] Thomas Hobbes, *Leviathan: With Selected Variants from the Latin Edition of 1668*, ed. Edwin Curley, Underlined, Notations ed. (Indianapolis: Hackett Publishing Company, 1994).

[41] Hobbes, *Leviathan*, 116.

[42] Hobbes, *On the Citizen*, 131.

[43] At least nearly everyone. Hobbes acknowledges that a few people will not sign the social contract and thus are enemies. Hobbes, *Leviathan*, 112. So too are foreign nations and criminals enemies. For further thoughts, see notes 63 and 96.

To achieve it, to break free of the feudal order, the people would have to be constructed outside of the current legal regime and outside of law itself. In the state of nature, this new people might be constructed. Hobbes asked his readers to imagine a world in which there was no government and everyone was an individual and equal; no social or legal distinction applied. For this world's inhabitants, the state of nature was a nightmare, a life that was "nasty, brutish, and short."[44] For Hobbes' reader, however, imagining the state of nature was an act of mental liberation to help realize his or her own interests. It liberated the individual reader from his or her attachment to particular groups or institutions that blinded them to reason and the common good. It was a thought experiment in which from "the very shadows of a doubt a thread of reason ... begins, by whose guidance [he] shall escape to the clearest light."[45]

Not only had Hobbes stripped away all social and legal distinctions, he also denies any significant differences in strength, intelligence, and interests. All are fundamentally the same: all have the fundamental motive of self-preservation, and all are equally threatened by the immediate and grave prospect of death. To survive and escape chaos, individuals rationally choose to enter into a social contract in which each agrees to obey the majority vote in all matters. Hobbes calls this majority, this new creation, "the people," and it has all power.[46]

Hobbes's social contract is not an agreement between distinct individuals with their own opinions and interests. Rather, it is based upon the homogeneity and rationality of individuals in the state of nature. Hobbes puts it best: the contract is "more than consent or concord; it is a real unity of them all, one and the same person."[47] As with all radicals, Hobbes's unity is achieved by positing a foundational and lawless commonality that outweighs and erases plurality.

Let us go into a little more detail about the transformation from the state of nature into the establishment of a people and state. Following the approach of Richard Tuck, I draw primarily on Hobbes's earlier work of *On the Citizen* rather than *The Leviathan* because only the former explicitly has a role for the people as a collective agent.[48] In *On the Citizen* and unlike later theorists of

---

[44] Hobbes, *Leviathan*, 76.

[45] Hobbes, *On the Citizen*, 5.

[46] Hobbes, *On the Citizen*, 77.

[47] Hobbes, *Leviathan*, 109.

[48] Indeed, *Leviathan* seems to deny that the people exist at all. The actors are individuals, the state, and the sovereign. Individuals, not the people, contract to establish the state and the sovereign. Unlike in *On the Citizen*, when the sovereign acts, he is not the people, but the representation

the constituent power, Hobbes's people are not a collective agent that exists before the creation of the state or constitution. In the state of nature, there are only individuals. Hobbes writes, "Prior to the formation of a common-wealth a People does not exist, since it was not then a person but a crowd of individual persons"[49] who lacks agency; it is impossible to attribute any action to this "crowd as *their action.*" If they all act together, it is still the re-flection of each individual's will. It cannot "make a promise or an agreement, acquire or transfer a right, do, have possess, and so on, except separately or as an individuals, so that there are as many promises, agreements, rights and actions as there are men."[50] However, after contracting the people become sovereign: "In every commonwealth the *People Reigns.*"

For Hobbes, the acts of the state are identical with the people: "[W]henever we say that a People or a number [of men] is willing, commanding or doing something, we mean a commonwealth which is commanding, willing and acting through the will of one man or through the wills of several men who are in agreement."[51] The first state, created with the unanimous consent of the people, must be democratic. At this early stage, whatever the majority of the democratic assembly vote for is what the people command.[52] Later, the people may choose to permanently alienate their sovereignty to a group of aristocrats or kings whose acts will then become the acts of the people.[53]

Although individual citizens have exited the state of nature, the state, which embodies the people, continues to reside in it. Whereas as in the state of nature, each individual was his own absolute judge on what measures were necessary for survival, now too the state is free to pursue any measure nec-essary for its own survival. This gives it power to regulate public debate and

---

of the state. Q. Skinner, "Hobbes and the Purely Artificial Person of the State," *Journal of Political Philosophy* 7, no. 1 (Mar. 1, 1999); Quentin Skinner, "Hobbes on Representation," *European Journal of Philosophy* 13, no. 2 (Aug. 1, 2005), 155–184. For a different reading of the exact relationship be-tween the multitude, state, and sovereign in *Leviathan* that nonetheless is consistent with it lacking a role for the people, David Runciman, "What Kind of Person Is Hobbes's State? A Reply to Skinner," *Journal of Political Philosophy* 8, no. 2 (June 1, 2000), 268–78. However, Murray Forsyth argues that the kernel of the idea of the people as a constituent power, as collective agent predating the existence of the state, is present in *Leviathan*. Forsyth's challenge is to counter the point that the social contract is established by individuals, not by a collective agent. Murray Forsyth, "Thomas Hobbes and the Constituent Power of the People," *Political Studies* 29, no. 2 (1981), 191–203.

[49] Hobbes, *On the Citizen*, 95.
[50] Ibid., 76.
[51] Ibid., 77.
[52] Ibid., 94.
[53] Hobbes, *On the Citizen*, 94–101. For an interesting discussion of how for Hobbes the people can be embodied by a small group of aristocrats or by a king, Richard Tuck, *The Sleeping Sovereign: The Invention of Modern Democracy* (Cambridge: Cambridge University Press, 2016).

religious doctrine; to declare and send individuals to war, and to redistribute property to ensure that individuals have the basics necessary for survival.[54] The absence of law is necessary for the creation of the people, and after their birth they persist outside of it. Although in the new sovereign state individuals are strictly bound by the law, the people continue to reside in their birthplace, in the state of nature. The lawless state of nature breeds absolutism.

Discussions of popular sovereignty, especially in relation to the French Revolution, often begin with Jean-Jacque Rousseau's *The Social Contract*, but his theory of the general will retains the basic radical framework established by Hobbes. Like Hobbes, Rousseau begins with homogenous individuals contracting in the state of nature to agree to abide by the majority vote, and this vote births the sovereign. After this initial and foundational state is completed, Rousseau makes two alterations to the Hobbesian foundation.[55] First, sovereignty becomes unalienable. In *De Cive*, Hobbes believed that the first contract births democracy or rule by the majority in an assembly. However, that assembly can alienate its sovereignty to a group of aristocrats or a king who may at a future date again alienate sovereignty. Rousseau believed this alienation to be "absurd and inconceivable" and that "[t]o say [this] of a whole people is to assume a people of madmen; madness does not make right."[56] The democratic assembly, composed of all members of the polity, would never give up its power so that according to Rousseau it should be that once a democracy always a democracy.

Second, whereas the Hobbesian sovereign can commit any type of act it wants, Rousseau believed that the people or general will could not execute or administer laws.[57] For Hobbes, pragmatic concerns will likely lead the sovereign to make general rules and then appoint individuals to interpret and execute them. However, the sovereign can choose at any time to instruct his subordinates exactly how to carry out his will or he can do so personally. His subordinates have no independence from him. Rousseau disagreed. Whereas Hobbes only sought to use the people to achieve order, Rousseau believed that the people embodied the public good, that they "could not err."[58] Rousseau connected the public good with generality. If the people

---

[54] Richard Tuck, *Hobbes: A Very Short Introduction* (Oxford: Oxford University Press, 2002), 80–8.

[55] For a similar account of the differences between Hobbes and Rousseau, Tuck, *The Sleeping Sovereign*, 124–42.

[56] Jean-Jacques Rousseau, *The Social Contract: And Other Later Political Writings*, trans. Victor Gourevitch (New York: Cambridge University Press, 1996).

[57] Ibid., 82–86.

[58] Ibid., 59.

tried to resolve particular disputes or execute the law, those affected would know that the decision reflects "nothing but a foreign, particular will which on this occasion is inclined to injustice and subject to error."[59] Therefore, to maintain the general will, the people, at regular intervals and composed of all assembled citizens, should limit itself to passing very general laws, choosing the form of government that would administer those laws, and electing that government's officeholders.[60] Rousseau's changes are crucial in the history of political thought, but they are not alterations to the basic Hobbesian framework of constructing the people as a lawless unity.

Later political theorists turned away from these hypothetical thought experiments featuring rational individuals. These theorists were embedded in and more directly addressed themselves to real political conflicts.[61] They were members of assemblies, committees, soviets, and secret societies. They contended with internal disagreements and external opposition. Unlike in the state of nature, in real politics, individuals are irrational and decline to give up their power to follow their enlightened self-interest. Unanimous consent is impossible, and conflict is inevitable. In these clashes, how can the people be forged? How can the "social contract be brought down to earth"?[62] These new theorists kept the foundations of Hobbes: the people were still outside law, and they still gained agency through unity. What changed was how this unity was constructed.[63]

---

[59] Ibid., 62.

[60] Ibid., 117. Our normal categories of executive and legislative do not match exactly onto Rousseau's thought. Our legislature's laws are far too detailed to satisfy Rousseau's criterion of generality. Indeed, much of the work of Rousseau's government would today be considered legislative. Frank Marini, "Popular Sovereignty but Representative Government: The Other Rousseau," *Midwest Journal of Political Science* 11, no. 4 (1967), 451–70.

[61] Of course, current political events influenced Hobbes, but his writings were less direct and more philosophical than Emmanuel Sieyès or Carl Schmitt. Nor did Hobbes play as direct a role in political events. I discuss the difference in more detail at the beginning of this chapter's discussion of Sieyès.

[62] The phrase is from Murray Forsyth, *Reason and Revolution: The Political Thought of the Abbé Sieyès* (Leicester: Leicester University Press, 1987), 54.

[63] I want to be precise here about how the two innovations of the friend-enemy distinction and top-down representation shift away from Hobbes. Both the enemy and representation are prominent themes in Hobbes's work, but the role they play is fundamentally different. First, there is no expulsion or destruction of an enemy by a group of friends in Hobbes. In the state of nature there are no friends and no groups; all are individuals and all are enemies. Unlike revolutionaries, Hobbes does not seek to heighten hatred of the enemy but rather to dissolve all friend-enemy relations. Whereas revolutionaries will call upon the people to destroy their enemies, the first law of nature for Hobbes is to seek peace. Through the social contract, all or nearly all citizens declare a truce in which they are neither friend nor enemies. To be sure, enemies still exist because individuals will break laws and foreign states lie outside the contract. He even declares that the few stray individuals who refuse to sign the social contract are an enemy. Hobbes, *Leviathan*, 112. But those individuals are not *necessary* for the social contract. It would be preferable if all signed it. Ultimately, the Hobbesian people is a nearly all inclusive entity that is formed through consent, not by setting itself against an enemy.

Post-Hobbesian theorists of the people turned to two innovations to construct the people: (a) exclusion based on the friend-enemy relation and (b) top-down representation.[64] In the first, a group identifies itself as universal, as the true embodiment of the general interest. Members are all friends and those who fundamentally differ from the group are an enemy. The enemy, the largest site of disagreement, is excluded from decision-making. But this is not enough to achieve unity; even "friends" disagree. That leads to the second step in which one part of the friend group is identified as representing the interests of all of them. It is both from and above them. From above, it can impose its will as the will of all. In a sense, it is not representative because they unproblematically embody and forge the people. Its decisions are the decisions of the people and those who disagree are wrong about its will.[65] These two combined maneuvers of exclusion and representation expel discord from the people. Indeed, in Chapter Three on Venezuela and Ecuador and in Chapter Five on Bolivia, I show how, consistent with the work of these radical theorists, Hugo Chávez, Rafael Correa, and Evo Morales all tried to forge a unified people through positing a friend/enemy distinction—specifically the urban poor vs. rich oil barons in Venezuela, the citizen vs.

In making this point about differences on the friend-enemy distinction between Hobbes and Schmitt, I build on Leo Strauss's essay. Leo Strauss, "Notes on Carl Schmitt, The Concept of the Political," in *The Concept of the Political: Expanded Edition*, rev. ed. (Chicago: The University of Chicago Press, 2007). For a thorough accounting of the friend-enemy relationship in Hobbes, Ioannis D. Evrigenis, *Fear of Enemies and Collective Action* (Cambridge: Cambridge University Press, 2007).

Second, although representation is prominent in Hobbes's story, it plays no role in the actual creation of the people. Each individual chooses to sign the social contract. No one does it on their behalf. Representation is important *after* the social contract in which an all-powerful sovereign comes to be the people. At this stage, whoever is sovereign—whether it be a single individual king, a small clique of aristocrats, or an open democratic assembly—is the people. However, the social contract itself that establishes the people is an act of individual consent. Consent, not representation, is necessary for the construction of the people. And even after the construction of the people, at the point at which they may act, the role of representation may be quite limited. The first form of government is a democracy where the assembled people, by majority vote, have sovereign control. This is a form of representation: the majority becomes representative of the people as a whole. Yet, this representation is far removed from later radicals' attempt to empower a small group or even an individual to embody the people. Whereas in Hobbes, representation entails that individuals may be outvoted, later radicals rob most individuals of any vote at all. Tuck, *The Sleeping Sovereign*, 106-111.

[64] These two categories come from Carl Schmitt's treatise, *Constitutional Theory*. Schmitt asserts these categories as the correct way to understand the construction of the people. However, for the most part he does not use them to analyze other theorists. That contribution is my own. The exception is Schmitt's use of the friend-enemy relationship to analyze Marxism and Sorel in *Crisis of Parliamentary Democracy*. Carl Schmitt, *Constitutional Theory*, trans. Jeffrey Seitzer (Durham: Duke University Press, 2008), 239–49. Carl Schmitt, *Crisis of Parliamentary Democracy*, trans. Ellen Kennedy (Cambridge, MA: The MIT Press, 1988), 51–77.

[65] In her classic work, Hanna Pitkin calls this the fascistic theory of representation, Hanna F. Pitkin, *The Concept of Representation* (Berkeley: University of California Press, 1972), 107–09.

the oligarch in Ecuador, and the indigenous vs. the mestizos in Bolivia—and through the top-down representation of a constituent assembly.

In the political theory cannon, Hobbes may have been the first to confront the problem of how to construct a unified people, but Emanuel Sieyès was one of the first to confront it in the context of real politics. Hobbes was reacting to and wished to influence current events, but he pitched his appeal at a high level of abstraction and appealed to the generic and individual reader's reason. By contrast, nearly all of Sieyès writings are concrete and topical; they were geared toward taking an action in response to constitutional events and crises. More specifically, Sieyès's most famous work on constituent power was written against the backdrop of a raging debate over the proper representation of the three different classes of mixed government in France. As a member of that government, he identified the Third Estate as the true people, the nobles as the enemy, and the Constituent Assembly purged of nobles as the representative tool in order to construct the unified will of the people.

Like Hobbes, Sieyès wanted a powerful centralized state to preserve peace, improve welfare, and defend against foreign attacks.[66] The countervailing and overlapping powers of the mixed government were inefficient and an impediment to these goals. As has been repeated often, the central feature of the modern state is its monopoly on force, but Sieyès and Hobbes also believed that the government that represented the state had to be unified; it had to have a "single, *unified* will."[67] One will had to be able to arrive rationally at a final decision and ensure its implementation. Anything else would be inefficient and stoke unnecessary conflict. As a political actor, Sieyès fought hard against any constitutional design that would hamper the formation of common wills, such as instructions, federalism, an executive veto, referendums, and checks and balances. At the root of government, there had to be the single unified will of the people in order for the state to act energetically to achieve its end. The unification of power in the people would buttress and legitimize a powerful central state.

But in late eighteenth-century France, there was no people, only feudal divisions. Sieyès also follows the Hobbesian strategy of overcoming them by

[66] Forsyth, *Reason and Revolution*, 140.

[67] Emmanuel Joseph Sieyès, "What Is the Third Estate?," in *Political Writings: Including the Debate between Sieyès and Tom Paine in 1791*, ed. Michael Sonenscher (Indianapolis: Hackett Publishing Co., 2003).

finding the people in the Hobbesian state of nature. From this site, they may be able establish a new order. Sieyès states:

> Every nation on earth has to be taken as if it is like an isolated individual outside all social ties or, as it is said, in a state of nature. The exercise of their will is free and independent of all civil forms. Since they exist only in the natural order, their will needs only to have the *natural* character of a will to produce all its effects. However a nation may will, it is enough for it to will. Every form is good, and its will is always the supreme law.[68]

Like an individual in Hobbes's state of nature, in the Sieyèsian state of nature, the nation's will is the highest law because there is no superior authority. Thus, the nation's "will is always legal. It is the law itself."[69] The nation is not bound by any positive law for "it would be ridiculous to suppose that the nation itself was bound by the formalities of the constitution to which it had subjected those it had mandated."[70] The nation's lawlessness is a logical deduction based on the nation's position at the apex of the hierarchy of law. Sieyès famously distinguished between the constituent and constituted powers, between the nation and the government.[71] The government or constituted powers should have no say in how it is constituted, on the content of a constitution. Rather, the people should create their own constitution.

Sieyès however goes beyond description and logic to prescription: not only is it impossible to subject the nation to law, one *should* not do so. The nation, "amidst so many perils" should "never leave[] the state of nature."[72] If the nation was subject to the laws of mixed government or any government, it would be powerless to overthrow it. Under those conditions, the nation would lose its rightful status as the sovereign ruler to a government that should be subordinate. It would have to follow the constitution that would irrationally empower the nobles and priests to outvote the Third Estate. Sieyès states:

---

[68] Sieyès, "What Is the Third Estate?," 149.

[69] Ibid., 136. In the next line, Sieyès states, "Prior to the nation and above the nation there is only natural law." This should not be misread as Sieyès advocating for some legally enforceable limit on the nation. Like Hobbes, the natural law seems to be unenforceable. And at other times, Sieyès seems to suggest that the nation itself is natural law and that this empowers it to be above all positive law. He states, "A nation is formed solely by *natural* law. Government, on the other hand, is solely a product of positive law."

[70] Ibid., 136.

[71] Ibid., 136.

[72] Ibid., 138.

But even if it could, a nation *should* not subject itself to the restrictions of a positive form. To do so would expose it to the irretrievable loss of its liberty. Tyranny needs no more than a single moment of success to bind a people, through devotion to a constitution, to forms which make it impossible for them to express their will freely and, as a result, to break the chains of despotism.[73]

To realize its own existence and to ensure its survival, the nation must be lawless. This raises the fundamental paradox that is at the heart of political theory of the people: Without law, without procedures, how do we know when and how the people have spoken? Who decides the myriad procedural questions, such as voter eligibility, approval thresholds, and district shape? Sieyès asks the same question, if not by law, "Where is the nation to be found?"

Sieyès constructed the people through top-down representation and the friend-enemy relationship. More specifically, an elected constituent assembly, purged of the nobles could embody the people's unified will on the contents of a new constitution.[74] In the midst of a financial crisis, King Louis XVI had summoned the Estates-General, composed of the three estates or classes of the Nobles, the Priests, and the Third Estate of the Commoners, to raise taxes. Sieyès wrote perhaps the most important pamphlet of the French Revolution, "What Is the Third Estate?," to address the problem within the Estates-General whether voting should occur by estate or by head. In other words, should each estate get one vote, or should each member of the assembly get one vote? The nobles and priests preferred voting by estate because it would allow them to outvote the Third Estate while the Third Estate preferred voting by head because they had a majority of the members. Eventually, the Third Estate prevailed, and a constitutional assembly composed of nobles, priests, and commoners voted by head to create the 1791 French Constitution.

For Sieyès, this rupture, this celebrated and foundational act of the French Revolution, was an unprincipled compromise that still gave the nobility power disproportional to their number in the population.[75] Although

---

[73] Ibid., 137.

[74] Sieyès's views in "What Is the Third Estate?" are not completely consistent with his political acts. For example, Sieyès was elected to the Third Estate, but according to his own principles as a member of the clergy he should have been ineligible. J.H. Clapham, *The Abbe Sieyes: An Essay in the Politics of the French Revolution* (London: P.S. King and Son, 1912), 67–68.

[75] Sieyès, "What Is the Third Estate?," 147–48. In his pamphlet, Sieyès was responding to the Third Estate's proposal that each estate vote by head. Since each estate had the same number of delegates, the First and Second Estate's total delegates could consistently outvote the Third Estate, the estate that

preferable to voting by estate, voting by head would still give disproportional representation to nobles and priests who were only voted in by their
own members rather than selected by all members of the estate.[76] Sieyès
summarizes the options: The Third Estate had been "nothing." A vote by
head would allow the Third Estate to be "something," but Sieyès demanded
that it become "everything."[77]

To do so, the Third Estate should break off to form a separate constitutional assembly and bar the nobles from entering as they were never voted on
by the majority of the country. However, even this self-transformation, while
satisfactory, would still not be ideal. The best course of action would be to
hold new free and fair elections for a constitutional assembly.[78]

Open elections for a constitutional assembly raises new question about
the nobles' participation. It's easier to justify excluding them when they have
reserved seats by virtue of a quota system that privileges their nobility as it
violates fundamental democratic principles. But would nobles be eligible to
participate if they ran under the same equal conditions as all other candidates
in open elections?

Sieyès's answer would have to be no. He never quite answers the question
of noble eligibility in elections for a constitutional assembly. He does, however, address the matter in the context of elections to a legislature. He states
that the nobles "can be neither electors nor eligible for election for as long as
their odious privileges exist." They should be "positively excluded" from the
legislature.[79] For Sieyès to be consistent, the same should hold true for a constitutional assembly as well.

Sieyès believed that nobles should be ineligible to be members of the assembly because they were the enemy while the Third Estate was the people
or the nation. The Third Estate is the universal class because of its economic productivity. It undertakes the public and private services necessary
for the nation's survival. It is the estate of farmers that cultivate the land, of

Sieyès favored. But this outvoting, what Sieyès calls "the proportion adopted between" the Estates, is
not really the root problem for Sieyès. Indeed, Sieyès maintains that no number of nobles or priests
should be allowed in the assembly by virtue of their position. He states, "In the light of true principle,
they cannot vote *in common;* they cannot vote either by head or by order. Whatever the proportion
adopted between them, it will not be able to meet the required objective, which is to bind and engage
the totality of representatives by *one* common will. Ibid., 116.

[76] Ibid., 115–16.
[77] Ibid., 94.
[78] Ibid., 116.
[79] Ibid., 158.

merchants and dealers that deliver the farmer's product to consumers, the army that defends the nation, and the administrators who run the state. It is the Third Estate that is "required to bear the whole burden of all the genuinely hard work."[80] For this reason, the Third Estate is a universal class whose interests stand for the will of all. As Sieyès states, "the will of the Third Estate will always be right for the generality of citizens, while that of the privileged orders will always be wrong."[81]

The nobles are an unproductive drain on the nation's resources. While "everything arduous" is done by the Third Estate, the nobles fill lucrative and honorific offices that serve no purpose. They "swell[]" the administration of government "beyond all measure, creating posts to meet the needs not of the governed, but of those who govern."[82] They unfairly enjoy monopolies that perform their services terribly and at an exorbitant cost. Sieyès summarizes the productive differences of these two estates: "Nothing can go well without the Third Estate, but everything would go a great deal better without the others."[83]

The nobility's lack of utility makes them not just an unfortunate economic cost but a foreign power, and Sieyès repeatedly labels them an "enemy" to the nation.[84] They are a "frightful disease devouring the living flesh of the body of its unhappy victim."[85] They are a "false people that, not being able to exist by itself, since it has no functioning organs, attaches itself to a real nation like one of those parasitic forms of vegetation that live off the sap of the plants they exhaust and desiccate."[86]

Sieyès maintained that the purpose of all assemblies, whether its goal is to pass a law or draft a constitution, is to deliberate to arrive at the nation's will or the public good. While individual citizens do have partial interests, they have a common interest in the general interest that is the nation's true will. As enemies of the nation with their own partial and corporate interest, nobles would distort the deliberative process and lead to legislation that does not reflect the interests of all. Sieyès sometimes speaks about this in the language of aggregation: "Without [the abolishment of noble privileges] it would be

---

[80] Ibid., 95.
[81] Ibid., 161.
[82] Ibid., 95.
[83] Ibid., 96.
[84] For instances of Sieyès calling the nobility the enemy, see the passages ibid., 28, 107–08, 157–59. Sieyès also labels the nobility a foreign power; ibid., 97–98, 107–8, 147, 158.
[85] Ibid., 157.
[86] Ibid., 97.

pointless to join the three orders together under the same denomination. They would still re-main three types of heterogeneous matter that it would be impossible to amalgamate."[87] More often, he talks about the problem of noble participation in the language of representation: "the right to be *represented* belongs to citizens only in respect to what they have in common and not to what serves to differentiate them."[88] An assembly represents the public good that is common to each citizen. An individual's selfish interest then cannot be represented as it is partial and unique to each. The same is true of the nobles' interest: "it is not *something that can be represented*."[89] Indeed, representation may only occur on the basis of one's citizenship and for a noble as an enemy of the citizen "that quality has been destroyed."[90] Regardless of whether Sieyès states it in the language of aggregation or representation, the root logic of his exclusion is that of friend-enemy relations as illustrated at the near end of the pamphlet when Sieyès returns to the issue of noble participation in free and fair elections. His statement is worth quoting in full:

> It might in the end be said that even if the privileged orders have no right to interest the *common will* in their privileges, they ought nonetheless to be able, as citizens, to enjoy their political right to representation together with the rest of the society. But I have already said that by adopting the mantle of privilege, they have become the real enemies of the common interest. They cannot therefore be entrusted with the task of providing for it.[91]

As enemies, nobles may not participate under any conditions in the Constitutional Assembly.

Let us pause for a moment to understand how Sieyès's inflexible stance against noble participation exemplifies the deeply exclusionary logic of the friend-enemy distinction. It targets not just formal political rights, such as quotas for particular groups in an assembly. No, it goes much deeper. It demands the renunciation of the very identity of the enemy class. Until they renounce their social affiliation or the constitution abolishes it, the

---

[87] Ibid., 128.

[88] Ibid., 155.

[89] Ibid., 157.

[90] The full quote reads, "A privileged class is therefore harmful not only because of its corporate spirit but simply because it exists. The more it has been able to obtain of those favors that are necessarily opposed to common liberty, the more it is essential to exclude it from the National Assembly. Anyone privileged is entitled to be *represented* only on the basis of his quality as a citizen. But for him that quality has been destroyed." Ibid., 151.

[91] Ibid., 161.

enemy should have no political privileges whatsoever. That's why for Sieyès the nobles are free to claim their political rights and "rejoin the veritable nation whenever they wish, simply by purging themselves of their unjust privileges."[92] For a noble to be eligible, he must no longer be a noble at all! To understand this, it might be helpful to glance at the same logic in a different example where the identity of the friend or the enemy is varied. For example, in a Marxist framework, as with the Soviet Constitution of 1918, political participation would be confined to the proletariat.[93] A bourgeoisie citizen would have to renounce his ownership of the means of production in order to participate. Regardless of the context, the desire for unity of the people risks the political elimination of entire classes that may compose significant minorities of the entire population.

But exclusion alone would not be enough to forge the unity. Here, Sieyès turned to the Constitutional Assembly as the site to create a consensus among the Third Estate. It's not obvious how an assembly, a place where individuals arrive divided between a variety of conflicting opinions, is a site of sudden consensus. Indeed, Sieyès asked himself, "How all members of a [constitutional] assembly might be able to join their individual wills together to form a common will that should be synonymous with the public interest?"[94]

Sieyès's answer was deliberation, an answer that anticipated the deliberative democracy movement. Although delegates might begin disagreeing with each other, deliberation was a "trial" in which "views that are useful and those that are harmful will be separated from one another. Some will fall while others will maintain their moment and will balance one another until, modified and purified by their reciprocal interaction, they will end up becoming reconciled with one another and will be combined together in a single view... "[95] Debate and discussion would forge unity.

This emphasis on deliberative unity turned Sieyès against the idea of instructing representatives and ratificatory referenda in constitution-making: the representatives of the Constituent Assembly should freely debate, and the assembly's word should be final. Instructions and referenda do not reflect the unified will of the people. In a large and commercial nation,

---

92 Ibid., 161.
93 Russian Federation's Constitution of 1918, art. 7.
94 Sieyès, "What Is the Third Estate?," 153.
95 Emmanuel Joseph Sieyès, "An Essay On Privileges," in *Political Writings: Including the Debate between Sieyès and Tom Paine in 1791*, ed. Michael Sonenscher (Indianapolis: Hackett Publishing Co., 2003). A common view is not necessarily a unanimous will. Sieyès often takes the majority opinion to be the common will.

all individuals cannot find the means and time to meet together to deliberate. Nor do they have the time or expertise to consider seriously the issues. Since both referenda and instructions to representatives lacked the filter of national deliberation, either device would end up creating votes that reflect representatives' individual or sectional interest rather than the common good. In other words, the vote would reflect the meaningless aggregation of individual wants rather than the people's will. However, by electing an assembly, the nation's extraordinary representatives could reach a common will through discussion and debate. Their unity would bestow itself upon the people. Outside the assembly, there was no common will.

The people's unity also leads to a more centralized state that could produce a unified will. But despite his emphasis on unity, it would be wrong to conflate Sieyès with Jacobin, Hobbesian, and Schmittian ideas of centralizing all power in one body to rule arbitrarily on the basis that it completely embodied the people.[96] Sieyès distinguishes the people from government, separates the latter's powers, and believes the government's powers must be used toward specific and higher ends.

Rather than centralizing all power in one body, Sieyès achieved unity through constitutional designs that would promote agreement and avoid gridlock between the different bodies of government. The system separated powers with separate bodies wielding the legislative, executive, and judicial power with each branch "limited to its special mission." A legislature would create the law, the executive would enforce it, and the judiciary would apply it in individual cases. At some points in his career, Sieyès embraced a separate constitutional court to ensure that these branches stuck to their assigned roles.[97] But the separation of powers should not be confused with checks and balances. For Sieyès, "within the sphere of their mission," each branch's powers would be "full and unlimited."[98] Hence, there was no executive veto,

---

[96] For an in-depth analysis of how Sieyès differs from Schmitt and other theorists of absolutely sovereignty, Lucia Rubinelli, Constituent Power: A History (Cambridge, United Kingdom; New York, NY, USA: Cambridge University Press, 2020), 56, 67–72, 128–135. My analysis is compatible with Rubinelli's. Yet, I place greater emphasis on key continuities and discontinuities between Sieyès and Schmitt on the friend-enemy distinction. On a separate note, although Hobbes and Schmitt are both radicals, they have important differences as I have repeatedly clarified. Hobbes does not want the sovereign to rule arbitrarily and believes they are still bound by natural law, but that natural law is unenforceable against the sovereign. Citizens also have the right to resist or retreat when their lives are in danger. Perez Zagorin, Hobbes and the Law of Nature (Princeton, NJ: Princeton University Press, 2009).

[97] Marco Goldoni, "At the Origins of Constitutional Review: Sieyès' Constitutional Jury and the Taming of Constituent Power," Oxford Journal of Legal Studies 32, no. 2 (June 1, 2012), 211–34.

[98] Emmanuel Sieyès, quoted in Reason and Revolution, 133–34. Even though Sieyès's designs became more and more complicated as time went on, at least in theory, the idea of a pure separation of

no judicial enforcement of a bill of rights, and no bicameralism.[99] And power would be centralized in the national government as Sieyès feared that federalism would "cut, chop and tear France into an infinity of small democracies."[100] While stopping short of Hobbesian designs for one sovereign body, Sieyès's understanding of the people still lends itself to a vision of a centralized form of government.

Like Hobbes, Sieyès embraced the idea of the people to overthrow a divided feudal order and centralize power in government. He also follows Hobbes in locating the people outside all current legal and social divisions and giving them agency through unity. However, the source of the unity has shifted for Sieyès. Whereas Hobbes located unity in unanimous consent, Sieyès finds it in the identity of members of the Third Estate and to their representation in a constituent assembly.

Decentralizers: Karl Marx, Vladimir Lenin, and Sheldon Wolin

Not all radicals are centralizers. Karl Marx, Vladimir Lenin, and Sheldon Wolin all sought to summon a lawless people to weaken the state. I call these thinkers, "radical democrats of the constituent power." Yet, each ultimately believes that centralization is necessary to enact the revolution. Their work is complex, and I cannot do justice to it here, but I will give a brief sketch of each.

For Karl Marx, the friend-enemy distinction ran along the lines of class: the conflict was between the proletariat and the bourgeoisie. The victory of the workers would spell the end of history; it was the class to end all classes. The revolution would "swe[ep] away the conditions for the existence of class antagonisms, and of classes generally and will thereby have abolished its own supremacy as a class."[101] The state would "wither

---

powers remained the same. What changed was the nature and number of these powers. For example, in his 1795 and 1799 proposed constitutions, the legislative power was divided into proposing on the one hand and on the other approving a law. While the underlying theory remains consistent, it is a separate question whether Sieyès's actual designs still accomplish a system of purely separated powers and whether they could achieve the unity he seeks. Ibid. See also Rubinelli, *Constituent Power*, 61-73.

[99] Ibid.
[100] Ibid., 137.
[101] Karl Marx and Friedrich Engels, *The Communist Manifesto* (New York: Penguin Classics, 2002), 244.

away"[102] and in its place each individual would have the freedom to engage in all spheres of life, to "rear cattle in the evening" and then "criticize after dinner."[103] Rather than a coercive state, there would be an "association, in which the free development of each is the condition for the free development of all."[104] However, to end the state, it had to first be bolstered to defeat the bourgeoisie and to augment production. Hence, before the proletariat is dissolved, its "first step in the revolution" is to "raise [itself] to the position of the ruling class." The oppressed becomes the oppressor. The proletariat will then "use its political supremacy to wrest, by degrees, all capital from the bourgeoisie, to centralize all instruments of production in the hands of the State." It will "centraliz[e] the means of communication and transport in the hands of the state."[105] To defeat the state, Marx strengthens it.

Lenin maintains the basic edifice of Marx. He too believes the central division is between workers and owners and that the just revolution of the former will end the state. Yet, he has less faith than Marx in the workers' capability to self-organize. Just as Sieyès uses a constituent assembly to impose a coherent will on the people, a vanguard, a highly centralized political party is necessary to give the workers collective agency.[106] And like Marx, Lenin too sought to strengthen the state to bring about the revolution. Indeed, revolutionaries must first "smash" the old state institutions, but then they must build up the state.[107]

Sheldon Wolin was not a Marxist. Class conflict was not central to his thought and he placed little faith in millenarian breaks. Nonetheless, he too thought of the people as a lawless unity. Even though he rejected this vanguardism as dictatorial, Sheldon Wolin still placed the people outside all law and thought of them as a unity. Drawing on the ideal of a state of nature, he searched for the "evanescent homogeneity of a broader politics," for a "community or perfect coincidence of (or between interests)" because "[h]eterogeneity, diversity, multiple selves are no match for modern forms of

---

[102] Friedrich Engels, "Anti-Dühring," in *The Marx-Engels Reader*, ed. Robert C. Tucker, 2nd rev. ed. (New York: W. W. Norton & Company, 1978), 720.

[103] Karl Marx, "German Ideology," in *The Marx-Engels Reader*, ed. Robert C. Tucker, 2nd rev. ed. (New York: W. W. Norton & Company, 1978), 160.

[104] Marx and Engels, *The Communist Manifesto*, 125.

[105] Ibid., 243.

[106] V. I. Lenin, *What Is to Be Done?: Burning Questions of Our Movement*, rev. ed. (New York: International Publishing, 1969).

[107] Vladimir Ilyich Lenin, *The State and Revolution*, ed. Robert Service, rev. ed. (London: Penguin Classics, 1993), 29.

power."[108] Even though Marx, Lenin, and Wolin seek to bolster local spaces of rule, they still fall into the trap of centralization because their agent of revolution is a lawless and unified people.

The loss of law and the invocation of unity play exactly into the hands of the centralizers but leaves radical democrats bitterly disappointed. At the heart of much radical democratic thinking lies a contradiction between the agent and the goal of revolution. The people would enact the revolution. The necessity of victory over the enemy drove the construction of the people. To seize power, the people would have to mirror their oppressors. To overthrow one tyranny, they would have to create another. Only the absolutism of the people would be powerful enough to overthrow the absolutism of the monarch.

Yet, the characteristics of the "people" were inappropriate for the democracy they sought. Means and ends were opposed. While democracy was local, plural and fluid, the people were a centralized, unitary, and unlimited juggernaut. New nouns multiplied to capture and characterize the absence of their internal division. More than a people, they were a nation, the volk, the masses, the proletariat, the vanguard, or even the leader.

When the dust cleared, radical democrats felt betrayed. The centralized agent of the revolution strengthened the power of the state. Once the unitary subject seized the reins of power, it refused to dissolve itself. The "people" perceived local units of democracy as challenges to its power. In the French Revolution, the Committee of Safety silenced the discussion of the Jacobin clubs.[109] In the Russian Revolution, to achieve the union of the soviets, the Soviet Union abolished them.[110] Revolutionaries promised local democracy but delivered centralization.

Carl Schmitt's Relativization of the Constituent Power

Sieyès, Marx, Lenin, and Carl Schmitt all tear down law to unleash the people and forge its unity through the friend-enemy relation and top-down representation. What distinguishes Schmitt though from his radical predecessors

[108] Sheldon Wolin, "Norm and Form: The Constitutionalizing of Democracy," in *Athenian Political Thought and the Reconstruction of American Democracy*, eds. J. Peter Euben, Josiah Ober, and John Wallch (Ithaca, NY: Cornell University Press, 1994), 24.

[109] Michael Kennedy, *The Jacobin Clubs in the French Revolution, 1793–1795* (New York; Oxford: Berghahn Books, 2000).

[110] Oskar Anweiler, *The Soviets: The Russian Workers, Peasants, and Soldiers Councils, 1905–1921* (New York: Pantheon Books, 1975).

is his "relativization" of the people.[111] With the notable exception of Hobbes, previous "radicals" sought to justify their choices as universal ones: the theorists chose the particular friend and its representation because they truly believed and gave reasons why their chosen group stood for the common interest of all. By contrast, for Schmitt, any choice of friend/enemy and any choice of representative that could forge the popular unity necessary for the survival of the state was justifiable. No valid normative criteria existed to distinguish between them. In this limited sense, he harkens back to Hobbes's near indifference to the identity of the sovereign people.

Let us work through Schmitt's thought to see exactly where he breaks with the radical tradition. Just as Hobbes and Sieyès called upon a lawless and unified people to overthrow the feudal regime, so too Schmitt thought that the regime of his era, liberalism, was ripe for popular overthrow. According to Schmitt, neutrality is at the heart of liberalism, and law is its means to achieve it. This is the meaning of the phrase the "rule of law, not men." Liberalism holds that law is neutral and rational, while the individual will is partial and irrational.[112] Government coercion is justified because it acts pursuant to the law rather than individual will.[113]

Schmitt argues that liberal law's neutrality is self-defeating. It paralyzes the modern state, leaving it vulnerable to attack. It saps the state of the will and energy necessary to prosecute wars against foreign enemies and to quell internal emergencies and insurrections.[114] Not only is neutrality self-defeating, but it is internally inconsistent because the irrational and willful people are the ultimate source of law's legitimacy. The very structure of law belies liberalism's claim to neutrality. Law is structured through a top-down chain of authorization. Every action of the state is legitimate because it is authorized by an entity higher than it. Administrative law is authorized by statutes, statutes are authorized by the constitution, and the constitution is authorized by the people. The people sit at the apex of the chain. But outside the chain of law, what authorizes and accounts for the existence of the people?[115] How

---

[111] In this sense, he is a return to Hobbes, who was more concerned that there was a sovereign than the particular identity of that sovereign.

[112] Scholars have questioned Schmitt's overly simplistic depiction of the relationship between law and liberalism. They argued that this results from his depiction of Kelsen as the culmination of liberalism and then generalizing from his thought to all other liberals. For that reason, I think his real target is legalism, not liberalism. William E. Scheuerman, "Carl Schmitt's Critique of Liberal Constitutionalism," *The Review of Politics* 58, no. 2 (Mar. 1996), 299.

[113] Schmitt, *Constitutional Theory*; Schmitt, *Crisis of Parliamentary Democracy*; Carl Schmitt, *Legality and Legitimacy*, trans. Jeffrey Seitzer (Durham: Duke University Press, 2004).

[114] Schmitt, *Concept of the Political*, 34–36.

[115] Schmitt, *Constitutional Theory*, 125–26.

does one know that the people have spoken? How do they coordinate so that they may act?

For Schmitt, the people are not authorized by law, but sheer will that makes "the concrete, comprehensive decision over the type and form of its own political existence."[116] This will is unified; it has no internal divisions or disagreements. Like Hobbes, Schmitt distinguishes this indivisible unity from mere agreement. In the Schmitt quote that follows, Rousseau is the central reference, but the words also capture the idea of unity for all other radical theorists of the constituent power. The quote is perhaps the best explanation of the radical idea of unity in political theory:

> [In Rousseau's Social Contract], the facade is liberal: the state's legitimacy is justified by a free contract. But the subsequent depiction and the development of the central concept, the "general will," demonstrates that a true state, according to Rousseau only exists where the people are so homogeneous that there is essentially unanimity. . . . According to Rousseau this unanimity must go so far that the laws come into existence *sans discussion*. . . . In short, homogeneity elevated into an identity understands itself completely from itself. But if unanimity and agreement of all wills with one another is really so great, why then must another contract be concluded or even construed? A contract assumes differences and oppositions. Unanimity, just like the general will, is either there or not and it may even be . . . naturally present. Where it exists a contract is meaningless. Where it does not exist, a contract does not help. The idea of a free contract of all with all comes from a completely different theoretical world where opposing interests, differences, and egoisms are assumed. This idea comes from liberalism. The general will as Rousseau constructs it is in truth homogeneity. That is a really consequential democracy. According to the *Contrat social*, the state therefore rests not on a contract but essentially on homogeneity, in spite of its title and in spite of the dominant contract theory. The democratic identity of governed and governing arises from that.[117]

Contracts and agreement, or as discussed in the next chapter, what Arendt calls "promises," arise from a meeting of two distinct minds. The range and moment of agreement is limited and circumscribed. The contract is one of

---

[116] Ibid., 125.
[117] Schmitt, *The Crisis of Parliamentarism*, 13–14.

many in the individual's life. It does not require or imply a commonality that is foundational and fundamental to the parties' very existence. And much of the need for the contract is based upon the likelihood of future disagreement because the contract provides a framework for adjudication. Indeed, a commitment to a procedure for settling future feuds might be the contract's entire content. Schmitt argues that a dramatically different logic is behind the radical's unity. In unity, individual differences are peeled away until a common essence is revealed that is the basis of unity. Differences may persist, but they are secondary and irrelevant to future behavior. On the most fundamental level, the people are homogenous and that homogeneity is decisive for future action. Since a unified people lacks disagreement, it no longer needs law to sort out its identity and agency.

The unified will exists prior to the creation of a constitution and therefore cannot be "bound by legal forms and procedures; it is always in the state of nature."[118] Since law does not regulate the will, it has no essential form. It is ever renewing its form and organization and refuses a conclusive one. Its existence is only "evident through the act" of constitution-making itself and "not through observation of a normatively regulated process."[119] Furthermore, as with Sieyès, the legal binding of the people is not only logically absurd but also a violation of their right to self-determination. Law cannot and *should* not stop the people from overthrowing oppressive regimes. The decision rule preexists and regulates the vote. The people cannot choose it themselves because it preexists their creation. Thus, for Schmitt such decision rules would be imposed violations on the people's right to self-determination.[120] Rather than neutral law, it is the people's biased will that ultimately legitimates the constitution. The people would supply the vitality that liberalism lacks and that is necessary for survival.

Schmitt's answer of unity does not resolve and raises again the question of the people's identity. A quick glance within any polity reveals deep and persistent divisions. Unity is not the natural state of human kind. How is it constructed?

Schmitt lays out the answer most systematically in *Constitutional Theory*. The expansive literature on Schmitt almost completely neglects and does not give sufficient attention to the key passage for understanding his method of

---

[118] Ibid., 128.
[119] Ibid., 131.
[120] See Schmitt, *Constitutional Theory*, 128.

forging unity.[121] Schmitt distinguishes "the two opposing formative principles," both of which are needed for the construction of a people.[122] The first is
bottom-up "identity" based on the friend-enemy distinction and lies behind
an ideal vision of democracy. Democracy is the "identity of the governing
and the governed."[123] Democracy depends upon the homogeneity of the citizens. This equality of the citizens is based on an inequality between friends
and enemies, between insiders and outsiders. No group of citizens is naturally homogenous but must constitute itself as such by defining itself against
an enemy. Everything the enemy is, they are not. The more similar a group of
citizens are, the more they are "factually and directly capable of political action" with a "minimum of government and personal leadership."[124] Identity
is an ideal that directly empowers the people to act on their own behalf.

Sieyès located the friend in the Third Estate while Marx and Lenin find it
in the proletariat. Each of them believed their choices were objectively justifiable; that they had found the sole force that had the right to wage revolution
for the common good of all. Not so with Schmitt. He relativizes the identity
of the universal class: it is circumstantial and subjective. It can be based and
draw upon any other set of oppositions that can divide people into two distinct and opposed groups that will fight to the death:

> Every religious, moral, economic, ethical, or other antithesis transforms
> into a political one if it is sufficiently strong to group human beings effec-
> tively according to friend and enemy. A religious community which wages
> war against members of other religious communities or engages in other
> wars is already more than a religious community; it is a political entity. . . .
> Also a class in the Marxian sense ceases to be something purely economic

[121] One exception is Andrew Arato, *Post Sovereign Constitutional Making: Learning and Legitimacy*
(Oxford: Oxford University Press, 2016), 26–29. John McCormick offers an excellent account of
Schmitt's theory of representation in his chapter on the subject in his book, John P. McCormick,
Carl Schmitt's Critique of Liberalism: Against Politics as Technology, 1st ed. (Cambridge: Cambridge
University Press, 1999), 157–206. The wide-ranging account puts Schmitt's theory of representation
into conversation with Max Weber, Walter Benjamin, and Jürgen Habermas, showing how they all
share the same narrative of the decline of medieval representation and for Schmitt and Weber it's
possible and desirable modern revival in plebiscitarian moments. Although my section benefited
from this account, my chapter places greater emphasis on the interdependency of "identity" and
"representation." This difference is partially a reflection of our different emphasis on the primary
material: I draw more heavily from *Constitutional Theory* while McCormick focuses on the *Crisis
of Parliamentarism*. Rubinelli also has an illuminating discussion of Schmitt on representation.
Rubinelli, *Constituent Power*, 123-24.

[122] Schmitt, *Constitutional Theory*, 240.

[123] Schmitt, *Crisis*, 15, 26.

[124] Schmitt, *Constitutional Theory*, 239.

and becomes a political factor when it reaches this decisive point, for example, when Marxists approach the class struggle seriously and treat the class adversary as a real enemy and fights him either in the form of a war of state against state or in a civil war within a state.[125]

Whatever distinction, whether based on religion, class, morality, or anything else that can muster the will necessary to unify the people, could be the basis of a friend-enemy distinction.[126]

Relativization, however, does not imply that Schmitt is completely indifferent to the identity of the friend and enemy. The basis of the choice had shifted: the search is no longer normative but sociological. As a partisan of the state and the people, Schmitt searched for the distinction most likely to charge and strengthen them given his time and place. He found his answer in ethnic nationalism, stating in the *Crisis of Parliamentarism*, "Since the nineteenth century, [unity] has existed above all in membership in a particular nation, in national homogeneity."[127] This evocation of nationalism is likely to quickly trigger associations of ethnic homogeneity, and the context of the quote confirms it. Shortly before the quote, Schmitt gives two ethnic examples of how to create homogeneity citing the examples of "contemporary Turkey," with its radical expulsion of the Greeks and its reckless Turkish nationalization of the country, and the Australian commonwealth, which restricts unwanted entrants through its immigration laws, and like other dominions only takes immigrants who conform to the notion of a "right type of settler."[128] Schmitt is coy about the basis of Australia's immigration policy, but it is clear the "right type of settler" was defined ethnically as the policy was aimed at restricting Asian immigration to maintain, as the official policy calls it, a "white Australia."[129] A page later, as he continues to elaborate on the theme of homogeneity, Schmitt comments that the British Empire could "not survive for a week" if it extended universal and equal voting rights to

---

[125] Carl Schmitt, *The Concept of the Political: Expanded Edition*, trans. George Schwab (Chicago: The University of Chicago Press, 2007). He also states, "The political can derive its energy from the most varied human endeavors, from the religious, economic, moral, and other antitheses. It does not describe its own substance, but only the intensity of an association or dissociation of human beings whose motives can be religious, national (in the ethnic or cultural sense), economic, or of another kind and can effect at different times different coalitions and separations."

[126] For more of Schmitt's analysis of Marx, see Schmitt's analysis of Sorel. Sorel is seen as taking a step in Schmitt's direction in which the friend and enemy are located in "myth" or sociological legitimacy rather than a normative one. Schmitt, *Crisis of Parliamentarism*, 65–77.

[127] Schmitt, *Crisis*, 9.

[128] Ibid.

[129] Ibid., translator's footnote 26.

all because "with their terrible majority, the coloreds would dominate the whites."[130] Lastly, in the *Concept of the Political*, in his list of antitheses from which the political can draw its strength, he cites the "national (in the ethnic or cultural sense)."[131] Based on its twentieth-century sociological legitimacy, ethnicity was Schmitt's favored means to accomplish unity.

Identity is a necessary condition for the formation of a people because at its base must lie an existential will to survival. However, identity or the friend-enemy distinction is not a sufficient condition to birth a people. A wide variety of decisions must be made, and the people lack the homogeneity and organization necessary to supply answers to all of them. They may agree on who their enemy is, but what about how to defeat the enemy? And what about all the other questions pertaining to political life that are not defined in relationship to an enemy? Even if they had the answers, the people are incapable of delivering them because it would require them to be constantly assembled. Schmitt concedes that this is unlikely in the modern state with its extensive territory and large population and that the people's weakness is their lack of definite form.[132] The first principle of identity, of the friend-enemy distinction, is incapable of fully delivering the unity Schmitt seeks.

Schmitt's second principle of "representation" provides the unity on the many remaining sites of disagreement. Schmitt's use of the term is very specific. Often, in modern discourse, representation consists of a representative advocating on behalf of those who elected him. Representatives act as delegates for their constituents. But, for Schmitt, this introduces division and discord into the heart of parliament and perverts it into a battle of interest groups. Representation must be "freed from any encumbrance from other concepts such as assignment, interest advocacy, business leadership, commission, trusteeship, etc."[133] Rather than represent an already preexisting entity, Schmittian representation produces it. It produces the "enhanced being" of "the political unity as a whole."[134] In the modern debate concerning whether representation is following the will of one's constituents, or pursuing the public good, Schmitt falls closer on the latter. Representation is top-down: it is not the ambassador representing the king's interests but the king's body giving unity to the entire realm.

[130] Schmitt, *Crisis*, 10.
[131] Schmitt, *Concept*, 38.
[132] Ibid., 131.
[133] Ibid., 241.
[134] Ibid., 243, 245.

For Schmitt, representation and identity are interdependent. Neither can "forgo" the other.[135] No group is ever so homogenous as to be able to achieve unity without representation.[136] At the time same, representation is incapable of substituting for or deciding the friend-enemy distinction. Both are necessary, but in what mix? How far away does reality fall from Schmitt's ideal of direct democracy through identity? How much must representation compensate for identity's deficiencies?

To some extent, Schmitt sees the mix of identity and representation as a continuum that will vary from state to state. Ultimately, however, Schmitt sides more with representation and against identity. Ironically, even as Schmitt celebrates the people, he is fundamentally skeptical about their agency. Although their formlessness is their strength, it is also their weakness, which means that "their expressions of will are easily mistaken, misinterpreted, or falsified."[137] To express their will, the people must be assembled and in large nation-states such assemblies "can only be held momentarily and intermittently."[138]

Even if it was possible to hold daily plebiscites, the people's faculties in these plebiscites are still greatly limited because they cannot deliberate. For Schmitt, "Acclamation" is "at the very center of the people's activity." It is the "natural form of the direct expression of a people's will." Since acclamation does not entail debate, the people themselves cannot set out the choice or question in the referendum. A referendum gives the people a binary choice:

> The people can only respond yes or no. They cannot advise, deliberate or discuss. They cannot govern or administer. They also cannot set norms, but only sanction norms by consenting to a draft of norms laid before them. Above all, they cannot pose a question, but can only answer with yes or no to a question laid before them."[139]

Referenda are notoriously susceptible to manipulation from those in power who set the rules for them, such as the timing and phrasing of the question.[140] Nonetheless, manipulation has its limits, and sometimes the

---

[135] Ibid., 239.
[136] Ibid.
[137] Ibid., 131.
[138] Ibid., 131.
[139] Schmitt, *Legality and Legitimacy*, 89. Schmitt makes the same point in *Constitutional Theory*, 302.
[140] Stephen Tierney, *Constitutional Referendums: The Theory and Practice of Republican Deliberation* (New York: Oxford University Press, 2012).

government loses in a referendum. The people are not completely helpless. The possibility of their answering "no" is very real. Schmitt argues that the people will answer "no" if the government lacks the sociological legitimacy, lacks the popularity necessary to represent the unity of the people. It must have "the authority to properly undertake the plebiscitary questioning at the right moment." Schmitt's formula is "authority from above, confidence from below."[141] Nonetheless, the people's power to act directly is not large. It may only decide occasionally through referendum in which it has no say over its format or question. Schmitt's people have limited self-rule through identity and acclamation, but ultimately most of the unity and decisions come from above and through the second principle of representation.

Whom do the people acclaim? Who poses the question to which they will "shout" yes or no? Just with the friend-enemy distinction, the identity of the representer is relativized: it is relative to the time and place. The representer should be whomever is capable of achieving the sociological legitimacy necessary for the unified state. Whomever the people consider legitimate at the moment may and should pose the question. The source of that legitimacy is irrelevant: the authority may come "from the effect and impression of a great political success; perhaps from the authoritarian residue of a pre-democratic time; or from the admiration of a quasi-democratic elite—of which the presently organized parties are at most only a surrogate or a caricature."[142] In the constitution-making context, Schmitt lists a wide variety of possibilities for who or what could be the proposer of a new constitution from constitutional assemblies to a singular person. In this context, Schmitt believed that a president who could act swiftly and was elected by the whole people was most likely to command the people's loyalty, but this was a matter of judgment and would vary from time to time and place to place.

---

[141] Carl Schmitt, *Legality and Legitimacy* 90 (quoting Emmanuel Sieyès).

[142] *Legality and Legitimacy*, 90. In *Constitutional Theory*, Schmitt lists and describes a variety of methods to create a constitution and in this section may misleadingly evince near-indifference to which method is best. The first he discusses is Sieyès's preferred method of an elected constitutional assembly, but Schmitt almost seems to mock it when he calls it the "so-called constitution-making assembly." In the same sentence, Schmitt puts the democratic characterization of the assembly in scare quotes, writing that the assembly ". . . developed as an accepted 'democratic procedure.'" While this passage is revealing, it should not be overread as evidence that Schmitt was or that his work is compatible with democracy and elected constitutional assemblies. Schmitt is repeatedly clear that acclamation is the natural form of expressing the people's will and many of the methods he listed do not involve any kind of public consultation or referendum. Indeed, Schmitt describes these examples not as instances of popular decision but rather as "the further execution and formulation of a political decision reached by the people in unmediated form" that "requires some organization, a procedure. . . ." Carl Schmitt, *Constitutional Theory*, 132.

This relativization is part and parcel of Schmitt's decisionism. For our previous thinkers, the decisions of the unity could be evaluated by some larger goal. Hobbes thought unity would create order and preserve life. Although they defined freedom and human flourishing differently, Sieyès, Marx, Lenin, and Wolin all thought unity would promote them. Not so with Schmitt. There is no higher criteria from which to gain perspective or evaluate the decision. What's important is that a decision is made, not its content or ends. This is not to say that the decision is an end in and of itself. As Leo Strauss points out, the affirmation of the decision is an attempt to preserve meaning, to ensure that there are some values for which individuals are willing to die.[143] However, Schmitt is clear that such values are illusions and "there exists no rational purpose, no norm however true, no program no matter how exemplary, no social ideal no matter how beautiful, no legitimacy nor legality which could justify men's killing one another for its own sake."[144] The decision is correct solely by virtue of it being taken.

In the context of the constituent power, Schmitt's decisionism is cashed out as the enshrinement of the people's will as the highest law. No higher norm can be used to evaluate a decision of the people. Schmitt's target in many of these passages is positivism's and natural law's attempts to impose its own norms on the people, but it also rubs against the radical thinkers on which Schmitt so often draws. He quotes Sieyès that "it is sufficient that the nation wills it."[145] Such a will in Sieyès, however, was only arrived at after deliberation in an assembly to ensure that the will had reached the correct answer. Its legitimacy lied in the fact that the means to achieve the will helped ensure that it was a good one. Schmitt dramatizes the distinction by casting it in theological terms:

> No less at issue is the traditional and eternal metaphysical dispute, which repeats itself in the most varied forms in the diverse areas of human thinking, whether something is good and just, because Gods will it, or whether God wills it, because it is good and just.[146]

For Sieyès and our previous radicals, the people will it because it is good and just. For Schmitt, something is good and just because the people will it.

---

[143] Strauss, "Notes on Carl Schmitt, The Concept of the Political," 116.
[144] Schmitt, Concept of the Political, 49.
[145] Schmitt, Constitutional Theory, 128.
[146] Ibid. 125.

Schmitt's promotion, in both texts and acts, of national ethnic unity are appalling. But we should not let this distract us from the disturbing fact that his solution of unity to the problem of the people's agency is widely held beyond his own fascist circle. Even if theorists of the people disagree on the source of unity, they all agree that unity is the answer. Schmitt's solution built on and radicalized the state-building theories of Hobbes and Sieyès, who both believed that in the state of nature it was, as Hobbes put it, the "Unity of the Representer, not the Unity of the Represented, that maketh [the people]."[147] Hobbes and Sieyès only differed on the identity of the representer: for Hobbes, it should be a monarch, and for Sieyès it should be a sovereign constituent assembly.[148] Left-wing enemies of the state shared with their statist foes the same solution of unity. For Marx, the common and universal interests of the proletariat made them one and capable of seizing and then overthrowing the state. When this proletariat failed to materialize, Lenin located the unity in the vanguard party.[149] Even though he rejected this vanguardism as dictatorial, Sheldon Wolin still groped for the "homogeneity" necessary to confront new forms of state power.[150]

Schmitt's insight is that debates about the correct source of unity are beside the point. It doesn't matter whether it is in the love or hate, the proletariat or the peasants, the masses or the vanguard: all are attempts to homogenize human diversity; all will concentrate and centralize power. Unity demonizes and shuns those who are different and those who disagree. It then centralizes power to defeat those enemies. Whether it is Hobbes's sovereign or the dictatorship of the proletariat, unity will empower an entity to rule over the people in its name. In Chapters 3 and 5, we'll see how Hugo Chávez and Evo Morales used Schmitt-like principles of the friend/enemy and top-down representation to try and forge a unified people in order to centralize power in the presidency. In Schmitt and in the Andes, breaking the chains of law is not liberation but a step toward a new form of tyranny. Schmitt and semi-authoritarian presidents celebrate this degeneration; I am devoted to staunching it.

* * *

[147] Thomas Hobbes, *Leviathan*, 104.
[148] Istvan Hont, "The Permanent Crisis of a Divided Mankind: 'Nation-State' and 'Nationalism' in Historical Perspective," in *The Jealousy of Trade: International Competition and the Nation-State in Historical Perspective* (Cambridge, MA: Belknap Press, 2010).
[149] Lenin, *What Is to Be Done?*
[150] Wolin, "Norm and Form: The Constitutionalizing of Democracy," 24.

Legalist opponents and radical proponents of the constituent power agree that the people are a lawless unity. This consensus has not served political theory well. The debate between the two camps has reached an impasse in which radicals dismiss legalists as too conservative and legalists fault radicals for empowering semi-authoritarian leaders. The consensus has created an interpretive bias in scholarship: it narrows our vision so that scholars are blind to, or miscomprehend, popular moments that do not conform to the lawless definition of the people. Most tragically, it leaves political actors who oppose the establishment of semi-authoritarian constitutions inadequately armed for battle. Invoking legalist arguments is a small shield against the tsunami of popular revolution because the letter of the law is unlikely to withstand the immense pressure for change in moments of crisis. Rather than completely oppose and crouch underneath the wave of revolution, political actors should channel it in new directions. To do so, they need new theorists and theoretical tools. Oddly, through frequent citation, legalists and radicals have given Carl Schmitt, a fascist enemy of democracy, the last word on its highest manifestation. In the next chapter, I shift focus from Schmitt to Hannah Arendt and Bruce Ackerman to redefine the people.

2

Extraordinary Adaptation

An Illegal and Plural People

In the previous chapter, I argued that both legalists and radicals, often drawing upon the work of Carl Schmitt, define the people as lawless, so that no law or institution regulates, limits, or sets boundaries on the people. What separates legalist and radicals then is not their conception of the people but their differences on its worth or value. They differ on whether the people should be summoned or banished. Legalists call for strict adherence to the law to prevent popular uprisings, and radicals try to accomplish the opposite end by invoking the people to overturn the old order. Both positions are untenable. Legalism would block the illegalities necessary for long-needed change, and the radicals' total abandonment of law and centralization of power in one sovereign body plays directly into the hands of would-be strongmen.

The fixation on lawlessness and on Carl Schmitt has blinded both groups to the alternative definitions of the people and to a more complex understanding of their cases of constitution-making. I turn to Hannah Arendt and the creation of the U.S. Constitution as guides to develop a theory of the relationship of the people to law called "extraordinary adaptation." Arendt shares with "radicals" the concern that law inhibits the people, but also fears that its destruction threatens their plurality. In "extraordinary adaptation," law is simultaneously transcended to break with the past and drawn upon to ensure the inclusion of multiple actors. Even as many of the specific rules of the old institutions are bent, reinterpreted, or broken, those institutions are still "extraordinarily adapted" to regulate the creation of the new constitution. The process may violate a law to realize a new beginning, but it does not plunge the country into a legal abyss. It may be illegal, but it is not lawless.

"Extraordinary adaptation" will not achieve a true revolution, a total break with the past, but it can radically alter the political order. The method seeks not to end the story of the regime but to begin a new chapter in its history. The break is momentous but still partial.

We, the Mediated People. Joshua Braver, Oxford University Press. © Joshua Braver 2023.
DOI: 10.1093/oso/9780197650639.003.0003

Extraordinary adaptation's bending and distortion of law is a realization of popular sovereignty when it adheres to the following three principles. The first is legal exhaustion or the failure of the legal system to enact a consensus about the need for far-reaching constitutional change. The second is open acknowledgment of and popular approval of the violation to enact the change. The last is the inclusion of all parties in the process so that the opposition can begrudgingly acquiesce to the result. These principles—legal exhaustion, popular vindication, and inclusion—compensate for and set out boundaries for how and when to violate the law in popular constitution-making.

This chapter has four parts. The first documents the pervasive and poisonous use of Schmitt in constitutional scholarship and how he offers few answers to the dangers of popular constitution-making. Part two shows how Hannah Arendt breaks away from the radical and Schmittian tradition of the constituent power to construct a plural people through law. Third, I use both Arendt and Bruce Ackerman as guides and play each off the other to develop the idea of "extraordinary adaptation." I use each to critique the serious gaps in the other's thought: Ackerman corrects Arendt by emphasizing the illegalities necessary for new beginnings, and Arendt supplements Ackerman by focusing on the importance of plurality and inclusion. Part three also develops the three principles of extraordinary adaptation: legal exhaustion, popular vindication, and inclusion. While the first three sections focus on how to create the people, the last focuses on their task of enacting a revolution. A plural people, one that internally grants limited concessions to "corrupt" actors from the old regime, requires a redefinition of revolution so that it is no longer understood as a total upending of all spheres of social and political life.

CARL SCHMITT'S UNFORTUNATE VICTORY OVER HANNAH ARENDT

This chapter seeks to loosen the stranglehold Carl Schmitt and the radical tradition of the constituent power has on the literature on popular constitution-making. Schmitt is perhaps the most cited constitutional theorist in the post-Cold War revival on the concept of constituent power. Both Schmitt and Arendt shared the fundamental insight that the people have the power to initiate extraordinary new beginnings by creating a new constitution. However, they disagreed over the identity and powers of the people. For

Schmitt, this power was absolute and outside the current constitution, while Arendt argued that it was limited and derived its authority from preexisting institutions.[1]

Schmitt's work has had far more influence than Arendt's in the analysis of constitution-making. Scholars have applied Schmitt, sometimes sympathetically, to understand constitution-making in Egypt, Russia, Chile, Colombia, the United States, Venezuela, Kenya, and the European Union.[2] The highest Constitutional Courts of Colombia and Peru have cited him favorably;[3] the German Constitutional Court may have wrestled with him secretly;[4] and he was a decisive influence on the constitutional advisers to Augusto Pinochet[5] and Hugo Chávez in the creation of their countries' respective constitutions.[6]

---

[1] Carl Schmitt, *Constitutional Theory* (Durham: Duke University Press, 1928); Hannah Arendt, *On Revolution* (London: Penguin Books, 1992).

[2] See, e.g., Paul Kahn, *Political Theology: Four New Chapters on the Concept of Sovereignty* (New York: Columbia University Press, 2011) (discussing the United States); Joel Colón-Ríos, "Carl Schmitt and Constituent Power in Latin American Courts: The Cases of Venezuela and Colombia," *Constellations* 18, no. 365 (2011); Renato Cristi, "The Metaphysics of Constituent Power: Schmitt and the Genesis of Chile's 1980 Constitution," *Cardozo Law Review* 21, no. 1749 (1999); Jan Muller, "Carl Schmitt and the Constitution of Europe," *Cardozo Law Review* 21, no. 1777 (1999); Richard Stacey, "Constituent Power and Carl Schmitt's Theory of Constitution in Kenya's Constitution-making Process," *International Journal of Constitutional Law* 9, no. 587 (2011); Lars Vinx, "Incoherence of Strong Popular Sovereignty," *International Journal of Constitutional Law* 11, no 1 (2013), 101–25; Joseph H.H. Weiler, "Does Europe Need a Constitution? Demos, Telos, and the German Maastricht Decision," *European Law Journal* 1, no. 219 (1995).

[3] See Colón-Ríos, *Carl Schmitt and Constituent Power in Latin American Courts*, 1.

[4] Vinx, *Incoherence of Strong Popular Sovereignty*, 114 (discussing Schmitt's influence on the court's *Lisbon* decision); Weiler, *Does Europe Need a Constitution?*, 223 (discussing Schmitt's influence on the *Maastrict* decision and arguing that the court's citation to Herman Heller is a secret allusion to Schmitt). Schmitt loomed in the background during many of the early debates about the role of the German Constitutional Court. Schmitt's disciple, Ernst-Wolfgang Böckenförde, became one of the most important justices of the court and a prominent intellectual of public law. Jan-Werner Müller, *A Dangerous Mind: Carl Schmitt in Post-War European Thought* (New Haven: Yale University Press, 2003), 63–75.

[5] *See* Cristi, *The Metaphysics of Constituent Power*, 1763–75.

[6] Ricardo Combellas had been the leading Venezuelan adviser in constitutional reform attempts for more than a decade and in the early stage was an important public voice and one of Chávez's most important advisers. He was deeply influenced by Schmitt. Ricardo Combellas, *Poder constituyente* (Caracas: En Cambio, 2000).Richard Combellas, *Byzantine Discussion*, El Universal, Apr. 23, 1999 (editorial defending Schmitt's conception of a sovereign constituent assembly). Jorge Olivarría, a lawyer, historian, and later a member of the Constituent Assembly, responded to the Combellas editorial and called attention to Schmitt's influence in a paragraph titled, "Tell me Whom You Quote . . . And I Will Tell You How You Think." See Jorge Olivarría, "The Darkest Hour," *El Nacional*, Apr. 25, 1999. In jail, Chávez read and in speeches has claimed to have adopted Antonio Negri's theory of constituent power from his early work, *Toni Negri in Venezuela*, Revolts Now, Mar. 7, 2013, https://revoltsnow.wordpress.com/2013/03/07/toni-negri-in-venezuela-socialism-of-the-21st-cent ury. Ricardo Combellas, *Qué es la constituyente?: Voz para el futuro de Venezuela* (Caracas: Editorial Panapo, 1998). Arcadio Delgado Rosales, a recent member of the Supreme Court, openly acknowledges Schmitt's influence. See *Reflexiones sobre el Sistema Político y el Estado Social*, Apertura de actividades judiciales del año 2012. *Tribunal Supremo de Justicia, No. 39, Serie Eventos*, Caracas (2012). His father had been the intellectual mastermind of the newly reconstituted Supreme Court, renamed the Supreme Tribunal of Justice under the new 1999 constitution, and has his own Leninist

Schmitt's writings are seductive: his distinctions are clear, sharp, and dramatic. As a trained lawyer, he could write in a style geared to the constitutional theorist, and indeed wrote a treatise on constitutional law. But underlying those more formal works are texts of political theory that cover a wide range of topics from Catholicism, Romanticism, and technology. He blended these two strands of his work so seamlessly that it could appeal to both audiences. By contrast, Arendt was trained as a philosopher, and her first work was on love and St. Augustine.[7] She was an outsider to constitutional theory. When she turned to the idea of the constituent power, her own categories sometimes threatened to swamp her object of inquiry, and they often confused the reader. Furthermore, the reviews of her work on the constituent power, *On Revolution*, were mixed, and it was overshadowed by that same year's publication of and controversy over *Eichmann in Jerusalem*.[8] No wonder then that Schmitt's influence has been so much greater than Arendt's in contemporary post-Cold War constitutional theory.[9]

Analysts of constitution-making most often cite Schmitt for his assertion that since the people are absolute sovereigns, they may ignore the old constitution's amendment rule and choose their own method of authorship.[10] But once the people realize they have the right to overthrow the old constitution and create a new one, how do they exercise it? What happens the morning after liberation? It is much easier to agree that the people have the right to make their own constitution than to answer the question of how this process should take place. How do you settle disagreement about the identity of the people, such as how to select individuals to the constituent assembly,

theory of unconstrained constituent power. See J.M. Delgado Ocando, *Problemas de Filosofía Del Derecho Y Del Estado: Hipótesis Para Una Filosofía Antihegemónica Del Derecho Y Del Estado* (Caracas: Vadell Hermanos Editores, 2004).

[7] Hannah Arendt, *Love and Saint Augustine* (Joanna Vecchiarelli, Scott and Judith Chelius Stark eds.), (Chicago: The University of Chicago Press, 1998).

[8] For a short take on the reception of *On Revolution*, Andreas Kalyvas, *Democracy and the Politics of the Extraordinary: Max Weber, Carl Schmitt, and Hannah Arendt* (Cambridge: Cambridge University Press, 2009), 187–90.

[9] Here, I am discussing Arendt's and Schmitt's influence on a particular literature, namely that of the constituent power and a related one on popular constitution-making. The influence of *On Revolution* outside of this literature is a separate question. It is also important to note that Arendt published the English edition of *On Revolution* in 1963, and Schmitt's *Constitutional Theory*, while originally published in 1928, was only translated into English in 2008. Hence, I am not stating that they have been competing for influence all these years and that Schmitt won out. The literature on constituent power began a soft revival in the early 1990s but has only really taken off over the last ten years, right about the time Schmitt's *Constitutional Theory* was translated.

[10] See, e.g., Colón-Ríos, *Carl Schmitt and Constituent Power in Latin American Courts*; Cristi, *The Metaphysics of Constituent Power*; Stacey, *Constituent Power and Carl Schmitt's Theory of Constitution*.

and what vote threshold is necessary in the assembly for approval of the draft constitution? If there are no limits on the people, may they arrest, imprison, or execute individuals at will? How do you prevent the new constitution-making process from degenerating into mob rule or charismatic dictatorship? These are questions confronting popular constitution makers, and ones to which Schmitt offers few or no answers.[11] For that, we must turn to Hannah Arendt.[12]

HANNAH ARENDT'S PLURAL PEOPLE THROUGH LAW

The Dangerous Freedom of the People

The normative foundation of my theory is rooted in Arendt's idea of a plural people. For Arendt, the people is the agent of our collective freedom to begin anew and create the future foundation of our political life in a constitution. Revolutions cannot be predicted or traced back to antecedent causes but rather exhibit the human capacity and power to generate its own terms of political existence. It radically breaks with the past to inaugurate a new future. The people deliberate and act together to start "anew," to begin "an entirely new story, a story never known or told before."[13] Indeed, Arendt believes this power is almost God-like, demonstrating a collective human capacity to perform a "miracle."[14]

But Arendt embraces a particular vision of the people, a plural one. Plurality refers to the inescapable diversity of human life. Indeed, it is that plurality that is the source of political freedom. Each birth or "natality" brings "some new" into the existing world, which is why humans can enact revolutions that "force open all limitations and cut across all boundaries."[15] To preserve that freedom, the people, as a collective agent, should reflect and protect that diversity. They are not one but many. There is no one group that

---

[11] Indeed, Schmitt is often cited to understand the establishment of dictatorships. See, e.g., Andrew Arato, "Conventions, Constituent Assemblies, and Round Tables," *Global Constitut ionalism* 1, no. 173 (2012); Cristi, *The Metaphysics of Constituent Power*.

[12] Andreas Kalyvas, *Democracy and the Politics of the Extraordinary* (Cambridge: Cambridge University Press, 2009), 195. My work is influenced by Kalyvas's comparison between Schmitt and Arendt.

[13] Arendt, *On Revolution*, 28.

[14] Hanna Arendt, "What Is Freedom?," in *Between Past and Future* (New York: Penguin Classics, 2006), 168.

[15] Ibid.

is universal; the people are everyone. Arendt's fear is that populist leaders will define the people as lawless and as one segment of the population to create a new constitution that centralizes power in the leader's own hands. Unlike Schmitt, she reminds the readers that after a revolution,

> constitutional government, if it came into existence at all, had a tendency to be swept away by the revolutionary movement which had brought it into power. Not constitution, the end product and also the end of revolutions, but revolutionary dictatorships, designed to drive on and intensify the revolutionary movement, have thus far been the more familiar outcome of modern revolution—unless the revolution was defeated and succeeded by some kind of restoration.[16]

All too often, triumph gives way to disappointment, and the revolution eats its own children.

Arendt explains that this is the direct consequence of positing the people as the ultimate and unified authority and then defining them as above and unbound by any law. Since the people are the source of legality for the entire system, it itself cannot be produced or controlled by law. Furthermore, not only are the people outside the preexisting political order but superior to it as well. To justify the overthrowing of the old institutions, they must not be bound by them. Arendt quotes Sieyès, writing that "it would be ridiculous to assume that the nation is bound by the formalities or by the constitution to which it has subjected its mandatories."[17] As Sieyès stated, the nation's "will is always legal. It is the law itself."[18]

For Arendt, this lawless understanding of the people posed two great dangers. First, new institutions are unstable because their creators lack legal authorization for their actions. They are "themselves unconstitutional."[19] Law provides a stable and objective source for locating authority. However, once we locate authority within a people that is outside law and all institutions, the identity of the people is continuously contestable. Each time a group claims to represent the people, others may object that they represent the people. Each time an institution tries to make a law or a constitution, groups will

---

[16] Arendt, *On Revolution*, 158–59.
[17] Ibid., 161.
[18] Emmanuel Sieyès, "What Is the Third Estate?," in *Political Writings*, ed. Michael Sonescher (Indianapolis: Hackett Publishing Company, 2003), 136.
[19] Arendt, *On Revolution*, 84.

claim a right to resist or even seize the power of the state because they act on behalf of or are the people. Arendt argued that no institution is able to lay a solid foundation on the "will of a multitude" because it is "ever-changing by definition, and that a structure built on it as its foundation is built on quicksand." Thus, revolutions often degenerate into chaos or mob rule.

The second danger is the potential tyranny of a centralized, unlimited, and arbitrary power. The rule of law limits the power of the state. The government can act only pursuant to and in the execution of a law. Inherent to the rule of law are protections against arbitrary executive action, such as the deprivation of rights without a fair hearing. As an unlimited power, however, the people may jail, imprison, and execute at will. Whoever then can sustain a claim to act on behalf of the people, be it an assembly or an individual, can seize and consolidate all power. As the representative of the people, it too is above the law. Arendt notes that "Napoleon Bonaparte was only the first in a long series of national statesmen who, to the applause of a whole nation, could declare: 'I am the *pouvoir constituant.*'"[20]

Underlying these two dangers is Arendt's paramount concern to preserve the plurality of the people. Without law, how does one identify who the people are? What adjudicates conflict? Arendt argues that the abandonment of law leads radicals to re-establish the people's agency by unifying them, creating "a multiheaded monster, a mass that moves as one body and acts as though possessed by one will."[21] Radicals expunge diversity from the people by identifying it with nonpolitical and natural entities.[22] More than a people, they are a nation, the *volk*, the masses, the proletariat, the vanguard, or even the leader. The cure of unity is worse than the disease. For Arendt, in the construction of the people, the question is not whether law, but rather what kind of law, may allow for a break with the past, while protecting against the homogenization of the people.

---

[20] Ibid.

[21] Ibid., 94.

[22] Ibid., 77–79. In the French context, Arendt identifies two methods of apolitical identification used to forge the people. First, she argues that Robespierre and other radicals invoked pity to create unity between the elite representatives and the poor, suffering masses. Second, she asserts that Rousseau and Robespierre identified enemies, both abroad in the form of foreign nations and within the heart of each citizen in the form of self-interest, because "only in the presence of the enemy can such a thing as *la nation une et indivisible*, the ideal of French and all other nationalism, come to pass." Ibid., 79–82. This may not be a historically accurate analysis of the French Revolution, but it captures radicals' attempts to forge the people into a lawless unity.

Law, Plurality, and Change

Radicals greet the state of nature with open arms; Arendt pictures the American pilgrims recoiling from it in horror. Upon landing on the shores of America, the pilgrims immediately feared "the untrod wilderness, unlimited by any boundary as well as the unlimited initiative of men bound by any law."[23] Whereas Jean Jaques-Rousseau believed that men were "good outside society, in some fictitious original state," the Americans believed they were sinners and that salvation lay in "checking human nature."[24] They immediately began building and compacting to form a wide variety of political bodies. By the time of the revolution they had "a hundred and fifty years of covenant-making behind them, rising out of a country which was articulated from top to bottom—from provinces or states down to cities and districts, townships, villages, and counties into duly constituted bodies, each a commonwealth of its own, with representatives 'freely chosen by the consent of loving friends and neighbors.'"[25]

These plural democratic bodies served as the foundation for the creation of the U.S. Constitution. Rather than acting outside all institutions, the framers started with a "working reality" in which the people "derive[d] its 'general authority . . . entirely from subordinate institutions.'"[26] The "great good fortune of the American Revolution was that the people of the colonies, prior to their conflict with England, were organized in self governing bodies, that the revolution . . . did not throw them into a state of nature." The townships elected the framers of state constitutions, and the framers of the American Constitution were tied to individual states. Hence, the people existed through and were organized by preexisting institutions, and they acted through them to create new constitutions. Without the American states, "the founders would have met immediately the perplexities of their French colleagues; they would have lost their *pouvoir constituant*."[27] Old institutions were "used as a foothold to secure the new beginning."[28]

Arendt believes that this institutionality of the U.S. people facilitated a plural constituent power. Schmitt and other radicals imagined one sovereign space of top-down representation would bestow unity on a fractured

---

23 Ibid., 167.

24 Ibid., 174–75.

25 Ibid., 176.

26 Ibid., 165.

27 Ibid., 165–66.

28 Kalyvas, *Democracy and the Politics of the Extraordinary*, 227.

people. We'll see in Venezuela and Bolivia that radicals believed that the Constituent Assembly should be that space of lawless unity. Law, however, creates and maintains divisions. It separates and divides individuals into different political entities and then coordinates between them. Those entities come to take on divergent identities. Since the United States possessed political spaces of deliberation, articulation and debate about the common good further distinguishes and transforms the social identities of the speakers and institutions while creating the basis for new agreements. Law creates juridical spaces between individuals, groups, and institutions that encourage them to articulate their differences and find new commonalities. It "relates and separates [them] at the same time."[29] Collaboration through different democratic institutions creates a *plural* people. A wide variety of actors comes together to create a new constitution that reflects their differences.[30]

The plurality exists before, during, and after the moment of agreement or the final ratification on the contents of the constitution. Let us begin with the before and after, as the middle moment of agreement is the most complex, taking Arendt's example of the United States. Before the agreement, the states came together to design a constitutional process. Since the states are the process's design, they ensure that they are amply represented in it. After the agreement ratification, the end product of the Constitution, as Arendt puts it, "preserves these bodies" rather than eliminating them. The Constitution grants new and broad powers to the national government, but the order is federal with a great deal of power still reserved to the states. Yet, isn't there still a moment of unity when the people have actually approved a constitution? Are radicals then not correct that unity is necessary for the creation of a people and a constitution?

This is a moment of agreement, but it is not the unity radicals seek. Schmitt and Arendt distinguished agreement from unity. Schmitt was deeply influenced by Thomas Hobbes who offered up the pithiest summary of the difference, writing that when individuals become the people it is "more than consent or concord; it is a real unity of them all, one and the same person."[31] Unity is based upon a deep and fundamental homogeneity

---

[29] Hannah Arendt, *The Human Condition*, 52.

[30] Arendt, *Love and Saint Augustine*, 168.

[31] *Thomas Hobbes, Leviathan: With Selected Variants from the Latin Edition of 1668* (Indianapolis: Hackett Publishing Company, 1994).

among its constituent parts. Radicals will attempt to justify one characteristic of all human beings as central. It is a foundation upon which all other differences may melt away so that in the moment of unity, the whole swallows up its parts so they no longer exist. The people becomes an unvariegated entity with no internal contours. With the loss of difference, discord is reduced or even completely annihilated. By contrast, agreement on a constitution, what Arendt would call a "promise," is reached by distinct individuals or political entities. It is not the action of one unified entity but "action in concert" among different ones. This difference needs to be negotiated. Arendt accuses the radicals of seeking to eradicate the give and take discussion needed for agreement and to replace it with a unified will, "[T]he very word 'consent,' with its overtones of deliberate choice and considered opinion, was replaced by the word 'will,' which essentially excludes all processes of exchange of opinions and an eventual agreement between them."[32]

Through such an agreement, the resulting constitution reflects rather than squeezes out the people's plurality. Its scope remains limited because many issues are incapable of being settled at the moment it is formed. But the constitution creates the foundations, institutions, and procedures over which more disagreement can be conducted. Arendt fears that attempts to reach beyond agreement or "promises" into unity smothers human plurality: "[t]he moment promises lose their character as isolated islands of certainty in an ocean of uncertainty, that is, when this faculty is misused to cover the whole ground of the future and to map out a path secured in all directions, they lose their binding power and the whole enterprise becomes self-defeating."[33] Unity, rather than agreement, produces constitutions that empower one individual, body, or group, to rule in the name of all.

Arendt's genius is to break from Schmitt's false glorification and deification of the people as outside any institution. They draw from the "working reality" of a plurality of democratic institutions to renew their ideals to give birth to a significant, but not total, break with the past. I supplement her work with an institutional account and correct her blind spot on the necessity of illegality to express this new conception of constituent power.

---

[32] Arendt, *On Revolution*, 76.
[33] Arendt, *Human Condition*, 244.

EXTRAORDINARY ADAPTATION

Those who seek a plural people to create a new constitution face the dilemma of needing both to transcend law for new beginnings and to preserve it to protect plurality. To create fundamental change, the people must be outside the old constitutional order. However, once you step outside the law, the people are homogenized into a dangerous unity to give them agency. How can the people be both inside and outside the law simultaneously? The theory of extraordinary adaptation attempts to roll with and take advantage of this contradiction by giving a plurality of forces input into the construction of the people through the legally questionable and even illegal uses of current institutions.

I develop my theory by putting Bruce Ackerman and Hannah Arendt in conversation with each other to critique the gaps in the other's thought. Ackerman corrects Arendt by emphasizing the illegalities necessary for new beginnings, and Arendt supplements Ackerman by focusing on the importance of plurality and inclusion. I argue that the illegalities of extraordinary adaptation must be principled: the violator must exhaust all other legal channels, openly acknowledge the violation in search of popular vindication, and concede enough to the opposition so that it may begrudgingly acquiesce to the new constitution.

Why do I use the term "extraordinary"? What makes this adaptation different from the rest? Adaptation always simultaneously breaks with and brings forward the past, but it can be quite mundane. Jacob Hacker, Paul Pierson, and Kathleen Thelen note that institutional adaptation is both "very common and very consequential."[34] They illustrate with examples of "conversion" in which "political actors are able to redirect institutions or policies toward purposes beyond their original intent." For example, whereas the Sherman Anti-Trust Act was originally intended to be wielded against corporations, years after its passage those same corporations successfully lobbied for it to be repurposed against unions. Conversion is ordinary and is orchestrated by interest groups and occurs "beyond the bright glare" of the public.[35] By contrast, constitution-making should be a rare act that is not

---

[34] Paul Pierson, Kathleen Thelen, and Jacob Hacker, *Drift and Conversion: Hidden Faces of Institutional Change*, in *Advances in Comparative-Historical Analysis*, ed. James M. Washington (Cambridge: Cambridge University Press, 2015), 180–81.
[35] Ibid.

dominated by any one interest or even a majority so that an inclusive people are its authors. It should not be banal but extraordinary.

Illegalizing Arendt and Pluralizing Ackerman

Extraordinary adaptation draws on, but also takes a step beyond, Arendt's insights into the tie between legal continuity and inclusion. Arendt captures the plurality, but not the illegality, of popular constitution-making. She often speaks of new beginnings as breaks and transgressions, but she never relates this insight to the illegality of the constituent power. Indeed, Jason Frank argues that in *On Revolution*, Arendt's story of the creation of the United States Constitution is one of the "persistence of formal legality."[36] Without further elaboration, her emphasis on subordinate authorities can be read as advocating for constitutional creation through the normal amendment method. This would be an act of the government, and it would not permit the revolutionary change that Arendt seeks. The potential for this reading exists because Arendt never directly addresses the role that illegality plays in the construction of a people.[37]

[36] Jason Frank, *Constituent Moments: Enacting the People in Postrevolutionary America* (Durham: Duke University Press, 2010), 54–57. Among quotes that support and interpret Arendt as believing the creation of the U.S. Constitution was legal, she writes that the U.S. people were "the organized multitude whose power was exerted in accordance with laws and limited by them." She also claims that the power of the states was not reduced in anyway by the process. This is important, as illegality was an important step necessary to reduce state power in the ratification process.

In contrast to Frank and in one of the most thorough accounts on Arendt's idea of the people, Andreas Kalyvas argues that she recognized the illegality of the constituent power, that "[f]or Arendt, the constituent power is effective only when it is firmly located in extra constitutional public spaces" and that even though they use "pre-constituted public bodies" those bodies "still remained antecedent and prior to the constitutional order." Kalyvas, *Extraordinary*, 229–30. However, he musters only one quote to support Arendt's supposed embrace of illegality, in which she writes, "The space of appearance comes into being whenever men are together in the manner of speech and action, and therefore *predates and precedes all formal constitution of the public realm and the various forms of government*, that is, the various forms in which the public can be organized." *Id.* There are two problems with this quote. First, it comes from the *Human Condition*, not *On Revolution*. In the former text, constitutions are built by an external craftsman or an extraordinary lawgiver, not by the people. Second, the quote does not confirm Kalyvas's interpretation that the constituent power is effective "only" when it is firmly located in extra constitutional space. In the quote, Arendt says that constituent power does not need a constitutional space to appear, not that it is required at all times or even some of the time. At most the citation shows that Arendt was open to the possibility of illegality, not that she had embraced it as necessary. Yet, the *Human Condition*'s embrace of expert-designed and externally imposed constitutions casts doubt on even this possibility.

[37] My assertion is that Arendt fails to grapple with the illegality of popular constitution-making, and therefore I have to develop the distinct concept of extraordinary adaptation. My claim does not obligate me to address the role of illegality in Arendt's larger corpus. Nonetheless, I do believe that Arendt often struggled to theorize the link between illegality and change. In addition to the problems in the *Human Condition* and *On Revolution*, both of which I discuss in this chapter, Arendt wrote

By contrast, illegality is one of the central driving points throughout Bruce Ackerman's magisterial narratives of constitution-making in the United States and abroad. Ackerman argues that creation of a new constitution often violates the old one. The norms and procedures of the old constitution are usually unfit for the creation of a new one that seeks to break them. An old constitution's method of amendment or change will likely reflect that old constitution's values and will privilege and empower the very actors that the people are seeking to overthrow. Ackerman's central example is the U.S. Articles of Confederation's enshrinement of equal state sovereignty. That enshrinement meant that any amendment had to be unanimously approved by the state legislatures. This power of state legislatures made it impossible to pass amendments that would weaken the states. Or to take

two other particularly relevant works. First, in the epilogue to *Eichmann in Jerusalem*, published in the same year as *On Revolution*, Arendt argues that the trial was completely legal. In doing so, she commits some odd legal maneuvers. She claims that the charge of crimes against humanity is not retroactive because it was the first time the crime had ever been committed. Even more peculiar, against the assertion that the Jerusalem court lacked jurisdiction, she claims that state territory is "a political and legal concept, and not merely a geographical term. It relates not so much, and not primarily, to a piece of land as to the space between individuals in a group." For a review and explanation of the implications of these legal arguments, including the definition of crimes against humanity, Seyla Benhabib, "Arendt's Eichmann in Jerusalem," in *The Cambridge Companion to Hannah Arendt* (Cambridge: Cambridge University Press, 2001), 76–80; David Luban, "Arendt on the Crime of Crimes," *Ratio Juris* 28, no. 3, (Sept. 1, 2015), 307–8, 313. Benhabib calls Arendt's defense of the Israeli court's jurisdiction "a curious claim," and Luban comments that it "is not legally serious." I am not suggesting that the trial was illegal. Rather, Arendt's work here shows that she would have been incapable of accepting and was greatly worried by the thought that it was illegal. Arendt does express concern that Eichmann was kidnapped in Argentina and faults the judges for misunderstanding the concept of crimes against humanity.

Ten years later, Arendt published the essay, "On Civil Disobedience," in *Crises of the Republic* (Boston: Mariner Books, 1972). There, her position on illegality is much more ambivalent than in *Eichmann*, but she again exhibits a strong devotion to following the law by seeking to legalize the practice of civil disobedience. Midway through the essay she accepts that civil disobedience will necessarily be in tension with law, asserting that "change itself is always the result of extralegal action," and she also writes that "[o]bviously, law cannot justify the violation of the law." Ibid., 80. She denies that First Amendment doctrine offers any protection for civil disobedience. Ibid., 82. These are Arendt's clearest and most strident comments in favor of illegality. However, at the end of the essay her position shifts and she ultimately strives to protect civil disobedience through something akin to law. She argues that although the practice is narrowly illegal, it is consistent with the "spirit" of American law because the Constitution is founded on a horizontal contract of consent and free debate. It can also be made "compatible with the institutions of government." Ibid., 85. What Arendt means by "institutions of government" is unclear, and she denies that it is the same as legalizing civil disobedience. In practice, however, her proposal seems to accomplish exactly that. First, it entails a constitutional amendment to shore up the First Amendment's lack of protection for free association. Whereas before, Arendt cited the First Amendment to argue that it is impossible to legally protect civil disobedience, now Arendt seems to believe that that was only as a matter of fact that is capable of being corrected. Second, she calls for obtaining "the same recognition for the civil-disobedient minorities that is accorded the numerous special-interest groups (minority groups, by definition) in the country, and to deal with civil-disobedient groups in the same way as with pressure groups." Ibid., 101. To sum up, it is difficult to reconcile Arendt's conflicting impulses about whether civil disobedience should be legal, but it is possible to argue that she attempts to legalize the tactic.

another example in eighteenth-century France, the Estates-General system reflected the values of feudalism and mixed government by giving each class of representatives one vote, which meant that nobles and clerics had far more power proportionate to their numbers and together could stymy the very large majority's desire for change.[38] The excessive legal blocking of constitutional replacements is still a problem today. Constitutions rarely provide for their own replacement. While amendment procedures are common, many theorists and constitutional courts have argued that it is illegal to use them for the creation of a new constitution. Even in the rare cases when replacement procedures exist, those in power in government can manipulate them to protect their power.[39] As Ackerman writes, "[f]orcing [actors] to play by the old procedures would . . . stifle the living voice of the people by manipulating legalisms that have lost their underlying functions."[40]

At the same time, Arendt puts Ackerman's work in a different perspective. The normative ideal of a plural people and its tie to law is Arendt's insight, and it is on it that both she and I differ or at least shift emphasis from Ackerman. Ackerman's work does not focus on key issues of inclusion, such as electoral or voting rules for constitutional assemblies, perhaps because he is not concerned by the dangers of popular constitution-making. His worry is that leaders are missing the rare opportunity to seize the moment and invoke the people to create a new constitution, so he does not focus on the issue of how this process should unfold.[41] He is so focused on egging on leaders to become more revolutionary that he fails to warn them and his readers of its many dangers. Hence, his work lacks the theoretical tools to condemn plebiscitarian forms of constitution-making and in fact sometimes unwittingly encourages it.

[38] William Doyle, *The Oxford History of the French Revolution*, 2nd ed. (Oxford: Oxford University Press, 2003).

[39] For example, in Venezuela, the constitution has a recall referendum clause: any elected official, including the president, may lose their office if they lose a recall referendum. The government is obligated to hold such a vote if 20 percent of registered voters petition for it. When citizens successfully gathered the required number of signatures in 2003 to hold a presidential recall referendum, Chávez delayed the referendum until he could regain his waning popularity. After he won, he created a blacklist barring all those who voted against him from government jobs, sending a clear deterrence message against future use of the method. Human Rights Watch, *A Decade Under Chávez* (New York: Human Rights Watch, 2008).

[40] *See* Bruce Ackerman, *We the People: Transformations* (Cambridge, MA: The Belknap Press of Harvard University, 1998), 12. [hereinafter *Transformations*].

[41] Bruce Ackerman, *Future of Liberal Revolution* (New Haven: Yale University Press, 1994), 64; Bruce Ackerman, *Revolutionary Constitutions: Charismatic Leadership and the Rule of Law* (Cambridge, MA: Harvard University Press, 2019).

Indeed, the differences between Ackerman and me are apparent in how we diverge on our readings of Arendt. This chapter argues that Arendt's great insight is that the people might become an organized multitude, rather than a lawless mass, by engaging with law. Ackerman never picks up on this distinction despite extensively discussing Arendt and despite her centrality to his enterprise. Ackerman draws from Arendt the idea that revolutions are popular acts that seek to break with the past, and that a constitution is an effort to institutionalize this collective act of redefinition.[42] This is an important point, but it is shared by many others, including by radicals like Carl Schmitt.[43] The reason Arendt is so valuable and distinctive is in the ways that she differs from Schmitt and the tradition of constituent power, and that is captured in her comparison of the U.S. and French constitution-making experiences, a comparison that Ackerman dismisses as fundamentally wrong-headed, attributing her anti-French revolutionary stance as a blindspot caused by her being caught up in "writing during the Cold War struggle against communism."[44]

Due to our differences in emphasis on the issue of how law ties in with inclusion, my concept of "extraordinary adaptation" diverges significantly from Ackerman's similar idea of "unconventional adaptation." To be sure, I owe a debt to his work, and both of our concepts seek to, as Ackerman states, "construct new higher-lawmaking processes out of older institutions, using them as platforms for an unconventional argument."[45] Yet, Ackerman never links the use of preexisting institutions to the inclusion of a variety of actors, including those from the old regime. Nor does he link the concept to any underlying principles as I do later in this chapter. Unconventional adaptation and inclusion are decoupled in Ackerman's work.

[42] Bruce Ackerman, *We the People Volume 1: Foundations* (Cambridge: Harvard University Press), 204–12.

[43] Indeed, Sandy Levinson and Andreas Kalyvas have argued that Ackerman's work on U.S. constitution-making is Schmittian. I think this is fundamentally unfair, as in contrast to Schmitt's unified site of will, Ackerman's U.S. work is concerned with extended deliberation and dialogue. This happens through multiple sites, whether it be the thirteen different states or the three branches of government. Kalyvas, *Politics of the Extraordinary*, 163–74; Sandy Levinson, "Transitions," *Yale Law Journal* 108, no. 2215 (1999).

[44] Ackerman, *Revolutionary Constitutions*, 41. Ackerman focuses only on one-half of the basis for the comparison between the two revolutions. He, along with many others, has rightfully hammered away at Arendt's idea that the French revolution failed because it sought to fulfill social needs while the U.S. revolution succeed because it was focused solely on political ends. But this still leaves two whole chapters—one-third of *On Revolution*—unaccounted for. In chapters four and five, Arendt turns away from the social question to the question of whether the people exist within or outside law. Ibid.; Ackerman, *We the People Volume 1*, 208–9.

[45] Ackerman, *Transformations*, 12.

In his seminal three volumes on the making and remaking of the U.S. Constitution, the idea of extraordinary adaptation appears only in the second volume. The discussion is brilliant, and I rely on it extensively, but it is also brief. Perhaps in this U.S. work, the concept of unconventional adaptation is undertheorized because in his U.S. case studies there are few proponents of lawless and exclusive constitution-making. Perhaps it simply was not particularly important to draw fine distinctions when there are few demagogues successfully centralizing power in the United States. But this is not the case when Ackerman goes abroad, where he is confronted with the possibility of semi-authoritarian constitution-making. But there, the concept of unconventional adaptation plays even less of a role than it does in his U.S. work, going unmentioned in his book on Eastern Europe and making only passing appearances in his wide-ranging study on revolutionary constitution-making.[46] In the very moment that his concept of unconventional adaptation is most in need of invocation, it falls by the wayside.

Indeed, at times Ackerman gives openings to semi-authoritarian leaders. Two moments are particularly worthy of note. The first is his openness to sovereign constituent assemblies, assemblies that wield all power. He states that there is nothing "sacrosanct about a special constitutional convention" that limits itself to only producing a constitution because "many plausible texts have also been produced by constituent assembles that have exercised plenary powers on normal legislative matters as well."[47] This is an invitation to disaster: sovereign constituent assemblies are the Schmittian tool for semi-authoritarian leaders to seize power and should be avoided whenever democratic institutions already exist. This problem rears its head a second time in Ackerman's discussion of Charles De Gaulle's plebiscitarian constitution-making in his newest book. De Gaulle is a milder but still potent version of Chávez or Erdoğan, but Ackerman never condemns his actions.[48] Ackerman documents at great length the many moments of dangerous

<hr>

[46] Ackerman, *Revolutionary Constitutions*, 34, 236, 246, 313, 372.

[47] Ackerman, *The Future of Liberal Revolution*, 59.

[48] One caveat to this statement is important. In the new book, *Revolutionary Constitutions*, Ackerman departs from the more normative approach of the *We the People* series to a more sociological approach in order to investigate the conditions under which a public will accept a constitution as legitimate. As I discuss in the introduction, my book is primarily normative, so it may be problematic to evaluate Ackerman's sociological project from that perspective. Yet, the normative seems to still creep into Ackerman's new book. It shares with *We the People* the goal of defending revolution from Marxists, and this time Ackerman also defends revolution against those who prefer more elite-style negotiations by showing that it sometimes damages the public legitimacy of the constitution (as in Poland) and that many examples of negotiated transitions are actually examples of popular constitution-making. Ackerman, *Three Paths to Constitutionalism*; Ackerman, *We the People: Foundations*, 202–3.

plebiscitarianism by De Gaulle in the process of constructing the current French Constitution. For example, once in power, De Gaulle signed an emergency decree giving his government unilateral power to rule by decree for the next six months. De Gaulle's next decree gave him unilateral power to design and propose a constitution, without elections to any assembly, and then gave the country only a yes or no vote.[49] He used such power to create a constitution that centralizes a great deal of power in the executive, in his office. Yet while Ackerman personally finds "De Gaulle's self-indulgent hero worship off-putting" and dislikes some of his rhetoric, none of De Gaulle's action raises a red flag for Ackerman.[50] The French process is held up as an example of successful constitution-making. Although Ackerman condemns egregious antidemocratic maneuvers like canceling elections or refusing to abide by election results,[51] his work provides few resources for dealing with the newest wave of democratic backsliding that comes from majorities who win elections and use their newfound power to systematically strip away the constitution's checks and balances, intimidate the press, and create an uneven playing field in future elections.[52]

Ackerman's main concern is to push leaders to "seize the moment" and not let "an ascendant movement fail[] to take advantage of its opportunity" for a constitutional revolution.[53] This was not a problem for the countries of this study that are part of a live and strong tradition of radical and revolutionary constitution-making. In South America, the question was not whether revolution but what type. The danger was that the charismatic presidents would leverage a unified and majoritarian vision of the people to establish highly centralized constitutions that undermined minority rights, the rule of law, and an equal playing field in elections. A more robust and a fully theorized understanding of when and what type of illegalities are justified can serve as an important countervailing force to such dangerous efforts.

---

[49] Ackerman, *Revolutionary Constitutions*.

[50] Ibid., 187.

[51] The main line Ackerman seems to draw between legitimate and illegitimate popular constitution-making is a willingness to abide by the election results. Thus, Ackerman asserts that Lenin crossed the line when he disbanded the Russian Constituent Assembly after his party lost the election to it. Ackerman, *We the People: Transformations*, 12. By contrast, Ackerman condones De Gaulle's plebiscitarianism because the general was "fully prepared to test his continuing popularity when his seven-year term came to an end" by "run[ing] for reelection." Ackerman, *Revolutionary Constitutions*, 191.

[52] Steven Levitsky and Lucan A. Way, *Competitive Authoritarianism: Hybrid Regimes after the Cold War* (Cambridge: Cambridge University Press, 2010).

[53] Ackerman, *Future of Liberal Revolution*, 112.

Extraordinary adaptation aims to do justice to both Arendt and Ackerman by providing a role for both continuity and break. There is continuity because revolutions use old institutions, but their rules are bent, reinterpreted, or even broken to create a new constitution. The action is illegal but not lawless. The constitution-making process violates specific rules but does not degenerate into a contest of strength or force. It is an extralegal process justified and constrained by the principles inherent to the normative ideal of a plural people. Old institutions are extraordinarily adapted to frame a collaborative process to create a new constitution.

The idea is abstract, but I will illustrate with the example of the creation of the U.S. Constitution. I use this example here and return to it throughout the chapter because the U.S. Constitution is the first example of popular constitution-making in the world, is therefore widely known, and is a paradigm case of extraordinary adaptation. The process was illegal. As Ackerman highlights, to ensure that authority derived from the people, the U.S. ratification process violated the amendment procedures for state constitutions and the Articles of Confederation by submitting the Constitution to specially elected state conventions with a new supermajority rule rather than with a unanimity approval rule. Furthermore, the drafting in the Philadelphia Convention disregarded the instructions of state delegates in the Continental Congress by choosing to create a new constitution rather than merely reforming the Articles.[54]

Nonetheless, even amid this break, there was continuity or adaptation: preexisting constituted institutions greatly influenced and organized the ratification of the American Constitution. The Continental Congress called for states to hold and organize ratifying conventions, and they complied. During ratification, both the Continental Congress and state legislatures continued in session. The Continental Congress certified the result and organized the transition to the new government.[55] This paradoxical drawing upon and violation of state authority is an example of extraordinary adaptation. When extraordinary adaptation occurs in other contexts, different preexisting institutions will be used, including the judiciary. Extraordinary adaptation not only prevents lawless voids but also ensures the people is composed of different groups and institutions deliberating together.

[54] Ackerman, *Transformations*, 33–68.
[55] Ibid., 11.

The Three Principles of Extraordinary Adaptation

Is extraordinary adaptation merely an unprincipled stopgap measure against the most egregious and blatant assertions of sovereign power? In South America, the threat was that through plunging the country into a legal void, presidents and constituent assemblies would declare themselves sovereign; this lawlessness would lead to dictatorship. In Venezuela, for example, President Hugo Chávez asserted, "there is no law or constitution, there are only the orders by yourself, the people for an all-powerful assembly."[56] Extraordinary adaptation is well-suited to combat these flagrant usurpations by preventing legal vacuums and by denying to any one institution a monopoly on the people's voice. But what about the less extreme cases? What about presidents who are more cunning and less open than Chávez about their contempt for the law and who use quasi-legal means to centralize power?

There is always a possible legal pretext for power grabs, grabs whose results are like those justified based on sovereign constitution-making. For example, the Supreme Court of Nicaragua ruled that the constitution's term limits on the president violated his human rights.[57] The decision was absurd, but at first glance it may seem to meet the definition of extraordinary adaptation as the bending and unconventional interpretation of legal rules. Even with no legal vacuum, the result is still the strengthening of executive power. Why are the differences between the processes of lawless constitution-making and extraordinary adaptation important if the result is the same?

The Nicaraguan Supreme Court's decision and many other ones like it are not examples of extraordinary adaptation but of derelictions of duty. They reflect not an attempt to wrestle with law in a moment of revolution but a total capitulation to presidential power. These capitulations are distinct from and opposed to extraordinary adaptation because the latter is an institutional expression of an inclusive vision of popular sovereignty. As such, it stands upon the three principles of legal exhaustion, popular vindication, and inclusion that distinguish it from thin legal pretexts for the undermining of checks and balances. The principles give guidance to prevent extraordinary adaptation

---

[56] Hugo Chávez, "Juramento en el acto de toma de posesión de la Presidencia 1999," in *La Construcción i Del Socialismo Del Siglo XXI: Discursos Del Commandante Supremo Ante La Asamblea Nacional* 1 (1999–2001), 139, 144 (2013).

[57] Sentencia [S.] No. 504, de las 5:00 p.m., Oct. 19, 2009, Corte Suprema de Justicia [CSJ] [Supreme Court of Justice], Boletín Judicial [B.J.] p. 21 Cons. VIII (Nicar.).

from degenerating into lawlessness and instead provide a foundation for the normative vision of a plural people.

The three principles of extraordinary adaptation address, from a particular angle, the broader question of how to violate law while still respecting its end, to give "fidelity to law" at "its outer edge."[58] Law deserves obedience when it is democratically enacted, when it respects fundamental human rights, and for the sake of maintaining order. When it no longer serves those ends, the obligation to obey is weakened and transformed. How does one seek to re-establish a more democratic system so that the violation of law does not merely substitute one tyranny with another? While this question has been wrestled with extensively in other contexts, so far the literature on constitution-making has not truly taken up this challenge. The debate has been between the extreme position of legalists who deny law should be violated and radicals who believe the people must exist in a lawless state of nature.

The literature on civil disobedience and emergency have confronted this challenge head-on. In both, important theorists and actors call out for illegalities but then lay out principles and guidelines to defend themselves against accusations of lawlessness. To distinguish himself from anarchists, revolutionaries, criminals, and violent segregationists, Martin Luther King committed his acts of civil disobedience in a peaceful, explicit, and public manner, and then accepted punishment. This method has become the dominant understanding of civil disobedience in public discourse and in political theory.[59] With executive emergency power, actors must balance the need for extraordinary measures while still preventing power from accumulating in the presidency. Living in extraordinary times, Thomas Jefferson argued that the president might have to violate individual provisions of the Constitution in order to save it as a whole. However, to combat the dangers of dictatorship, the president should openly admit the violation and throw themselves at the mercy of the public for absolution.[60] To be sure, I am citing

---

[58] The phrase comes from John Rawls in his discussion of civil disobedience. John Rawls, *A Theory of Justice* (Cambridge, MA: The Belknap Press of Harvard University, 1999), 322.

[59] The dominant liberal and Rawlsian account of civil disobedience is coming under heavy attack by those who seek to legitimize more radical forms of protest as civil disobedience. See, e.g., Erin Pineda, "Civil Disobedience and Punishment: (Mis)reading Justification and Strategy from SNCC to Snowden," *History of the Present* 5, no. 1 (2015).

[60] On Jefferson, see Clement Fatovic "Constitutionalism and Presidential Prerogative: Jeffersonian and Hamiltonian Perspectives," *American Journal of Political Science* 48 (2004), 431. For a more general theory that is in the spirt of and incorporates Jefferson's insights, Oren Gross and Fionnuala Ní Aoláin, *Law in Times of Crisis: Emergency Powers in Theory and Practice* (Cambridge: Cambridge University Press, 2006).

and simplifying only one strand of a vast literature. What's striking, however, is that no such similar strand exists on popular constitution-making. I provide it. My account is based on the three principles of extraordinary adaptation. In discussing the principles, when illuminating, I note some of their similarities to the liberal account of civil disobedience. I also show how these principles manifested themselves in the first example of extraordinary adaptation—the creation of the U.S. Constitution. These principles legitimized the U.S. process's multiple illegalities, illegalities that I discussed earlier in the chapter.[61]

One preliminary note: extraordinary adaptation requires institutional integrity. Without independent courts or other institutional resistance, there might be little hope for staunching democratic decay. Indeed, at a certain point it may be too late if the rot has deeply permeated institutions. In the post-Cold War Andes, before the creation of the new constitution, the normal legal system possessed adequate tools to resist change. The countries were hobbled but functioning liberal democracies. Public trust was low, corruption plagued the bureaucracy, the political branches were often unresponsive, and the processing of cases in the judicial system was painfully slow. Nonetheless, the judiciaries were independent and ruled with integrity. They and the legislatures had tenaciously fought against perceived presidential attempts to undermine checks and balances through constitutional change.[62] If, as in Nicaragua, these new presidents had filed lawsuits against the constitutionality of term limits, the legislatures would have denounced the suits, and the Supreme Courts would have laughed the suits out of court. The systems possessed sufficient powers to resist these blunt and clumsy power grabs. Countries without these resources fall outside the purview of this study.

The first principle of legal exhaustion addresses when it is appropriate to engage in extraordinary adaptation. Legal exhaustion requires both that there is almost a widespread consensus about the need for far-reaching constitutional change and that attempts to achieve it through legal channels have failed. Crisis is usually the driver of this agreement. For example, in the eighteenth-century United States, both Federalists and Anti-Federalists believed that significant changes to the Articles of Confederation were

---

[61] Bruce Ackerman, *Transformations*, 34–39.

[62] On the conflict between courts, legislatures, and presidents in Colombia, see Gabriel L. Negretto, *Making Constitutions: Presidents, Parties, and Institutional Choice in Latin America* (Cambridge: Cambridge University Press, 2013).

necessary so that more power would reside in the national government to confront the pending crises to the national economy and to the nation's defense. It was not the need for, but the extent of, that centralization that divided the two parties.[63] So too did Venezuela, Bolivia, and Colombia all suffer from profound crises of representation and governance. Very few principled participants denied the need for a constitutional overhaul, and indeed many had been seeking it for decades.

The first principle also holds that revolutionaries must first exhaust traditional legal routes for change. Only once the ordinary method has failed may the extraordinary one begin. If possible, one should avoid breaking the law. The danger is a slippery slope: once one law is broken, why not others? Without a common baseline of law to adjudicate disagreement, there is a risk of chaos and disorder. This risk is worth bearing when the legal system is incapable of reforming itself to confront a brewing crisis. The same logic is at play in civil disobedience. In his fight for racial equality in Birmingham, Martin Luther King first sought to follow the law because it was "the better path." But it was the city's leaders' "failure to negotiate in good faith" and failure to uphold one's promise that meant King had "no alternative except that of preparing for direct action."[64] In the eighteenth-century United States, the amendment method required a proposal by the Continental Congress and then ratification by all thirteen states. The Congress's proposed amendments were blocked in 1781, 1783, and 1786, each time by one state legislature, usually Rhode Island. Subsequently, the Annapolis and Mount Vernon Conferences' proposed amendments met even more resistance.[65] Only after these failures did James Madison, the most influential delegate to the Constitutional Convention, seek a method of change that would violate the Article's unanimity rule. Similarly, constitutional activists in Bolivia, Venezuela, and Colombia tried the legal route of amendment first. It failed; once in Bolivia, thrice in Venezuela, and five times in Colombia.[66]

[63] Michael J. Klarman, *The Framers' Coup: The Making of the United States Constitution* (Oxford: Oxford University Press, 2016), 73–126.

[64] Martin Luther King, "Letter from a Birmingham Jail," in *A Testament of Hope: The Essential Writings and Speeches*, ed. James M. Washington (San Francisco: HarperOne, 2003), 291.

[65] Bruce Ackerman, *We the People: Transformations* (Cambridge, MA: The Belknap Press of Harvard University, 1998), 40–44.

[66] For Bolivia, see Carlos Romero Bonifaz, *El Proceso Constituyente Boliviano* (Santa Cruz: CEJIS, 2005), 155–237; Gustavo Rodríguez Ostria, "Marco Histórico: La Larga Marcha a la Asamblea Constiuyente," in *Enciclopedia Histórica Documental del Proceso Constituyente Boliviano*, ed. Juan Carlos Pinto Quintanilla, vol. 1 (Bolivia: Estado Plurnacional de Bolivia, 2009), 108–23. On Venezuela, Kornblith, "Legitimacy and the Reform Agenda in Venezuela," 13–15. In Colombia, in total, there were seven failed attempts at constitutional reform. Five followed legalist formulas, but the first two attempts by Barco in 1988 disregarded the legalist route of the traditional amendment

While the first principle concerns *when* to violate law, the second and third principles are about *how* to violate law. Under the second principle of extraordinary adaptation, the violation must be done in a definite, explicit, and public manner so that it may be popularly ratified. For King, civil disobedience required that the illegality be committed "openly, cheerfully," and even "lovingly."[67] With constitutional creation, the open acknowledgment of illegality dramatizes the need for popular ratification and excusal of the acts. It shifts the burden to those who seek constitutional change to prove that the people side with them. Famously, in *Federalist 40* Madison conceded that the proposed constitution was an "unauthorized interposition," but justified it based on popular sovereignty, on the basis that the "approbation of the people would blot out all antecedent errors and irregularities."[68] So too we'll see in post-Cold War South America, where supreme courts and presidents call attention, to varying degrees, to the illegality of the process in order to explain their appeals to the people.

We should not always expect completely full-throated admissions of illegality. Even Madison's concession in *Federalist 40* that the Constitution was illegal is not totally forthcoming. Legalists have noted that *Federalist 40* begins with a defense of the Constitutional Convention against the charge that it violated its instructions and the Articles of Confederation.[69] Only after defending the convention as legal does Madison explore how "duty arising out of the case itself *could* have supplied any defect of regular authority," with the word *could* signifying that addressing the illegality may not even be necessary.[70] In other words, Madison argued in the alternative: yes, the creation of the Constitution was legal, but even if it was illegal it would be justified. For a politician, it is difficult to not leave some wiggle room to appeal to multiple audiences and to soften the blow of any partial concession.

---

method in favor of referendums. John Dugas, *Explaining Democratic Reform in Colombia: The Origins of the 1991 Constitution* (Bloomington: Indiana University Press, 1997), 267–303.

[67] King, *Letters from a Birmingham Jail*, 294. Gross and Ní Aoláin, whose theory of emergency power is in the same spirit as the principles of extraordinary adaptation, argue that in Jefferson's purchase of the Louisiana territories, Jefferson sought to or at least believed he notified the public that he had "done an act beyond the Constitution." Oren Gross and Fionnuala Ní Aoláin, *Law in Times of Crisis: Emergency Powers in Theory and Practice* (Cambridge: Cambridge University Press, 2006), 123–25.

[68] *Federalist No. 40* (James Madison).

[69] Andrew Arato, *The Adventures of the Constituent Power: Beyond Revolutions?* (Cambridge: Cambridge University Press, 2017), 114–20; William Partlett, "American Tradition of Constituent Power," *International Journal of Constitutional Law* 15, no. 4 (2018).

[70] *Federalist No. 40* (James Madison) [Emphasis added].

Rarely is a principle realized perfectly in politics. We must not be too exacting in applying the second principle of confessing illegality, and Madison comes close enough. Indeed, even with the initial equivocation, Madison's language about the illegality of the process is so strong that it is almost overwhelming. In his section on the convention's choice to completely rewrite the new constitution and choose a new method of ratification, he speaks of the "liberty assumed" by the convention, its "assumptions" and "usurp[ation] of powers 'wholly foreign to their commission,'" and its "irregular and assumed privilege." Madison calls the proposed constitution an "informal and unauthorized proposition[]" and an "unauthorized interposition."[71] He not only asserts that popular sovereignty is a sufficient remedy, but twice asserts that "forms ought to give way to substance" so that an illegal constitution may be ratified.[72] Given the vehemence of this language, it is hard to read Madison's arguments about the legality of the process as completely sincere. While full openness is always preferable, the reality of politics means that there will always be some hedging on and some ambiguity about the illegality of the action. Hence, *Federalist 40* fulfills the second principle's call for openly avowing the illegality so that the people's "approbation" may become a necessary requirement for legitimacy.

In what "does the approbation" of the people consist? Under the second principle not only must the revolutionary avow the illegality, but that illegality must also be popularly ratified. What fulfills this requirement is contextual and will have to be worked out through politics. In general, though, multiple victories by historic margins show an enduring choice for a new constitution. One referendum is not enough. Citizens are fickle: polls show that after further consideration, voters change their minds. And indeed, in closely timed subsequent elections, they sometimes vote in ways that seem to rebuke their previous choice.[73] Nonetheless, we can establish a floor of at least

---

[71] *Federalist No. 40* (James Madison).

[72] Ibid. Madison ends the essay by throwing down the gauntlet: he implies that those who criticize the process on legal grounds are betraying the revolution itself. These Anti-Federalists are either disingenuous or hypocrites for this same method, as an illegal convention was used to win the U.S. revolution and it "could [not] have been forgotten that no little ill-timed scruples, no zeal for adhering to ordinary forms, were anywhere seen, except in those who wished to indulge, under these masks, their secret enmity to the substance contended for." Anti-Federalist legalists are hypocrites because they supported the same method during the revolution and they are disingenuous because their true motive is opposition to the content of the constitution, not its ratification method.

[73] For example, U.K. citizens voted "yes" to leaving the European Union in June 2016. Less than a year later, in a snap election called to strengthen the mandate for "Brexit," the Conservative Party lost its majority in parliament. Steven Erlanger, Katrin Bennhold, and Stephen Castle, "The British Election That Somehow Made Brexit Even Harder," *The New York Times*, June 9, 2017, https://www.nytimes.com/2017/06/09/world/europe/uk-theresa-may-minority-government.html.

two elections, one of which is for a constitutional assembly. This is enough to distinguish the South American experiences from most of the cases in the recent rise of ostensibly popularly created semi-authoritarian constitutions in Turkey, Hungary, Poland, Egypt, central Asia, and perhaps many of the examples that legalists cite of "constitution-making gone wrong."[74] In most of these cases, a president or his appointed assembly either directly offers amendments or offers the draft of the constitution to be approved in a single referendum. That falls short of the standard pattern in South America, which consists of four moments: (1) presidential election in which a central issue was a new constitution, (2) referendum on whether to have a constitutional assembly, (3) elections to the constitutional assembly, and (4) referendum on the text of the constitution. Certainly, these four moments would be sufficient to fulfill the requirement of popular ratification.

The third principle is inclusion. This issue, not legal exhaustion or popular approval, most strongly distinguishes between and was the greatest source of conflict within the South American cases. It requires that the opposition be given input or at least enough concessions so that they can begrudgingly acquiesce to the new constitution. In their quest for revolutionary change, today's populists and radicals denounce the opposition as enemies of the true people so that they may exclude them from participation in the constitutional assembly. Including the opposition would moderate the political and economic transformation sought by new insurgent majorities. The people, however, is not a segment of the population; it is everyone. Since the constitution will bind all citizens, all have a right, through their duly constituted representatives, to contribute to its content.

Extraordinary adaptation then denies the radicals' division of the country into friends and enemies. Although Evo Morales, Hugo Chávez, and Rafael Correa won elections by stunning and historic margins, a significant portion of the country still opposed them. Even if we take Chávez's greatest electoral victory, his candidates' earning of 65.8 percent of the vote for the Constitutional Assembly, this still leaves more than one-third of the country in the opposition. These almost nine million individuals are part of the people too.[75] These numbers reflect that we live in a diverse and pluralistic society. Any attempt to homogenize it are normatively illegitimate. Furthermore,

---

[74] Partlett, "American Tradition of Constituent Power"; David Landau, "Constitution-Making Gone Wrong," *Alabama Law Review* 64 (2012), 923.

[75] This number is illustrative and far from exact. I am basing this number on the total population. https://www.populationpyramid.net/venezuela-bolivarian-republic-of/1999/.

such exclusions empower one party to dominate the assembly and write a semi-authoritarian constitution. This in turn invites resistance by the opposition leading to domestic unrest or even civil war. The people are not a part but the whole.

Centrists and the opposition should be included in the design of the constitution-making process and inside the constitutional assembly itself. The design stage, sometimes called the "pre-assembly" moment, is the decision on basic framework for how a new constitution will be created, such as the election rules for the constitutional assembly and the voting thresholds inside the assembly.[76]

Inclusion in the design stage occurs through the participation of multiple preexisting constituted institutions, which is the central idea of extraordinary adaptation. In the design stage, radicals tend to place all power in the president as a vessel of the people. While the president will later claim subservience to the constituent assembly, at this point the assembly does not yet exist. The president's claim is based on winning a nationwide election by historic margins, and because he is a singular figure, he can embody the unity of the people. But again, the electoral victories are never anywhere near the total population. And that singular unity, the fact that the president is a winner-take-all office, is why the president cannot speak for the diversity of the entire country. By contrast, a legislature and a federal system can capture that diversity because its multiplicity allows it to include minority forces. And it is not infrequent that a president wins his office, but his party still lacks control of one or both houses of the legislature, calling into question the idea that he is the people. For those reasons, to truly represent a diverse people, in addition to the president, multiple preexisting institutions must participate in deciding how a new constitution will be created.

In the creation of the U.S. Constitution, federalism's continuity created significant inclusion. The danger was that one majority or segment of the country might design a constitution that completely favored their own interests. Since selection for the Continental Convention happened under the state-centric Articles of Confederation, each state was given equal representation in the Philadelphia Convention. Many of the key divisions among citizens were represented, such as the division between the large and small states and between the plantation and slave economies of Virginia and those

---

[76] For the term pre-assembly moment, Renata Segura and Ana María Bejarano, "¡Ni una asamblea más sin nosotros! Exclusion, Inclusion, and the Politics of Constitution-Making in the Andes," *Constellations* 11 (2004), 217–36.

of the northern urbanizing states. Even though Rhode Island ultimately chose to not participate in the drafting of the Constitution, and while the convention was more nationalist than the country as a whole, the convention still made significant concessions in anticipation of needing Rhode Island and other states to approve or at least accept the result. The convention's proposed constitution did not reflect the median preferences of the convention's members because they knew they had to win the vote of moderate citizens and not completely alienate even those who would vote against the project.[77] The approval requirements of a supermajority and that each state would hold its own separate convention to assent ensured that each state's voice would be heard.[78]

This inclusion of old constituted institutions should not be taken too far. They are too tarred and delegitimized to directly create the constitution. Any constitution they produce will lack legitimacy from the get-go. Rather, they should lay the groundwork for the creation of a constitutional assembly that will attract new political actors.

The next stage is the meeting of the constitutional assembly, which will draft the constitution. An inclusive constitutional assembly is not causally mysterious; it follows naturally from the previous round of inclusion. As political scientists have shown, inclusion of the constituted institutions at the design stage leads to an inclusive electoral rule.[79]

All significant political parties and movements should have a presence in the actual assembly. To achieve this, the electoral rule should be inclusive. Winner-take-all rules, such as the Venezuelan first past the post rule, that give the majority nearly all of the seats are per se illegitimate. Winner-take-all is exclusive: it gives to the majority political party nearly all the power, beginning the descent into semi-authoritarianism. Such majoritarian rules may have their place in normal politics. However, with elected constitutional assemblies, the stakes are higher and the number of checks and balances is lower. The stakes are the very foundation for the entire polity. Among other things, the constitution will semipermanently entrench the conditions for all political competition in the future; indeed, it might determine whether there will be any such competition at all. In normal politics, bicameralism,

---

[77] Klarman, *The Framers' Coup*, 135.

[78] Ibid.

[79] Todd A. Eisenstadt, A. Carl LeVan, and Tofigh Maboudi, *Constituents Before Assembly: Participation, Deliberation, and Representation in the Crafting of New Constitutions* (Cambridge: Cambridge University Press, 2017); Segura and Bejarano, "Exclusion, Inclusion, and the Politics of Constitution-Making in the Andes."

federalism, and judicial review offset the risk of majoritarian constitution-making. In a unicameral constitutional assembly that drafts a constitution, fewer of these checks are present. Courts can try to check a constitutional assembly, but they are more likely to be effective in the design stage, acting before the constitutional assembly is composed to make it diverse. Once the constitutional assembly is gathered, courts are unlikely to withstand a face-off against this highly regarded, singular body. The best bet against tyran-nical constitutional assemblies is to ensure there are countervailing minority forces within the assembly itself that can fight back against the majority's at-tempt to declare the assembly sovereign.

Even though badly outnumbered, the meaningful inclusion of the minor-ities in the constitutional assembly will greatly decrease the chances of a semi-authoritarian constitution by changing the median member of the entire assembly. If only the revolutionaries are present in the assembly, the constitution will reflect the preferences of the median member of the revo-lutionary party since that member is the pivotal vote. The constitution will likely concentrate power in the executive. However, if centrists and the op-position are present, the range of preferences is much wider. The median of the assembly is shifted to a more moderate member of the revolutionary party. On certain issues, that moderate revolutionary may collaborate or threaten to collaborate with centrist members of the other party. Inclusion then not only empowers the opposition but centrists as well. It opens up the possibility of cross-party compromise that is not available when only one party dominates the assembly.[80] The constitution then will reflect the preferences of the average voter rather than a more radical supporter of the majority party.

Still, inclusion should not empower the opposition to block the revolu-tion, to block extraordinary adaptation itself. After repeated electoral victo-ries, new political forces have earned the right to create a new constitution. Inclusion is a warm and fuzzy term evoking the notion that all participants will leave uplifted and content. Nothing could be further from the truth.

---

[80] This idea of cross-party compromise is my own hypothesis and what I assert occurred in Bolivia. In formulating the hypothesis, I drew upon the debates in American political science about whether the pivotal vote in the House of Representatives is the median member of the House as a whole or the majority political party. Gary W. Cox and Mathew D. McCubbins, *Setting the Agenda: Responsible Party Government in the U.S. House of Representatives* (Cambridge: Cambridge University Press, 2005); Eric Schickler, "Institutional Change in the House of Representatives, 1867–1998: A Test of Partisan and Ideological Power Balance Models," *American Political Science Review* 94, no. 2 (June 2000), 269–88.

Inclusive constitution-making will leave many dissatisfied, and in extraordinary adaptation, the old guard will be especially upset that they wield less power in the new order. The goal is to give enough to the substantial minority that they will be willing to live with the change. The minority may not vote for the constitution, but there will be enough concessions that they are willing to accept the result and become a loyal opposition.

Think about the opposition's preferences in terms of three variables: (1) status quo, (2) new constitution, and (3) civil war. Given these options, the opposition's strongest preference may be the status quo. However, the majority's numerical, electoral, and governmental power makes that untenable. The goal then is to ensure that for the opposition the new constitution is preferable to civil war or domestic unrest. Given the right design of the constitution, the opposition's preferences will be status quo > constitution > civil war. If a new constitution is made, the opposition will be frustrated because they prefer politics to stay the same. Since the status quo, however, is not a realistic option and since civil war is the worst outcome, the opposition will accept the constitution as a necessary evil.

Inclusion is on a continuum. The least desirable possibility is a single-party constitutional convention as was held in 1999 Venezuela. This allows the party to create a constitution that centralizes power in its hands. By definition, a multiparty convention is more inclusive, but this may still leave many important groups out. While the U.S. process included both Federalists and Anti-Federalists, it excluded women, African Americans, and British loyalists. In 1991 Colombia, although the main political parties and urban guerillas compromised on a new constitution, the rural peasants and their demands for land redistribution were left aside. It is in creation of the Bolivian Constitution that we will find a fully inclusive process that included all relevant stakeholders.

My burden though is not merely to lay out principles but to show they are plausible and realistic ones. It is easy to call for inclusion but harder to show that it is feasible during a revolution. The principles emanate from and amplify tendencies already preexisting within the South American stories I recount. Not only should actors follow these principles, but they possess the means and incentives to do so.

They would not possess such means in lawless constitution-making. Some radicals make an ad hoc call for inclusion, but they do not address the impediments their embrace of lawlessness creates for inclusion. For example, based on the origins of the word "constituent power," radical Joel-Colon Rios argues that by definition it should be inclusive.[81] An etymology will not persuade populists, and it fails to arm their opponents. Lawlessness, the radical definition of constituent power, is tied to exclusion, which in turn leads to higher concentrations of power. If successful, declaring the people outside all law strips any institution of the power to check actors. To give total power to a political actor and then trust them to share it with their enemies is foolish. By incorporating law into popular constitution-making, extraordinary adaptation gives multiple actors leverage and power to ensure their own inclusion. Since law is not dead, since the old constitution still lingers on, and since no one institution may embody the people, congress, the courts, and state governments all have the right to participate in the creation of the new constitution. Rather than follow the approach of inclusive radicals and ask those seeking to centralize power to share it with their rivals, extraordinary adaptation empowers the rivals themselves to fight back; it helps them help themselves.

REVOLUTIONARY CHANGE

Extraordinary adaptation will likely fall short of delivering the radicals' vision of revolution, especially in the economic sphere. The political theory of popular revolutions has two related components: (1) the change and (2) the agent. Radicals sought change in the form of a total break with the past that cuts across all domains. Since they thought the people stood outside the current order, they were the ideal agent to achieve it. However, once extraordinary adaptation connects the people to law and current institutions, they are no longer capable of total upheaval. They will draw on old institutions whose rules will be biased against change and in favor of their own survival. Even as some of those rules are broken, powerful traces of the old regime will persevere.

Another way to explain how the utilization of old institutions will limit change is from the perspective of plurality or inclusion. Radicals empower the group most eager for change by giving them complete dominance over one sovereign site of change, such as the party or the constitutional assembly. Exclusion of those who oppose change promotes change. By contrast, extraordinary adaptation includes older institutions in which the old guard will

---

[81] Colón-Ríos, *Carl Schmitt and Constituent Power in Latin American Courts.*

have a foothold, as it served as the foundation for their power. Once these conservatives are part of the process of constitutional change, their input will water down the revolution. As a minority pinned against the wall by powerful and mobilized majorities, they will likely prove incapable of stopping change completely, but they may scale back its reach.

What does this inclusion of extraordinary adaptation mean for the dream of revolution? I bite the bullet and accept that extraordinary adaptation will likely fall short of delivering justice, a justice fit not only for the gods but for men on earth. Theorists, such as Hannah Arendt, Bruce Ackerman, and Gary Jacobsohn want to defend political or constitutional revolutions as true revolutions, and they all defend them as renewals and rebirths of old regimes.[82] These three thinkers argue that Marxists expect too much when they call for a total overturning of the old order that ends all scarcity and conflict. Revolutions occur in one domain at a time, and a constitutional revolution is a mighty achievement.[83]

I disagree. New constitutions should not be fetishized; they do not exist in a political realm shielded from all others. Constitutional revolutions are not neutral outside their own sphere; they have profound effects in all domains. A constitutional revolution will arrest, consolidate, or spur social change. And besides, most social revolutionaries, the political actors rather than the theorists, have far more modest goals than their Marxist counterparts. The slogan from the French, Russian, and the recent Egyptian revolutions was some variation of "Peace, Land, and Bread."[84] They sought economic redress through a restructuring of class relations. The constituent assembly occurs at

[82] Arendt, *On Revolution*; Ackerman, *We the People Volume 1*; Gary Jeffrey Jacobsohn, "Making Sense of the Constitutional Revolution," *Constellations* 19, no. 2 (June 1, 2012), 164–81; Gary Jeffrey Jacobsohn, "After the Revolution," *Israel Law Review* 34, no. 2 (July 2000), 139–69.

[83] In addition to defending constitutional revolution, on the related issue of speed of a revolution, Jacobsohn with co-author Yaniv Roznai has embraced the idea of revolution as the culmination of a slow evolution. I think this will deliver even less change than extraordinary adaptation because of its even slower speed. The window of opportunity for change is short, and revolutionaries must strike while the iron is hot. See Gary Jefrey Jacobsohn and Yaniv Roznal, *Constitutional Revolution* (2020); Joshua Braver, "Balkinization: What's the Rush? Why Revolutionaries Love Speed," *Balkin* (Jan. 15, 2021), https://balkin.blogspot.com/2021/01/whats-rush-why-revolutionaries-love.html.

[84] This variation of the slogan is from the Russian Revolution. In Egypt, it was "bread, dignity, and social justice." Although the French revolution is most famous for "Liberty, Equality, and Fraternity," the San-Culottes in March and May of 1795 printed on their caps the slogan, "Bread and the Constitution of 1793." Thanassis Cambanis, *Once Upon A Revolution: An Egyptian Story* (New York: Simon & Schuster, 2016), 51; George Rude, *The French Revolution: Its Causes, Its History and Its Legacy After 200 Years* (New York: Grove Press, 1994), 116; John J. Vail, *"Peace, Land, Bread!": A History of the Russian Revolution* (New York: Facts on File, 1995).

the height of popular mobilizing, making it an ideal moment to seize the momentum to overcome powerful enemies to redistribute wealth.

Inclusion of the opposition in the constitution-making process will obstruct this kind of radical change, especially in the economic sphere. The change will still be significant, but its intensity will be watered down by extraordinary adaptation. Revolutions occur in a wide variety of spheres, and extraordinary adaptation is likely to affect them differently. I am particularly interested in the constitutional one, but since this sphere is linked to others, I must ask how extraordinary adaptation's constitutional revolution will affect other spheres. Cultural revolutions re-evaluate the worth of oppressed groups' practices and heritage, which in turn gives them fuller access to the public sphere. In the sprawling and open public sphere, there are few formal barriers to a mobilized and self-conscious majority reclaiming its self-worth. Extraordinary adaptation might augment the cultural revolution as majorities often succeed in creating constitutional clauses to reinvigorate native languages, and the preamble often contains strong language about cultural worth. The constitution itself becomes a symbol or testament of cultural strength and worth. In the political sphere, extraordinary adaptation will give the majority dominance over the most central institutions but leave safeguards against egregious abuses, such as judicially enforceable rights and federalism, in order to entice the opposition to at least passively consent to the constitution.

The biggest source of disappointment to radicals will be the lack of an economic revolution. The opposition may be able to accept their loss of political power, but they will fight tooth and nail to protect their property. Defeating these economic elites will be costly. In addition to the elites' own ability to resist, redistribution will likely incur international opposition from countries allied with these elites and from international institutions like international arbitration courts and the International Monetary Fund, which are against nationalizations. Redistribution also poses a risk to the smooth functioning of the economy as it can be disruptive to production, to foreign investment, and the new owners might be less productive. In both my examples of extraordinary adaptation, Colombia and Bolivia, presidents settled for land redistribution that fell far short of radicals' goals, with Colombia avoiding the redistribution issue altogether and Bolivia leaving the most valuable lands to their owners.

The strength of extraordinary adaptation is that it avoids the establishment of semi-authoritarian constitutions. Its use of old institutions allows for the inclusion of the old guard that will push to ensure that the future opposition has some leverage against any government. Its weakness is the mirror image of its strength. The inclusion forces painful compromises that protect the old guard's wealth, wealth that was often plundered and stolen from the majority. The cost of extraordinary adaptation is the loss of a just economic revolution.

* * *

The dominant tradition in political theory and in analyses of popular constitution-making has led us astray. It feeds upon romantic and terrifying images of the people as marauding hordes rising up against their oppressors. Radicals foment the upheaval and legalists condemn it. The debate has become predictable and is at a stalemate. Radicals are right that many constitutional systems are incapable of reforming themselves, and that the people legitimately desired change. Yet, legalists are also correct that such change should not come at the cost of basic liberal and democratic values.

To change the terms of the debate, we must redefine the people's relationship to law. Since they annihilate law to achieve great change, radicals must construct a unified people to give them agency. Extraordinary adaptation grants to radicals the need to push the boundaries of legality, but by seeking a more modest revolution, it can still utilize the old institutions to include the opposition and adjudicate their differences with the majority. The people will be a plural entity. Hence, this approach avoids the radical danger of centralization and the legalist one of choking needed change.

Extraordinary adaptation might ultimately satisfy the legalists, but it will be a bitter pill for radicals to swallow. Legalists will be unnerved by the method's toleration for irregularity, but at their best, legalists do not fetishize the law as an end in itself. They seek its preservation as a means to protect liberal democracy, a task that extraordinary adaptation can fulfill. The method, however, will be of less comfort to radicals because it comes at a high cost to their aspirations for an economic revolution. Extraordinary adaptation is not the best of both worlds, but it may be the best we can hope for in this one.

3

The Enemies Clash

Lawless Constitution-Making in Venezuela and Ecuador

Venezuela and Ecuador are examples of lawless constitution-making. In both countries, the constitutional assemblies declared themselves to be sovereign or above all law because they embodied the people. On the basis of their sovereignty, the assemblies then purged or seized control over rival government institutions and then established semi-authoritarian constitutions. What can we learn from these failures so that they may be prevented in the future?

For Ecuador, the answer is nothing. No theory of the people or law could constrain the massive power that Correa commanded by virtue of his party's singular and massive win in the elections to the Constitutional Assembly. Sometimes, pure electoral firepower will overwhelm nearly any constraint.

That exceptional situation wasn't the case in Venezuela, however. Venezuela's story offers hope for an alternative theory of constituent power that I call extraordinary adaptation. For that reason, this chapter begins with and mostly discusses the creation of the 1999 Venezuelan Constitution before turning to the Ecuadorian story.

The scholarly consensus holds that Venezuela is an example of lawless or sovereign constitution-making, but scholars disagree over whether this feature should be praised[1] or condemned.[2] Radicals celebrate the process,

---

[1] For praise, Ricardo Combellas, *Poder constituyente* (Caracas: En Cambio, 2000); Roberto Viciano Pastor and Rubén Dalmau Martínez, *Cambio Político Y Proceso Constituyente En Venezuela (1998–2000)* (Valencia: Tirant Lo Blanch, 2001); Joel I. Colón-Ríos, "Carl Schmitt and Constituent Power in Latin American Courts: The Cases of Venezuela and Colombia," *Constellations* 18, no. 3 (2011), 365–88.

[2] For condemnation, Andrew Arato, *The Adventures of the Constituent Power: Beyond Revolutions?* (Cambridge: Cambridge University Press, 2017), 310–33; Allan R. Brewer-Carías, *Dismantling Democracy in Venezuela: The Chávez Authoritarian Experiment* (New York: Cambridge University Press, 2010); Allan-Randolph Brewer-Carias, *Poder constituyente originario y Asamblea Nacional Constituyente: (comentarios sobre la interpretación jurisdiccional relativa a la naturaleza, la misión y los límites de la asamblea nacional Constituyente)* (Caracas: Editorial juridica venezolana, 1999); Lolymar Hernández Camargo, *El proceso constituyente venezolano de 1999* (Caracas: Academia de Ciencias Políticas y Sociales, 2008); David Landau, "Constitution-Making Gone Wrong," *Alabama Law Review* 64 (2012), 923.

We, the Mediated People. Joshua Braver, Oxford University Press. © Joshua Braver 2023.
DOI: 10.1093/oso/9780197650639.003.0004

rightly pointing out that the constituent power opened up a sorely needed avenue for constitutional change.[3] Legalists strike back and observe that the country changed for the worse by replacing a liberal democratic constitution with a semi-authoritarian one.[4] For them, Venezuela is one more in a long list of cases that show that constituent power is a threat to stability and democracy.[5] Both sides are half right: the radicals understand the strengths of the constituent power, and the legalists know its pitfalls. The question then is how to achieve the best of both worlds: how to follow the radicals in empowering the people to create a new constitution while heeding the legalist call to prevent excessive centralizations of power in the executive.

This chapter lays out Venezuela as an example of "constitution-making gone wrong."[6] In this sense, I agree with the legalists that it vividly exemplifies all the dangers of constituent power. Yet, I draw different lessons from it. In contrast to legalists who cite Venezuela as a justification for discarding the idea of the constituent power entirely, I use it as an occasion to reformulate it.

For this reformulation of the constituent power, I draw upon the jurisprudence of the Venezuelan Supreme Court. For ten months and across nine cases, the Supreme Court pitted its vision of extraordinary adaptation against Hugo Chávez's lawless vision of the people. Legalists and radicals are both so fixated on defining the constituent power as a radical, lawless force that they mistakenly project this understanding onto the court's jurisprudence. In actuality, the court asserted its right to collaborate in the structuring of the constitution-making process by extraordinarily adapting the preexisting statute law on referendums. To be sure, the court's reasoning was not always clear, and most importantly it sealed its own fate by failing to force Chávez to have an inclusive rule for the assembly. This book is an attempt, under conditions of calm and reflection, to extrapolate from the court's and the other political actor's efforts and actions a more coherent and effective vision of constituent power.

---

[3] Combellas, *Poder Constituyente*; Pastor and Rubén Damau Martínez, *Cambio Político Y Proceso Constituyente En Venezuela (1998–2000)*; Colon-Rios, "Carl Schmitt and Constituent Power in Latin American Courts."

[4] Brewer-Carías, *Dismantling Democracy in Venezuela*; Brewer Carías, *Poder Constituyente Originario Y Asamblea Nacional Constituyente*; Lolymar Hernández Carmago, *El Proceso Constituyente Venezolano* (Caracas: Academia de Ciencias Politicas y Sociales, 2008). Landau, "Constitution-Making Gone Wrong."

[5] Landau, "Constitution-Making Gone Wrong"; William Partlett, "Constitution-Making by 'We the Majority' in Egypt," *The Brookings Institution*, accessed Jan. 4, 2015, http://www.brookings.edu/blogs/up-front/posts/2012/11/30-constitution-egypt-partlett.

[6] Landau, "Constitution-Making Gone Wrong," 923.

This chapter begins by documenting the legal exhaustion or the inability of the Venezuelan constitutional system to reform itself. Both Hugo Chávez and the Supreme Court recognized that "legal exhaustion" justified the need for invoking the people to create a new constitution in legally questionable ways, but they disagreed about the identity of the people. I then compare and contrast Chávez's and the Supreme Court's understanding of "the people." In doing so, I show how Venezuela might have pulled off extraordinary adaptation, including fulfilling its three principles of legal exhaustion, popular vindication, and inclusion. Lastly, I turn to Ecuador and concede that due to Rafael Correa's enormous electoral victory in elections for the Constitutional Assembly, there was little hope for extraordinary adaptation.

LEGAL EXHAUSTION

Building a new constitution is a dangerous endeavor: it unleashes the possibilities of both chaos and despotism. Such extreme measures should be reserved for the direst of situations.

For that reason, the first principle of extraordinary adaptation is legal exhaustion in which there is a widely held consensus that a new constitution is necessary and experience has shown that legal methods are insufficient to achieve the necessary change. In 1999, Venezuela met this criterion.

Most accounts of the creation of the 1999 Venezuelan Constitution begin with Hugo Chávez's 1998 presidential campaign in which constitutional revolution was a central plank.[7] But it would be a mistake to reduce the plan for a new constitution to one individual or group. By the early 1990s, all sides of the political spectrum had called for substantial constitutional change because the political system's legitimacy had long been in crisis. The crisis was intertwined with a widely held perception that the 1961 Venezuelan Constitution was complicit in and had created the foundations for a system

---

[7] Some of these accounts mention previous political systems and the 1961 constitution, but they rarely discuss reform efforts predating Chávez. Perhaps the most widely read account that essentially begins with Chávez's presidential campaign is Landau, "Constitution-Making Gone Wrong," 940. Other prominent ones include Brewer-Carías, *Dismantling Democracy in Venezuela*; Colon-Rios, *Weak Constitutionalism*; Rosalind Dixon and David Landau, *Abusive Constitutional Borrowing: Legal Globalization and the Subversion of Liberal Democracy*, (Oxford: Oxford University Press, 2021). 122-24. Pastor and Rubén Damau Martínez, *Cambio Político y Proceso Constituyente En Venezuela (1998–2000)*; Renata Segura and Ana María Bejarano, "¡Ni Una Asamblea Más Sin Nosotros! Exclusion, Inclusion, and the Politics of Constitution-Making in the Andes," *Constellations* 11, no. 2 (2004), 217–36.

in which two essentially identical parties dominated the government in order to enrich themselves and their allies.

The 1961 constitution was built around the consensus of the centrist political parties. The consensus was informed by the previous failure to transition to democracy. A few years after the transition, in 1945, the democratic government collapsed, and the country fell back into dictatorship because of the intense infighting among the political parties.[8] When the parties restored democracy in 1958, they committed to compromise. Reflecting this commitment, most of the political parties struck a pact to share power and limit policies called the Pact of Punto Fijo. The pact ensured that for the next five years, or the first presidential period, there would be a multiparty presidential cabinet shared by the parties to the pact.[9] The pact also ruled out the pursuit of the most radical leftist policies in agrarian reform, education, and the oil sector.[10] Shortly after the first elections, a bicameral committee, composed of members of Congress in proportion to their electoral performance, including the members of the Communist Party, drew up a new constitution that was approved by the Congress and all provincial governments.[11] The pact and the ensuing constitution enshrined a basic framework of consensus and moderate governing that would be supported by most of the major sectors of society, including the Catholic Church, the business community, and urban workers as well as by the United States.

For those on the radical left, both within the Acción Democrática party (AD) and in the separate Communist Party, the pact and the constitution was a conspiracy against them. While the Communist Party was still able to compete in elections and did so successfully in the 1958 elections, their polices and the policies of the radical wing of the AD were ruled out by those in power, and both groups lacked representation in the cabinet.[12] In response, and following the recently established Cuban example, the Communist Party and the radical factions within the AD took up arms and established one of the largest guerilla organizations in Latin America, which resulted in a ban on the communist party and their continual exclusion from

[8] Steve Ellner, *Rethinking Venezuelan Politics: Class, Conflict, and the Chávez Phenomenon* (Boulder, CO: Lynne Rienner, 2008), 42. Ellner's chapter is a wonderful overview of this period.

[9] Ana Maria Bejarano, *Precarious Democracies: Understanding Regime Stability and Change in Colombia and Venezuela* (Notre Dame, Ind: University of Notre Dame Press, 2011), 109.

[10] Ibid., 111–13.

[11] Ibid., 159; Miriam Kornblith, "The Politics of Constitution-Making: Constitutions and Democracy in Venezuela," *Journal of Latin American Studies* 23, no. 1 (1991), 72.

[12] Bejarano, *Precarious Democracies*, 159.

mainstream politics.[13] By the late 1960s, the rebellion had collapsed, and the government granted amnesty to the rebels and repealed the ban on the Communist Party.[14] Restrictions on policies or the composure of the cabinet had long expired after the first election. Still, even with these changes, the two centrist political parties continued to dominate the political system further cementing the belief that the constitution at root was responsible for limiting political competition.

In the 1970s, political scientists hailed Venezuela as a "model democracy" but the system's legitimacy began a deep descent in the 1980s. The Venezuelan economy and social programs were heavily dependent on oil, and the drop in its price led to a deep economic depression. Against the wishes of the voters and in contradiction to their campaign platforms, presidents elected in 1989 and 1993 embraced neoliberal policies that cut government support and privatized national companies. These measures led to a wave of political turmoil. In response to a raise in public transport fares, on February 27, 1989, riots broke out first in the capital of Caracas and then spread around the country.[15] The government's brutal response left an estimated 396 civilians dead and created a widespread resentment toward those in power.[16] Twice in 1992 segments of the armed forces attempted coups, both of which failed. Hugo Chávez led the first of these attempts, which garnered significant sympathy among the population and made him a hero to many. Once captured, Chávez gave a televised address calling on his soldiers to lay down their arms, but he also stated that they have only failed "por ahora" or "for now," which became a common and ironic catchphrase among Venezuelans.[17] As the coup winded down, Senator Rafael Caldera gave a blistering speech in Congress, expressing sympathy for Chávez's cause and legitimating his grievances. The speech propelled Caldera to the presidency at which point Caldera pardoned Chávez. In 1993, Congress impeached and

---

[13] Ibid, 105–6, 109, 160; George Ciccariello-Maher, *We Created Chávez: A People's History of the Venezuelan Revolution* (Durham: Duke University Press, 2013), 29. Maher argues that the turn to revolutionary violence by the PCV and the MIR occurred in response to government oppression, citing the arrest of six of MIR's members by the government, which "sparked an escalating cycle of student demonstrations and further repression; ibid., 26–27.

[14] Bejarano, *Precarious Democracies*, 160.

[15] Margarita López Maya, "The Venezuelan 'Caracazo' of 1989: Popular Protest and Institutional Weakness," *Journal of Latin American Studies* 35, no. 1 (2003), 120.

[16] Ibid., 130. For a discussion of the difficulties of knowing the number of the dead, including because of the refusal of the government to cooperate and a possible cover-up, see Ciccariello-Maher, *We Created Chávez*, 97.

[17] Richard S. Hillman, "Intellectuals An Elite Divided," in *The Unraveling of Representative Democracy in Venezuela*, ed. David J. Myers (Baltimore: Johns Hopkins University Press, 2006), 121.

removed the president, a first in Venezuelan history. By this time a torrent of "editorials television talk shows, academic writing and even televised soap operas" portrayed the political system as "closed, pathologically corrupt, and beyond redemption."[18]

In the early 1990s, there was widespread agreement that the old political system was broken and that radical constitutional change was necessary. What remained an open question was whether the 1961 constitution could provide a legal route for constitutional transformation. In addition to a method for small amendments, Venezuela's then 1961 constitution provided an additional route for more ambitious "general reforms" of the constitution. Furthermore, its threshold requirement of multiple approvals by Congress and a general referendum were not unreasonably burdensome. Could the old constitution's "general reform" method resolve the crisis?

The answer turned out to be "no." The two significant attempts to change the constitution failed. The first reform attempt began with a special bicameral commission in June of 1989, and it had modest goals and the support of all the major political parties. Since then Senator and soon to be president Caldera was the chair of the committee, his thundering speech in response to Chávez's 1992 coup attempt thrust the committee into the public spotlight. Constitutional reform became a major national issue, and the proposed changes to the constitution became more far-reaching. Just as deep as the agreement that reform was necessary was the disagreement over what that reform should entail. The media, in particular, spearheaded the opposition because they objected to measures prohibiting media monopolies, barring the offense of public decency, and requiring pluralistic representation of views. The media's opposition was soon joined by state governors and influential members of the judiciary. Eventually, the public too turned against these changes, and the measure died in the Senate in late September of 1992.[19]

The second attempt made even less progress than the first. One of the most important planks in Caldera's presidential campaign was constitutional reform and upon becoming president he pressured Congress to develop a proposal. Accordingly, a Senate committee took up the issue, but the committee

---

[18] Ibid., 121.

[19] Miriam Kornblith, "Legitimacy and the Reform Agenda in Venezuela," in *Reinventing Legitimacy: Democracy and Political Change in Venezuela*, eds. Damarys J. Canache and Michael Kulisheck (Westport, CT: Praeger, 1998), 14. For a review of different amendment methods based on the intended level of constitutional change, Richard Albert, *Constitutional Amendments: Making, Breaking and Changing Constitutions*, (Oxford, United Kingdom, 2019), 175-194.

worked "unevenly and intermittently, with little public involvement" in the debate.[20] With little public buy-in and little confidence that Congress would be able to do any better than before, the committee never set forth any proposals. Even a more limited attempt to fix an ineffective judiciary went nowhere.[21]

The problem was that the Congress lacked the credibility and will to enact reform. Any attempts at change will elicit great opposition from those who fear it. But this obstacle is expected and not insuperable. In Venezuela, however, since the political parties were at their weakest, they were unable to act as a negotiating space to forge compromises between competing interests and rally the public against those who stood in their way. As Miriam Kornblith summarized writing shortly after the failed attempts, "Although the parties were the original promoters of the reform, they failed to present an organized and coherent front, coordinate a solid defense of the substantive innovations of the different bills, or assert convincingly Congress's legitimate right to propose constitutional reform. The political parties appeared bewildered and isolated, and failed to defend what was, after all, their own project."[22] Even if the Senate had approved the proposals, Kornblith was skeptical that voters would approve anything Congress proposed in a referendum: "In Venezuela's present condition a referendum could well be interpreted more as a plebiscite on the system, the government, or the proponents of the reform, than on the content of the proposal; rejection or indifference are highly probable outcomes in any case."[23] Venezuela fulfilled extraordinary adaptation's first principle of legal exhaustion because the constitutional system could not enact the consensus about needed change through the amendment method.

Hugo Chávez's Radical Constituent Power

Upon winning election to the presidency, Chávez stood at a new juncture in Venezuelan constitutional history. A constitutional revolution was almost inevitable; the question was what form it would take. All previous

---

[20] Ibid., 14.

[21] Ibid., 16; Lawyers Committee for Human Rights (U.S.), *Halfway to Reform: The World Bank and the Venezuelan Justice System* (New York: Lawyers Committee for Human Rights, 1996).

[22] Miriam Kornblith, "Political Crisis and Constitutional Reform," in *Lessons of the Venezuelan Experience*, eds. Louis W. Goodman et al. (Washington, D.C.: Baltimore: Woodrow Wilson Center Press, 1995), 346.

[23] Kornblith, "Legitimacy and the Reform Agenda in Venezuela," 15.

constitutional assemblies had been established after military insurrections or other calamitous events, and as a result those assemblies had wielded absolute power. As Chávez had learned the hard way in 1992 when his own attempt to topple the government failed, the era of coups was over. Instead, the revolution would come through elections in an ailing, but still alive, constitutional order. In just such a setting, extraordinary adaptation is a live possibility. Would Chávez take advantage of this new opportunity and follow the Colombian example by extraordinarily adapting old institutions, or would he take the traditional Venezuelan path of creating sovereign constitutional assemblies that concentrated power in the executive? Chávez chose the latter. In the terms of constitutional theory, he chose to follow the well-trod Schmittian path at a moment of real possibility for extraordinary adaptation.

In this section, I will first discuss how Chávez and the Venezuelan Constituent Assembly successfully purged or seized control of all rival institutions and then show how these events reflect Chávez's radical vision of constituent power.

The Sovereign Constituent Assembly in Venezuela

In December of 1998, riding a wave of popular discontent with the political system, Hugo Chávez was elected president of Venezuela with 56.20 percent of the vote, the most decisive presidential victory since 1947, the first year of electoral democracy in twentieth-century Venezuela.[24] The central promise of his campaign was to hold elections for a constituent assembly to write a new constitution. The problem was that the 1961 constitution's amendment method did not involve or permit a constituent assembly.[25] Furthermore, although Chávez won a landslide in the December 1998 election, the legislative elections occurred a month before, and Chávez lacked the votes in Congress necessary for general reform.[26] He claimed a right, however, to call

---

[24] Michael Coppedge, "Venezuela: Popular Sovereignty vs. Liberal Democracy," in *Constructing Democratic Governance in Latin America*, eds. Jorge I. Domínguez and Michael Shifter (Baltimore: Johns Hopkins University Press, 2003), 167.

[25] The constitution specified two exclusive methods of formal constitutional change: either amendment or "general reform." The latter referred to the radical change or perhaps even the creation of a new constitution through a multi-step process that included the supermajority vote of a joint sitting of the two houses of the legislature and subsequent approval through a popular referendum. This process did not involve a constituent assembly, and it is nowhere else provided for in the constitution. See Venezuelan Constitution, 1961, Arts. 245, 246; Brewer-Carías, *Dismantling*, 49–50.

[26] Coppedge, "Venezuela: Popular Sovereignty vs. Liberal Democracy," 178.

the referendum on whether to have a constituent assembly because "sovereignty resides in the people," and Chávez could act as their vessel to initiate the process to create a new constitution.[27]

On February 2, 1999, on the day of his inauguration, and as his first official act of government, Chávez issued a decree calling for a referendum with two separate questions on the ballot: (1) whether to hold elections for a constituent assembly to draft a new constitution and (2) whether to authorize Chávez to unilaterally decide the method of election for the assembly. If the voters said yes, elections to the constituent assembly would go forward, the assembly would draft the constitution, and the process would culminate in another referendum in which the people would vote on whether or not to approve the constitution. The referendum decree was challenged in the Supreme Court of Venezuela, and a struggle ensued between Chávez and the court that spanned ten cases and nearly nine months.[28]

Chávez ultimately prevailed. The court authorized the referendum on whether to have elections to a constituent assembly. However, they ruled that the second question, as formulated, was unconstitutional. The second question should offer voters the opportunity to approve or disapprove of a specific electoral rule for the constituent assembly.[29] Chávez complied, and put on the referendum ballot a first-past-the-post method of aggregating votes for future elections to the Constituent Assembly. Consistent with the standards for a fair referendum and fair elections, the questions were separated, intelligible, and neutral.[30]

The referendum was held on April 25, 1999, and voters answered yes to both questions, yes to the proposition to have a constituent assembly and

---

[27] Hugo Chávez Frías, "Discurso de toma de posesión como Presidente Constitucional de la República de Venezuela," in *Hugo Chávez: La construcción del socialismo del siglo XXI: discursos del comandante supremo ante la Asamblea Nacional (1999–2012)*, 2013, 32; Hugo Chávez, "Presentación de Hugo Chávez ante la Academia de Ciencias Políticas y Sociales," in *Asamblea Constituyente y Proces Constituyente 1999. Coleccion Tratado de Derecho Constitucional, Tomo VI*, ed. Allan R. Brewer-Carias (Caracas: Fundacion Editorial Juridical Venezolana, 2014), 73, 76–77).

[28] For an overview of the struggle, see Brewer-Carías, *Dismantling*; Landau, "Constitution-Making Gone Wrong."

[29] Corte Suprema de Justicia [C.S.J.] [Supreme Court], Sala. Politico Administrativa enero 19, 1999, M.P. H. La Roche, *Revista del Derecho Publico* (Nos. 77–80, p. 56) (approving the referendum); Corte Suprema de Justicia [C.S.J.] [Supreme Court], Sala. Politico Administrativa marzo 18, 1999, M.P.H. Harting, *Revista del Derecho Publico* (Nos. 77–80, p. 73) (reiterating the approval of the referendum, but requiring Chávez to specify the electoral rule).

[30] For a thorough discussion of fair rules for a referendum, Stephen Tierney, *Constitutional Referendums: The Theory and Practice of Republican Deliberation* (New York: Oxford University Press, 2012), 229–34. For the rules for the Venezuelan referendum, Brewer-Carías, *Dismantling Democracy in Venezuela*, 55.

yes to Chávez's chosen electoral rule. In the elections to the Constituent Assembly, Chávez's chosen electoral rule converted his 65.8 percent of the vote into 93.1 percent of the seats in the Constituent Assembly.[31] Despite repeated Supreme Court rulings to the contrary[32] and with Chávez's support, the Constituent Assembly declared itself sovereign. As a testament to the assembly's sovereignty and to prove that his powers derived from the assembly rather than the "moribund constitution" of 1961, Chávez asked the assembly to ratify him his as president.[33] On August 9, 1999, the Constituent Assembly voted unanimously with three abstentions to select Hugo Chávez as the president,[34] and he was re-sworn in on August 11.[35]

Logically, if they had the power to ratify Chávez's presidency, they too possessed the power to fire the holders and limit the powers of other offices. The next day, on the basis of its sovereign power, the Constituent Assembly declared a state of emergency "declaring the reorganization of all the organs of public power" and authorized itself to "take, execute and order the measures dealing with the competence of the public powers of the state . . . that are necessary and indispensable to overcome the situation of emergency confronting the nation." Through a series of decrees in August and then later in December, the Constituent Assembly purged the opposition in virtually every level of government.[36] Most notably, and among other purges,

---

[31] Coppedge, "Venezuela: Popular Sovereignty," 187; Segura Bejarano, "¡Ni Una Asamblea Más Sin Nosotros!," 230..

[32] See, e.g., Corte Suprema de Justicia [C.S.J.] [Supreme Court], Sala. Politico Administrativa abril 13, 1999, M.P. H. Harting, *Revista del Derecho Publico* (Nos. 77–80, p. 85); Corte Suprema de Justicia [C.S.J.] [Supreme Court], Sala. Politico Administrativa julio 21, 1999, M.P. H. Rondón de Sanso, *Revista del Derecho Publico* (Nos. 77–80, p. 104).

[33] Hugo Chávez, "Discurso con motive del reconocimiento del Ejecutivo Nacional al character originario de la Asamblea Nacional Constituyente y entrega de propuestas para la nueva Constitución," 43, 44, 58, 61, 62, 68, 80, 83, 86 (repeatedly declaring the assembly to be "most sovereign" at his speech at the opening of the assembly).

[34] *Gaceta Constituyente (Diario de Debates), Agosto–Septiembre 1999*, No. 5, Aug. 9, 1999 [hereinafter *Gaceta Constituyente*, No. 5].

[35] See *Gaceta Constituyente (Diario de Debates), Agosto–Septiembre 1999*, No. 6, Aug. 11, 1999.

[36] Carias, *Dismantling*, 57–60; Landau, "Constitution-Making Gone Wrong," 948. To be more precise, the process proceeded in two stages, with the ratification of the constitution occurring in between. In the first stage, through a series of decrees on August 12, 19, 26, 28, the assembly effectively neutered Congress and the judiciary through a combination of limiting their powers, reorganizing their structure, shrinking their size, as well as asserting a right to veto their decisions, and fire individual members. David Landau summarizes the changes, "[The Constituent Assembly] issued a decree suspending the functioning of the plenaries of the House and Senate and reducing Congress down to its delegated commission (which normally stayed in session during congressional recesses) and several other committees. It also approved a short list of activities that the Congress was allowed to work on, established that some of these actions were subject to ratification by the assembly, placed all other legislative powers in the assembly itself, and established a Commission of Investigation charged with auditing the budgetary and other operations of the Congress. Finally, the resolution similarly reduced all state legislative assemblies down to designated commissions composed of no more than seven members and decreed a list of matters on which they and even town councils were

in December it formally dissolved the Congress and state legislative assemblies, placed mayors and municipal councils under supervision, replaced the National Electoral Council, and removed a large number of judges—including many members of the Supreme Court. The assembly replaced Congress with a "Congressito" or "Little Congress" whose members were chosen by the Constituent Assembly.[37] The opposition had not only been excluded from the process of drafting the constitution, but also from all other possible positions of power at every level of government.[38] On October 23, 1999, a newly reorganized judiciary, meeting in plenary session, ruled that the decrees were valid as acts of sovereign power. The judges from the political-administrative chamber, who had participated in the earlier decisions on the constitution-making process, dissented on the basis that the people, not the assembly, were sovereign. On December 15, 1999, with a low turnout of 30.4 percent, 71.8 percent of participants in a referendum voted yes to approve the new constitution.[39]

The Constituent Assembly, stacked with Chávez allies, became a despotic and all-powerful actor that illegitimately usurped the constituted powers. For almost a year, starting from the mid-August 1999 decrees until the first round of elections under the new constitution on July 30, 2000, the Constituent Assembly and its appointed allies ruled and dominated the country. Similar to the French Jacobin Convention of 1793, the Constituent Assembly justified this claim on the basis that it was sovereign since the people, as embodied in the March referendum and elections to the Constituent Assembly, had

---

forbidden to take any action on until further notice." David Landau, "Constitution-Making Gone Wrong," 947. See also Pastor and Dalmau, *Cambio Politico*, 150–51. On December 15, 1999, with a low turnout of 30.4 percent, 71.8 percent of participants in a referendum voted yes to approve the new constitution Five days later, as David Landau has well-summarized, the Constituent Assembly issued a transitory decree that removed a large number of judges, formally dissolved the Congress and state legislative assemblies, and placed under supervision mayors and municipal councils. The assembly replaced Congress with a national legislative commission whose members were chosen by the Constituent Assembly. The assembly also chose a new national ombudsman, chief prosecutor, and members of the National Electoral Council. It replaced many members of the Supreme Court with allies of the regime and set up a commission to remove judges throughout the country. Lastly, it created a National Commission of Unions to purge the leadership of the labor unions, who were dominated by the old political parties. Carias, *Dismantling*, 57–60; Landau, "Constitution-Making Gone Wrong," 948.

[37] The assembly also chose a new national ombudsman, chief prosecutor, and members of the National Electoral Council. It also created a National Commission of Unions to purge the leadership of the labor unions, who were dominated by the old political parties. Carias, *Dismantling*, 57–60, and Landau, "Constitution-Making Gone Wrong," 948.

[38] Carias, *Dismantling*, 57–60, and Landau, "Constitution-Making Gone Wrong," 948.

[39] Michael Coppedge, "Venezuela: Popular Sovereignty vs. Liberal Democracy," 167.

risen up against and overthrown the old regime.[40] This is Hannah Arendt's greatest fear: the claim to sovereign and total authority based upon embodiment of the people.

As the Supreme Court repeatedly pointed out, sovereignty lies with the people, and not with the assembly. Indeed, no one institution or individual can embody the people, but only represent it. Hence, any one body's claim to sovereignty is always a usurpation because of the very logic of representation itself.[41] The assembly was not identical with the people. Rather, just like Congress and state governments, the assembly represented the people, and for that reason could only have limited and delegated powers. In the March referendum and elections, as stated on the ballot, the people delegated to the assembly the sole task of drafting a constitution. The Constituent Assembly had exceeded this mandate.

Furthermore, the process created the conditions for near complete executive dominance over government. For at least most, if not all, of Chávez's time as president, elections were meaningful, frequent, and contested events in Venezuela with accurate tabulation of votes.[42] What was lacking were meaningful checks on presidential power during the term of office. To be clear, this is not the fault of the constitution itself. While it did strengthen the presidency by permitting one consecutive re-election and extending the term from four to six years, it also provided for a presidential recall, an independent judiciary, and the protection of a generous list of human rights.[43]

[40] Luis Milquena, president of the Constituent Assembly's opening speech. *Gaceta Constituyente* (Diario de Debates), agosto–septiembre 1999, No. 5, Aug. 9, 1999. To be clear, Chávez's constitutional advisers did not argue that the sovereignty of the assembly gave it completely unlimited powers. It could not violate human rights or international treaties, for example. See Combellas, *Poder Constituyente*, 32. *Senate Speech of Hermann Escarrá, in* Hermann Escarrá Malavé, *Chávez y El Proceso Constituyente de 1999* (2013). Malavé was a key constitutional adviser to Chávez.

[41] See Bryan Garsten, "Representative Government and Popular Sovereignty," in *Political Representation*, eds. Ian Shapiro et al., 1st ed. (Cambridge: Cambridge University Press, 2010); Hanna F. Pitkin, *The Concept of Representation* (Berkeley: University of California Press, 1972). Thee illegitimacy of one body's claim to represent the people does not exclude the idea of a people as embodied in the acts of multiple representative bodies coming to agreement as occurs as in extraordinary adaptation.

[42] See, e.g., Carter Center, *Final Report on Venezuela's April 2013 Elections* (2013); Human Rights Watch, *Countries at the Cross Roads: Venezuela* (2011). For example, Chavistas won in the 2006 presidential election and the 2009 referendum, but lost in the 2007 referendum and performed below expectations in the 2008 and 2010 legislative elections. Maduro barely managed to win his first election to the presidency in 2013, and Chavistas lost control of Congress in the 2015 elections. However, there are valid concerns about unequal access to public and private media, harassment of opponents, and illegitimate use of state media for campaign purposes. Since Maduro has become president, elections have become much less free and fair to the point where office holders have little electoral legitimacy..

[43] Landau, "Constitution-Making Gone Wrong," 941, fn 66; for an opposing view, Allan-Randolph Brewer-Carias, *Constitutional Law in Venezuela*, 2012. For a summary and analysis

However, the assembly's liquidation of the opposition gave Chávez near complete dominance over the process of implementation of and transition to the new constitution. This allowed him to manipulate the system to undermine the powers and independence of Congress and the judiciary.[44] There are also serious, though heavily contested, accusations that Chávez abused his power to seriously hinder, though not make it impossible, for the opposition to compete in elections through various forms of blacklisting, harassment, "legal" persecution for speech and broadcasting violations, illegitimate use of state resources to support incumbents in elections, and occasional arrest or exile.[45] There is a straight line from the sovereign constitutional assembly to these problems of executive aggrandizement.

The Lawless People

While it would be naive to deny that the aggrandizement of power was an important drive for Chávez, it would also be wrong to use that basis to dismiss the coherent and principled view of popular sovereignty that undergird Chávez's actions. Chávez acted in accordance with a radical theory of constituent power that goes as far back as Thomas Hobbes and was crucial for the enactment of the French Revolution. Without understanding this venerable vision, it is impossible to combat it.

Although Chávez's actions embody a long tradition, his reference points were much closer to home. Chávez and his advisers had in mind both the 1991 Colombian precedent and Venezuelan history, both of which were

of the contradictions of the Constitution English, Phoebe King, "Neo-Bolivarian Constitutional Design: Comparing the 1999 Venezuelan, 2008 Ecuadorian and 2009 Bolivian Constitutions," in *Social and Political Foundations of Constitutions*, eds. Denis J. Galligan and Mila Versteeg (New York: Cambridge University Press, 2013), 375–78.

[44] Coppedge, "Venezuela: Popular Sovereignty vs. Liberal Democracy," 178; Landau, "Constitution-Making Gone Wrong," 940–41, 949.

[45] Human Rights Watch, "A Decade Under Chávez" (2008); Letter, "More than 100 Latin American Experts Question Human Rights Watch's Venezuela Report" (2008), Dec. 17, 2008, available at http://venezuelanalysis.com/analysis/4051. See also Steven Levitsky and James Loxton, "Populism and Competitive Authoritarianism in the Andes," *Democratization* 20, no. 1 (Jan. 1, 2013), 107–36 (arguing that Venezuela is a competitive authoritarian regime where "formal democratic institutions are viewed as the primary means of gaining power, but in which incumbent abuse skews the playing field to such an extent that the opposition's ability to compete is seriously compromised"); David J. Myers, "Venezuela: Delegative Democracy or Electoral Autocracy," in *Constructing Democratic Governance in Latin America*, eds. Jorge I. Dominguez and Michael Shifter, 2013.(2008) (arguing that even though Chávez has respected freedom of speech, the government has been used to discredit opposition groups and undermine their ability to organize).

partial models. Chávez visited Colombia in 1994 to learn about the country's Constitutional Assembly[46] and left impressed, later stating in an interview that "We were very aware of what happened in Colombia, in the years of 1990–1999, when there was a constitutional assembly—of course." From it, he and his advisers took the strategy of winning a presidential election and then calling for a referendum on a constitutional assembly by executive decree. But Chávez thought the Colombians hadn't gone far enough because the participation of the old political parties in the Constitutional Assembly obstructed revolutionary change. To Chávez, the Colombian process "was very limited because in the end it was subordinated to the existing powers. It was the existing powers that designed Colombia's Constitutional Assembly, and got it going, and therefore, it could not transform the situation because it was a prisoner of the existing powers."[47] Chávez would not repeat Colombia's mistake. He would break free of the "existing powers" through election rules that helped his party completely dominate the Constitutional Assembly and by having that assembly declare itself to be free of all constraints from other institutions of power.

Carl Schmitt's work here also had a role. Ricardo Combellas had been the leading Venezuelan adviser in constitutional reform attempts for more than a decade and in the early stage was an important public voice and one of Chávez's most important advisers. He was deeply influenced by Schmitt and invoked his work publicly to defend the idea of a sovereign constituent assembly.[48] He counseled Chávez to radicalize in a Schmittian fashion the Colombian process.[49] Lawyer, historian, and later a member of the Constituent Assembly, Jorge Olivarría responded to the Combellas editorial, and called attention to Schmitt's influence under a paragraph titled, "Tell Me Whom You Quote . . . And I Will Tell You How You Think."[50] In jail, Chávez read, and in speeches has claimed to adopt, Antonio Negri's theory of constituent power, which is descended from and influenced by Schmitt's work.[51]

---

[46] Nicolás Figueroa, "A Critique of Populist Jurisprudence: Courts, Democracy, and Constitutional Change in Colombia and Venezuela," PhD diss. (New York: New School for Social Research, 2016), iv.

[47] Hugo Chávez, *Understanding the Venezuelan Revolution: Hugo Chávez Talks to Marta Harnecker* (New York: Monthly Review Press, 2005), 32.

[48] Combellas, *Poder constituyente*.Richard Combellas, "Byzantine Discussion," *El Universal*, Apr. 23, 1999 (editorial defending Schmitt's conception of a sovereign constituent assembly).

[49] Ricardo Combellas, "El Proceso Constituyente y La Constitucion de 1999," *Politeia* (2003); Ricardo Combellas, *El proceso constituyente: una historia personal*, 2010; Ricardo Combellas in interview with the author Caracas, Aug. 31, 2014.

[50] See Jorge Olivarría, "The Darkest Hour," *El Nacional*, Apr. 25, 1999.

[51] "Toni Negri in Venezuela," *Revolts Now*, Mar. 7, 2013, https://revoltsnow.wordpress.com/2013/03/07/toni-negri-in-venezuela-socialism-of-the-21st-century. Negri shares with Schmitt a conception of the constituent power as outside all law. But whereas Schmitt believes lawlessness

And last, as I discuss in more detail later in this chapter, the Venezuelan Supreme Court also seems to cite to Schmitt's work.

Chávez's thinking also conformed in spirit to past Venezuelan constitutional history, a history that had no experience with and therefore no theory of extraordinary adaptation. Instead, Venezuelan jurists describe the constituent power as "original," which means that it is sovereign and above all law. It is normally exercised after the complete overthrow of the old order through a civil war or violent revolution.[52] The old government and constitution has been dissolved and power must be re-established for day-to-day governance. The Constituent Assembly is tasked then, not only with drawing up a new constitution, but also with governing the country. All remnants of the old regime are subordinated to its power. All previous examples of constitution-making in Venezuela occurred under the circumstances of original constituent power which overthrows the old order by brute force.[53]

But 1999 was different, or at least could have been. In 1999, no violent revolution or other explosion of the old system had occurred. Six years before his election, Hugo Chávez had tried to overthrow the government by military force, counting on the people to flood the streets to support him, but no uprising materialized. That Cuban or Bolshevik style attempt at revolution

leads to centralization in a singular site such as a president or sovereign constituent assembly, Negri thinks it leads to a radically decentralized people, which in later work he calls the "multitude." Antonio Negri, *Insurgencies: Constituent Power and the Modern State*, trans. Maurizia Boscagli (Minneapolis: University of Minnesota Press, 2009); Michael Hardt and Antonio Negri, *Multitude: War and Democracy in the Age of Empire* (New York: Penguin Books, 2005).

Furthermore, Schmitt's influence persisted after the promulgation of the Venezuelan Constitution. Arcadio Delgado Rosales, a current member of the court, openly acknowledges Schmitt's influence. See "Reflexiones sobre el Sistema Político y el Estado Social", Apertura de actividades judiciales del año 2012. Tribunal Supremo de Justicia, No. 39, Serie Eventos, Caracas (2012). His father had been the intellectual mastermind of the newly reconstituted Supreme Court, renamed the Supreme Tribunal of Justice under the new 1999 Constitution, and has his own Leninist theory of unconstrained constituent power. See J.M. Delgado Ocando, *Problemas de Filosofía Del Derecho y Del Estado: Hipótesis Para Una Filosofía Antihegemónica Del Derecho y Del Estado*, 2nd ed (Caracas: Vadell Hermanos Editores, 2004). Nicolás Figueroa drew my attention to this development and writes about it in "A Critique of Populist Jurisprudence: Courts, Democracy, and Constitutional Change in Colombia and Venezuela," 27–28 (unpublished and on file with the author)

[52] Pedro Vega Garcia, *La Reforma Constitucional Y La Problemática Del Poder Constituyente* (Tecnos, 1985). Original constituent power contrasts with derived constituent power, which refers to constitutional asmendments. The distinction is originally from French public law. For the first two texts that first used the term, see Roger Bonnard, "Les actes constitutionnels de 1940" [The Constitutional Acts of 1940], *Revue du Droit Public* 48 (1942); George Vedel, *Cours de droit constitutionnel* (Paris, 1953).

[53] Elena Plaza and Ricardo Combellas, eds., *Procesos constituyentes y reformas constitucionales en la historia de Venezuela: 1811–1999* (Universidad Central de Venezuela, Facultad de Ciencias Jurídicas y Políticas, 2005).

failed, and indeed had become outmoded in Latin America more generally. In 1999, the constitution of 1961 was still intact, elections were held under it across the country for a wide variety of positions, and Congress was in session.[54]

Nonetheless, Chávez and his constitutional advisers still maintained that even though there was no violence, this new peaceful rupture would be just as lawless and radical. Chávez's constitutional adviser, Ricardo Combellas, recognized that the situation was "exceptional" and "*sui generis*." But he maintained that "even though the origins are distinct, the effects are similar."[55] Different means still led to the same end of an original constituent power. In his swearing-in ceremony to become president, Chávez began to recite the traditional oath, "before God, before the homeland and before the people" but then altered the remaining portions, "and upon this *moribund* constitution, that I will complete and propel the democratic transformations necessary for the Republic, a new Magna Carta adequate to the new times."[56] The Congress and the Supreme Court had no role to play in the establishment of a new Republic because they existed only under the 1961 constitution, which was "moribund." Even though this was not a violent rupture, the referendum had still activated the original constituent power.

Indeed, Chávez repeatedly narrowed the distance between this peaceful moment and the physical upheavals of the past by arguing that he was the only bulwark against the kind of violence traditionally associated with constituent power. In the presidential debate on constitutional reform, Chávez stated that in response to the crumbling of the old order, the people or the "constituent power" had "awoken from their slumber" and were now "unleashed" in the "streets, the avenues, the neighborhoods, the hamlets, the barrios and the suburbs of all of Venezuela." His hope was to give this "wild" force of nature a "peaceful channel." He ominously warned though that if the constituent power were not "given space, it would occupy it." Without "canals" to guide the people, Venezuela would likely arrive "at new violent facts" and "events much more tragic than what has passed."[57]

---

[54] Carías, 10, of the Constituent Assembly records, August 7, 1999.

[55] Combellas, *Poder Constituyente*, 29.

[56] Hugo Chávez Frîas, "Juramento en el acto de toma de posesión de la Presidencia 1999," in *Hugo Chávez: La construcción del socialismo del siglo XXI: discursos del comandante supremo ante la Asamblea Nacional (1999–2012)*, 139.

[57] Hugo Chávez, "*Presentacion de Hugo Chávez Ante La Academia de Ciencias Políticas y Sociales*," 76–77 (2014). See also Cristina Marcano, Alberto Barrera Tyszka, and Moises Naim, *Hugo Chávez: The Definitive Biography of Venezuela's Controversial President*, trans. Kristina Cordero (New York: Random House, 2007), 118-19. ("'We are advancing toward the exercise of power

Chávez drew "a dichotomy, it is reform or the constituent power." At this late point, "[R]eform is not viable in Venezuela" because "[y]ou cannot reform that which is rotten; an edifice that is rotten to its base cannot reform."[58] Since the current system was totally "rotten," no part of the current government could participate in the process of the making of the new constitution. Even if reform was possible, it was not Chávez's goal: his hope was for a radical revolution.

The constituent power needed to be "original" so that the Constituent Assembly could enact this revolution. The revolution meant "radical change, total change of a model of society of politics, economics, etc."[59] While the revolution was total, its "central axis" was political, to create a "new participatory" democracy.[60] Chávez proclaimed, "It is the end, also, of the paradigm, of liberal democracy and its age."[61] Chávez rejected the participation of the opposing parties because, as in Colombia, these enemies of the people would diminish the scale of the revolution. Indeed, not only would the old guard have to be excluded from the assembly, but any institution in which the old guard had a foothold had to be neutralized or destroyed.

Who were the people that were enacting this revolution? There must be some official and final procedure mark when and how they spoke. In his opening speech to the Constituent Assembly and in words that echo Thomas Hobbes's formulation, Chávez depicts the problem this way, "There has to be something more for that mere human conglomerate, that is a crowd, to be a true people . . . What are the necessary conditions, the essential conditions for a group of individuals to be considered a people?"[62]

---

through the peaceful path', [Chávez] said, but a bit later on, close to the two-year anniversary of his release from prison, he noted that 'if forced, we are willing to achieve it through force.' ") Chávez's supporters echoed a similar line. "There was a peaceful constitutional rupture . . . and if we don't undertand [that] . . . [it] is going to carry this country onto the path of violence." See *Senate Speech of Hermann Escarrá Malavé*, Hermann Eduardo Escarra Malavé, *Chávez y el proceso constituyente de 1999: La revolución bolivariana*, 2013. *Escarrá Malavé* was one of Chávez's most important constitutional advisers.

[58] Hugo Chávez, "*Presentacion de Hugo Chávez Ante La Academia de Ciencias Políticas y Sociales*, 76–77 (2014).

[59] Hugo Chávez Frías, *Habla el Comandante* (Caracas: Catedra Pio Tamayo, 1998), 115.

[60] Ibid.

[61] Ibid., 121.

[62] Chávez Frías, "Discurso con motivo del reconocimiento del Ejecutivo Nacional al carácter originario de la Asamblea Nacional Constituyente y entrega de propuestas para la nueva Constitución," in *Hugo Chávez: la construcción del socialismo del siglo XXI: discursos del comandante supremo ante la Asamblea Nacional* (Caracas: Fondo Editorial de la Asamblea Nacional, 2013), 45.

As I discussed in Chapter One, radicals forge the people in a two-step process. First, they divide the population into friends and enemies, designating the former as the people. To a degree, Chávez follows the same playbook identifying the friends or the people as the poor and the enemy as members of the old party establishment, the "partyocracy" who he denounced as "snakes" and "thieves." He ended his closing campaign speech by declaring, "the rotten elites of the parties are boxed in, and soon they will be consigned to the trash bin of history."[63]

However, compared to his populist presidential counterparts of Evo Morales in Bolivia and Rafael Correa in Ecuador, Chávez is far less specific about what groups constitute the people. While Evo Morales and Rafael Correa emphasize the common identity of the people to start giving them agency, Chávez still regards them as chaotic. Perhaps for that reason, Chávez seems to place even greater emphasis on the radical's second step of top-down representation, in which the people's unity are forged by claiming that one person or institution embodies the people. That institution would be the Constituent Assembly.

To Chávez, the people are an "unplannable and unstoppable" force, a "crowd that invades everything," that is always on the verge of blindly unleashing its rage against anything in its path.[64] He continuously draws upon metaphors of nature calling the people a "wild horse," a "tempest," or a "tsunami."[65] While Chávez lauds the people's rising, he also warns that without guides, without leaders, and without institutions, the people will become destructive. Chávez quotes Bolivar, "If we do not melt the mass of the people into a whole, if we do not fuse the national spirt into a whole, the Republic will be chaos and anarchy."[66]

While there is "no revolution without the people," the "people are looking for captains because the people do need that: true navigators, true leaders who are able to take the lead and give their all for the people."[67] Chávez pairs each metaphor of the people as a force of nature with a corresponding way of leading that force. A rider directs the horse with reigns, a surfer will try to "ride on the wave, trying to guide it" always aware that the "wave can swallow

---

[63] Kirk A. Hawkins, *Venezuela's Chaivmo and Populism in Comparative Perspective* (Cambridge: Cambridge University Press, 2010), 86.

[64] Ibid., 44.

[65] Ibid., 49, 60, 61.

[66] Ibid., 46. Directly after the Bolivar quote, Chávez continues, "And the people, I would add, would cease to be a people and simply become the sum of living human beings."

[67] Ibid., 45.

us," and Chávez even suggests that he will fly on the wind so as to "navigate in the eye of the hurricane." At the very end of speech, he gives his most important pairing in which the constituent ssembly is revealed as the ultimate site of the people's unity. The assembly pairing is developed by paraphrasing Shakespear's the *Tempest* where the captain in a storm shouts, "And now wind, blow, blow hard, do what you will, 'I can maneuver with you.' I say today like Shakespeare: strong wind blow, blow tempest, the Assembly can maneuver with you."[68]

Chávez does not elaborate why the Constituent Assembly is the right institution to embody the people. The idea has an intuitive appeal because of the revolutionary heritage of the constituent assembly that begins in France and has a long tradition in Latin America. But this is not enough as Chávez rejected the Colombian Constituent Assembly as too "subordinate" to the preexisting government. What is it about the Venezuelan Constituent Assembly specifically that makes it an instrument by which the people will speak?

The two key features of the assembly were exclusion and a mandate. The electoral rule of first past the post (FPTP) was key to achieving these two goals. In the Republican tradition in political theory, an assembly is superior to a president because its multiple members can better reflect the diversity of a political community than a king or president.[69] However, the radical tradition prizes unity and hence seeks to constrict the diversity of the assembly. Recall that Emmanuel Sièyes, perhaps the founding theorist of the constituent assembly, advocated banning any nobles from participating in the assembly. So too for Chávez, since the opposition were part of the "partyarchy," they should be excluded from the assembly so that it would not replicate the Colombian process.

While Chávez could not outright exclude through an outright ban on the opposite political party, the electoral rule would minimize their presence. FPTP is inherently exclusionary. It awards all of the power to the individual or party that wins the plurality of the votes. The minority receives no representation. In Venezuela, it would ensure that the oligarchs would not hold back the tide of the revolution.

---

[68] Ibid., 89

[69] For a good summary and examination of this theory in the U.S. context, Eric Nelson, *The Royalist Revolution: Monarchy and the American Founding* (Cambridge, MA: Belknap Press, 2017), 12, 148.

By contrast, proportional representation (PR) was associated with the very party elites that Chávez sought to overthrow. PR is a voting system that, in comparison to FPTP, awards seats more proportionally to the casted votes. Within Venezuela, closed list PR had allowed the traditional political bosses to maintain their grip upon the party by excluding from the list those who challenged their power. It was also associated with the ostensibly elite usurpation of the revolutionary constitution-making process in Colombia, a story of extraordinary adaptation that I discuss in the next chapter.[70] In Venezuela, PR would have enabled the oligarchs to water down the intensity of constitutional change..

Once the people's allies dominate the assembly through the first step of exclusion, the next step for constructing unity is a mandate. A mandate is a command delivered through an election from the people to their representatives to carry out a particular action. The mandate seeks to obliterate any gap between the represented and the representer, turning the latter into a mere delegate who acts without discretion and in accordance with the belief of their constituents.

Through a mandate, the people themselves would create a new social and participatory democracy. Chávez and the Constitutional Assembly would merely carry out their will. As Chávez stated, "The elections to the Constituent Assembly are not the mandate of the Constitution or of any law, it is the mandate by all of you, the sovereign, that you said yes to it in a referendum." Chávez argued, "When I say, as a citizen and as a soldier, I am subordinate to the mandate of the Constituent Assembly, it is because I am firmly convinced that the assembly decides that which is cried out for in the streets, that which is begged for in the roads, . . . that which the people say galloping towards the revolution."[71]

FPTP would be the tool to create the mandate. As political scientists have established, for a mandate to be plausible voters must have the option of choosing a single cohesive party who will then wield "unblocked control of the policy-making process." Usually, FPTP voting establishes these conditions by facilitating the establishment of two main political parties and giving to the victor a disproportionate share of the seats after the

[70] For a review of the pre-1999 electoral system and the discrediting of party-list PR in Venezuela, Jose E. Miriam Molina, "Electoral Systems and Democratic Legitimacy in Venezuela," in *Reinventing Legitimacy: Democracy and Political Change in Venezuela*, eds. Damarys J. Canache and Michael Kulisheck (Westport, CT: Praeger, 1998).

[71] Hugo Chávez, "Discurso con motive del reconocimiento del Ejecutivo Nacional al character originario de la Asamblea Nacional Constituyente," 83.

election.[72] In other words, since Chávez wanted the Constituent Assembly to have a mandate to create a constitution that would overthrow the Venezuelan oligarchs, FTPT voting was the necessary electoral rule.

A mandate is impossible in a PR system. PR disperses power among numerous parties who must negotiate policy decisions. The site of policy decisions is not taken by the people at the election, but by representatives afterward. The representative is not a delegate or mouthpiece for the people, but must have discretion to make independent judgments about how best to represent them in the bargaining process.[73] Chávez's preference for FPTP voting was a principled choice consistent with his long-held populist and majoritarian vision of democracy and the people. By choosing FPTP, Chávez sought a constitutional assembly that would mirror his exclusionary vision of the Venezuelan people.

THE SUPREME COURT'S EXTRAORDINARY ADAPTATION

The Supreme Court fought back against Chávez's radical vision of the people, but this effort has been misunderstood or not fully appreciated. Within the constitutional theory literature on Venezuela, both supporters and critics of Carl Schmitt's idea of an unlimited and lawless constituent power argue that the court accepted that definition.[74] Indeed, for these writers that seems to be the only definition of the constituent power of importance in Venezuela. Jose Colón-Rios argues that the Venezuelan Supreme Court drew heavily on Schmitt, which led it to rightly approve the referendum and recognize that a "more democratic and participatory process was about to take place, as opposed to a naked exercise of power."[75] He argues that the court's decision contains an unattributed quote from Schmitt's book *Constitutional Theory*, and Rios's own theoretical work relies heavily on that text.[76] Nicolas Figueroa agrees that the court's

---

[72] G. Powell Jr., *Elections as Instruments of Democracy: Majoritarian and Proportional Visions* (New Haven, CT: Yale University Press, 2000), 4-17.

[73] Ibid..

[74] One important exception is Allan Brewer-Carías. However, he maintains that the court initially only allowed for a consultative referendum and gave no real weight to a constituent power at all. Brewer-Carías, *Poder Constituyente*, 146–50.

[75] Colon-Rios, *Weak Constitutionalism*, 371; Colón-Ríos, "Carl Schmitt and Constituent Power in Latin American Courts."

[76] Colon-Rios, *Weak Constitutionalism*, 84–88.

decision is Schmittian, and traces the intellectual history of one justice whose father was a radically Marxist revolutionary theorist of constituent power. However, unlike Rios, Figueroa argues that the constituent power is too dangerous, and that by accepting it the court signed its own death warrant.[77] Both Rios and Figueroa are so determined to either praise or condemn the constituent power that they miss the complexities of the court's conception of it. Another legalist critic of popular constitution-making, David Landau briefly notes that the court conceived of the constituent power as inherently limited, but he is skeptical that the court's doctrine had much potential to restrain Chávez.[78]

Contrary to these authors, I argue that the court developed a promising and nascent concept of extraordinary adaptation. While these authors focus on the court's January decision on whether to allow the people to speak in a referendum on whether to convoke a constitutional assembly, I shift emphasis to the subsequent and more foundational moment in the construction of the people. In other words, I focus on who will decide post-referendum what steps are necessary for the creation of the constitution that will count as the legitimate expression of the people's will. The key step and the true "turning point" was the establishment of first-past-the-post electoral rules for the Constitutional Assembly. On this issue and based on the continued survival of the old order, the Supreme Court "extraordinarily adapted" preexisting statute law on referendums to regulate the process. I trace how the court used the three principles of extraordinary adaptation to permit the referendum on whether to hold a constitutional assembly, but tried to place guardrails so that the process would not degenerate into lawlessness.

The guardrails faltered. They faltered because the court failed to fully develop the implications of the third principle of inclusion so as to make the crucial decisions about the content of the electoral rules necessary to restrain Chávez. The court needed to take some action to increase the likelihood that the electoral rules would be inclusive and permit a more proportionate representation of the opposition in the Constituent Assembly.

---

[77] Nicolás Figueroa, "A Critique of Populist Jurisprudence: Courts, Democracy, and Constitutional Change in Colombia and Venezuela," 96.

[78] Landau, "Constitution-Making Gone Wrong," 948. Landau calls the court's limiting principles of the constituent power "a vague doctrine that was difficult to enforce" and argues that "it is difficult to see how [the court] could have succeeded.

Legal Exhaustion

In its January decision, the Venezuelan Supreme Court ruled that the president could issue a decree calling for a referendum on whether to have a constitutional assembly because the people were the ultimate authority. For legalists, this was an egregious mistake; the Venezuelan Constitution's process for large-scale amendments was the only appropriate means to enact legal change and no invocation of the people could justify violating the law.

Legalists fail to account for the court's own argument, which was that there was a consensus in favor of legal change, but traditional routes of repairing the constitution had repeatedly proven themselves inadequate.. Illegality was necessary. I call this justification "legal exhaustion," and it is the first principle of extraordinary justification. I discussed the previous attempts at constitutional reform in detail in the first section of the chapter, but I briefly re-center them again to show how they were an explicit part of the reasoning for why the Supreme Court permitted the Constitutional Assembly.

In its January decision upholding Chávez's decree calling for a referendum on a constitutional assembly, the Venezuelan Supreme Court noted the consensus in favor of a constitutional assembly: "All without exception, the most diverse national sectors—political, economic and social—have expressed a common conviction: the new realities, Venezuelan and world, demand an update of the constitutional text of 1961." After Chávez's electoral victory, an elected constitutional assembly could accomplish what Congress could not: rally support for badly needed constitutional reform to re-democratize and broaden the base of the political system. The court's best path forward was not to deny the people their rightful power, but to participate in the creation of the people themselves by structuring the process.

Indeed, the alternative option of ruling against Chávez would also have resulted in the destruction of the court. Having failed to repair itself, the legitimacy of the old constitution and even the judiciary was at a breaking point. By contrast, Hugo Chávez was at the height of his popularity, even earning the vote of the bourgeoisie, and had made the creation of a new constitution the central promise of his presidential campaign. His election was, and the creation of the constitution would be, the result of the "channeling" of the people through peaceful means, but Chávez repeatedly warned the "moribund Congress" and Supreme Court that, even though he prayed for "a transition without trauma" the "warrior's sword ... is unsheathed ... [We] will not hesitate, we will not tremble or shed a tear to use it in favor of the original National Constituent Assembly . . against any who wants to hinder or disturb" it.[79] If the court had ruled against Chávez, he would have purged the court and incurred little political cost. In terms of a new constitution and the activation of a new constituent power, the train had already left the station. The best the court could do is help construct the right tracks.

Extraordinary Adaptation and Popular Vindication

In every case, the first question any court must answer is jurisdiction, or whether the court has the power to hear the case. The implications of such jurisdiction are broad: if the court has the right to participate in the creation of the constitutional assembly, so too might other parts of the government, such as the Congress and nonpartisan agencies. The dominant understanding of the Venezuelan Supreme Court's rulings as "Schmittian" and "point[ing] toward an *unlimited* constituent power" is inconsistent with the court's assertion of jurisdiction.[80] If the people are outside all law, including and especially the old constitution, then the court should dismiss the case without even reaching the merits. Indeed, Chávez often made this exact point to resist the court's rulings, claiming, "there is no law that regulates elections to the Constituent Assembly, that is clear, there is no law . . . This election campaign is not governed by law."[81] But the court repeatedly and stridently asserts its right to rule in cases on the constitution-making process, including whether to hold a referendum, the electoral rule for the assembly, the identification of a candidate's party on the ballot, and the rules for campaigning for the assembly. How did the Venezuelan Court justify its role in regulating the creation of the people?

The answer was that the lack of a legal abyss meant that preexisting laws, specifically the law that regulated referendums, could be extraordinarily adapted so as to give a legal hook for current institutions to collaborate in structuring the constitution-making process. The challenge for the court was how to harness, channel, and constrain the constituent power. Like Chávez, the Venezuelan Supreme Court believed that as the ultimate source of

[79] Chávez, "Discurso con motive del reconocimiento del Ejecutivo Nacional al character originario de la Asamblea Nacional Constituyente," 81–82.

[80] Colón-Ríos, "Carl Schmitt and Constituent Power in Latin American Courts," 365.

[81] Quoted in Corte Suprema de Justicia [C.S.J.] [Supreme Court], Sala. Politico Administrativa julio 21, 1999, M.P. H. Rondón de Sanso, Revista del Derecho Publico (Nos. 77–80, p. 104).

authority, the people were not obliged to follow the old amending procedure. But they disagreed fundamentally about the role of preexisting institutions in the construction of the people. They disagreed about the implications of constitutional continuity for the constituent power.

In Venezuelan history, every exercise of the constituent power had been preceded by the complete breakdown of the old government, often by coups or wars. In 1999, however, the constitution of 1961 was still intact, elections were held under it, and Congress was in session. For Chávez this fact, this novelty, was irrelevant: he argued that Venezuela would take the peaceful road to the same original and unlimited constituent power that had shaped all previous Venezuelan constitutions.[82] By contrast, for the court, the continuity gave shape to a new type of constituent power:

> What is novel and for that reason extraordinary—is that the current Venezuelan constitutional process is not the consequence of a successful event (civil war, coup, revolution, etc.), but on the contrary, was conceived as a "constituent process of law," that is, it is treated as a process framed in the current Venezuelan juridical system.[83]

Just as extraordinary adaptation theorizes, the people both transcended and were bound by the Venezuelan constitutional system. Even though the people need not follow the 1961 amendment rule, this singular violation did not create a legal vacuum. The current constitution had not been overthrown. All constraints, laws and preexisting institutions did not fall by the wayside.

The court took advantage of the lingering old constitution by extraordinarily adapting its statute on referendums, a statute entitled the Organic Law of Participation and Suffrage. In the March 18th decision, the court began by clarifying that Article 181 of the Organic Law of Participation and Suffrage was the source of authority for violating the old amendment rule and for conducting a referendum on whether to elect a constituent assembly.[84] Article 181 was a recent statute, one of a series of reforms passed in the late 1980s and 1990s in response to pressure for democratization. Article 181

---

[82] See text accompanying notes 52–61.

[83] Corte Suprema de Justicia [C.S.J.] [Supreme Court], Sala. Politico Administrativa julio 21, 1999, M.P. H. Paradisi Leon, *Revista del Derecho Publico* (Nos. 77–80, p. 109).

[84] Ibid. ("The pronouncement of this Sala on the 19th of January 1999, was circumscribed to determine the conformity with article 181 of the Organic Law of Suffrage and Participation with the convocation of a constituent assembly.")

authorized the president, with the support of his ministers, to call referendums to decide issues of "special national transcendence."[85]

The Venezuelan Supreme Court attempted to structure a process that simultaneously violated the constitution's amendment procedure, while still drawing upon the Organic Law within that constitutional order to structure the constitution-making-process. We'll see in the next chapter how the Colombian Supreme Court tried following a similar logic of violating and drawing upon that country's state of emergency provisions. Returning to Venezuela, let's first discuss how the court's adaptation of the Organic Law violated the 1961 Constitution and then how it established continuity with it.

It is unconstitutional to use the Organic Law, essentially a statute, to authorize the creation of a new constitution. The constitution is the highest law and thus outranks the Organic Law. As a statute, the Organic Law was created pursuant to the 1961 constitution, and hence the Organic Law lacks authority to overthrow that old constitution. Through the Organic Law, the people can use a referendum to pass a statute. Like any other statute, if it violates the constitution, it is null and void. Furthermore, the constitution of 1961 provides its own exclusive method of creating a new constitution "called general reform." Its exclusivity serves a purpose: the requirements for general reform are more burdensome than that of the Organic Law, and thus the latter should not be used to circumvent the former.[86]

However, this unconventional use of the Organic Law is justified because the people are acting together to create a new beginning, or as the court stated in its March decision, quoting Chávez, to "transform the state and create a new judicial order."[87] As the court states, "Sovereignty resides in the people who undoubtedly retain the power to decide for those matters which they have not delegated."[88] This ties in with extraordinary adaptation's second principle of popular vindication. Although the court often alludes to popular sovereignty, the court does not spend much time showing that popular

[85] Julia Buxton, The Failure of Political Reform in Venezuela 82–105 (2001). The Organic Law was one component of a reform attempt to democratize the Venezuelan political system. The elites of the two political parties dominated politics. Under considerable strain from economic crises and brutal neo-liberal reforms, in 1989, Congress began a series of reforms to the main election and federalism Organic Laws. Most significant for our purposes, in response to Chávez's coup attempt two years earlier, in 1994 Congress added the word, "participation" to the Organic Law of Suffrage and created the referendum provision. In addition to permitting the President to call a referendum, Congress or citizens through signatures could call referendums as well.

[86] Venezuelan Const. 1961, arts. 245–246.

[87] Corte Suprema de Justicia [C.S.J.] [Supreme Court], Sala. Politico Administrativa marzo 18, 1999, M.P. H. Harting, Revista del Derecho Publico (Nos. 77–80, p. 79).

[88] Ibid.

vindication is actually present, but it could have easily cited how Chávez campaigned for the presidency on the promise to create a new constitution and how he then won the highest percentage of the vote in the history of modern Venezuelan democracy. It could have then noted that the court's decision only facilitates a first step for the principle of popular vindication. The court does note that Chávez's support will be tested again in the referendum on whether to have a constitutional assembly,[89] and it should have also noted that it would be tested again in the elections to the Constitutional Assembly, and in a final referendum on the assembly's proposed constitution.

The court's use of the Organic Law of Participation as Suffrage empowers it and other actors to check Chávez's attempt to unilaterally control the creation of the people. First, it justifies the court's jurisdiction. As the court notes, its power is to "determine the reach of and interpret legal texts."[90] Since the Organic Law is a legal text, the court must interpret it. Second, the continuity empowers bipartisan bodies to carry out the referendum to ensure that it is honest and competitive. The Organic Law lays out specific procedures for how the referendum should proceed and who should carry out those procedures. Thus, the court concludes that the "referendum must proceed by following ordinary procedures provided for in the current legal order, through the competent Public Authorities."[91] Lastly, the rest of the constitution remains intact. As the constitutional assembly proceeds, the normal institutions still operate. Thus, the assembly is limited to the sole task of proposing a draft constitution, and daily governance remains with the three branches of government.

Inclusion

We know the ending: Chávez and his Constituent Assembly triumphs over and purges the Supreme Court to establish a semi-authoritarian constitution. For most legalists, the court's defeat is evidence that the court's invocation of the constituent power and its permitting of an illegal referendum in its January decision was an egregious error that led to its own destruction. For Nicholas Figueroa, in the first referendum decision in January, the court

[89] Ibid.
[90] Ibid.
[91] Ibid.

"shot itself in the foot" and "provided Chávez's quest for the consolidation of a new political hegemony with a very suitable doctrinal basis."[92] For Landau, "once [the court] abandoned the formal limits in the constitutional text, they were left with a vague doctrine that was difficult to enforce."[93] And writing shortly after the January referendum decision, Allan Brewer-Carías subtitled his article responding to the decision, "How the Guardian of the Constitution opened the road to its own violation and to its own extinction."[94] For legalists, once the court opened up the Pandora's box of the people, it deprived itself of any means to control Chávez.

I disagree. The court was right to invoke the people. The problem was that it did not uphold the third principle of extraordinary adaptation, inclusion, in order to ensure that the opposition was represented in the Constitutional Assembly. In my reading, the key turning point then was not the January decision to authorize the referendum on the holding of a constituent assembly, but the March and April decisions on the assembly's electoral rule. In other words, the court's mistake was not its recognition of the people's sovereignty, but its insufficient push over their identity, an identity that should be inclusive of all groups that earned substantial votes in the election. Acting under great pressure and with little theoretical guidance and precedent, the court buckled too soon to Chávez's chosen exclusive electoral rule that allowed his allies to dominate the assembly. An inclusive assembly, as empirical research shows, might have likely scaled back the level of presidential power in the 1999 Venezuelan Constitution.[95] If the court had fought back and if the Constitutional Assembly represented the full diversity of the vote, it is less likely that the assembly would have declared itself sovereign.

Recall that Chávez's planned referendum had two questions. The first concerned whether to convoke a constitutional assembly and had essentially already been approved by the court in January. The second question was the central issue for the court in its March and April decisions. Originally, the second question asked voters to authorize Chávez to choose the electoral rule after the referendum. In March of 1999, the court ruled that this formulation

[92] Figueroa-Garcia, "A Critique of Populist Jurisprudence: Courts, Democracy, and Constitutional Change in Colombia and Venezuela," 14.

[93] Landau, "Constitution-Making Gone Wrong," 949.

[94] See Allan R. Brewer-Carías, "La configuración judicial del proceso constituyente o de como el guardian de la Constitucion abrió el camino para su violación y para su propia extinción," 77–80 *Revista de Derecho Publico* 453 (1999).

[95] Gabriel L. Negretto and Mariano Sánchez-Talanquer, "Constitutional Origins and Liberal Democracy: A Global Analysis, 1900–2015," *American Political Science Review* (2021).

of the second question was unconstitutional. The court required that in the second question Chávez specify the proposed electoral rule on the referendum ballot so voters could accept or reject it. The decision was based on a distinction between a plebiscite and a referendum and how they relate to the rule of law. In both the January and March decisions, the court argued that § 181 authorizes only a referendum and not a plebiscite. As the court stated in its January decision and reiterates in the March one, "[b]oth figures tend to be confused theoretically. While the referendum refers to a text or project, the plebiscite tends to ratify the confidence in a person or ruler."[96] A referendum addresses a discrete issue and is regulated by law. If approved, it is executed by the normal executive and judicial structures, preserving the separation of powers. By contrast, a plebiscite empowers an individual or a group to both create and execute laws or to rule outside of the law in the name of a more direct representation of the people. For example, a popular vote to transfer all legislative or judicial powers to the executive is a plebiscite that violates the separation of powers.

Since electoral rules can easily be manipulated, empowering Chávez to unilaterally decide the electoral rule is tantamount to giving him great power over the membership of the Constitutional Assembly, and therefore over the content of the constitution and the powers of his office. Rather than a deliberative and inclusive process, Chávez proposed that the people delegate to him the task of single-handedly creating the constitution. That is a plebiscite, not a referendum, and hence the court ordered Chávez to specify the electoral rule on the ballot.

Would Chávez choose an electoral rule that would give fair representation to all segments of Venezuelan society, or would he choose one that would likely give him near total dominance over the assembly?

Chávez chose the latter. He complied with the court ruling, but chose a first-past-the-post electoral rule, which would give him a disproportional number of seats in the assembly. The assembly would have 131 members. Three seats were reserved for the indigenous, 24 were to be elected in a national constituency, and the remaining 104 were to be elected in regional constituencies corresponding to the preexisting political subdivisions of the territory. The number of candidates in each regional constituency

---

[96] Corte Suprema de Justicia [C.S.J.] [Supreme Court], Sala. Politico Administrativa enero 19, 1999, M.P. H. La Roche, Revista del Derecho Publico (Nos. 77–80, p. 63); Corte Suprema de Justicia [C.S.J.] [Supreme Court], Sala. Politico Administrativa marzo 18, 1999, M.P. H. Harting, Revista del Derecho Publico (Nos. 77–80, p. 81).

corresponded to the population of each state and district. In the spirit of the prevailing anti-party sentiment, candidates ran as individuals, and each required a certain number of signatures to be on the ballot.

Most importantly, the block vote was the system of allocating seats. In it, candidates run as individuals in multi-member districts. Voters have as many votes as there are seats but cannot vote for the same candidate twice. Whichever candidates have the greater number of votes are elected. All plurality systems tend to create disproportional outcomes, but this danger is particularly acute with the block vote.

The next significant court decision addressed the constitutionality of the electoral rule. On April 13, 1999, the court accepted this electoral rule as in compliance with its previous decision. However, it also struck down a phrase on the ballot that referred to the Constituent Assembly itself as an original constituent power. If this claim was correct, the assembly would be all-powerful and could supplant all the constituted powers, including the court and Congress.

Elections proceeded and through the electoral rule Chávez transformed his victory of 65.8 percent of the votes cast into 94 percent of the seats in the Constituent Assembly. Despite earning one-third of the vote, the opposition received only six seats. Four of these seats were earned by luck because Chávez ran only twenty candidates out of the twenty-four available national seats. Despite repeated rulings from the court to the contrary, the Constituent Assembly called itself sovereign and on this basis essentially purged the Supreme Court, the legislature, and all other sources of opposition.

What could the court have done differently? What can it do if the Constituent Assembly will defy its rulings? This is the classic problem of what Jon Elster calls "constitutional boot-strapping, the process by which a constituent assembly severs its ties with the authorities that have called it into being and arrogates some or all of the powers to itself." Once the constituent assembly is convoked, it becomes very difficult for the old regime to control or limit it because "almost, by definition, the old regime is part of the problem that a constituent assembly has to solve. But if the old regime is flawed, why should the assembly respect its decisions."[97]

Since an assembly cannot be controlled once it has been convoked, the solution is to choose a selection method that obtains the right members. If

---

[97] Jon Elster, "Constitutional Bootstrapping in Philadelphia and Paris," 14 *Cardozo Law Review* (1992), 549, 564.

courts cannot hold the assembly accountable ex-post, they should focus on the ex-ante method of selection. More specifically, the electoral rule should be inclusive giving representation to minority, opposition parties. A more inclusive assembly will be less likely to defy the Supreme Court's rulings.

Here, the Venezuelan Supreme Court flopped, greatly ceding control over the electoral rules to Chávez. The court failed to fully develop extraordinary adaptation's third principle of inclusion so as to fulfill the court's role in defining the identity of the people. The people are plural. For Arendt, one danger of popular constitution-making is that one entity, such as a convention or dictator, will be perceived as a complete embodiment of the people. No matter the identity of the claimant, its singularity violates the plurality of the people. This violation occurred in 1999 in Venezuela when the Constituent Assembly, dominated by Chávez's party, exercised sovereign power on the basis that it was the people. Arendt's solution was to multiply representations of the people and have those representations deliberate together. The exact means of multiplication will vary based on context. In the United States, federalism was key as each state's equal representation in the assembly ensured that the assembly was diverse.

In Venezuela, the electoral rule for the assembly was key method for creating a singular people. Chávez's FPTP electoral rule facilitated a unified constituent assembly that purged rival representations of the people and privileged the Constituent Assembly as the true popular and sovereign site. A more inclusive electoral rule would have helped fragment and diversify the Constituent Assembly making it difficult to claim that it mirrored a unified will of the people. The minority within the assembly would have constantly contested the majority's claim to carry out the will of the people. It would have called national attention to the usurpations of the assembly and the more executive-centered features of the constitution. It might have allied with majorities in Congress and state governments. An inclusive electoral rule had the potential to create a minority faction that would contest the sovereign claim of the Constituent Assembly, allowing other actors to assert themselves and preserve the plurality of the people.

Even more importantly, it might have also created the potential for issue-specific coalitions with either more moderate or more radical minority factions of Chávez's big tent party. Even under the highly unlikely possibility that the distribution of electoral seats matched exactly the proportionality of votes, Chávez's candidates would have still outnumbered the opposition nearly 3 to 1. Skeptics might argue then that the electoral rule would make no difference to the dynamics within the assembly. However, since Chávez's coalition was heterogeneous, with a significant number of liberals and moderates, an inclusive electoral rule might have created centrist parties that would have held the balance of power in the assembly. Or perhaps it would have facilitated coalitions that cut across party lines on specific issues with the opposition peeling off moderates on some issues. Under an electoral rule, this moderate minority may have joined forces with the opposition to stop the purge and the concentration of power in the executive branch.

The Court's Four Options

The Venezuelan Supreme Court should have intervened to facilitate a more inclusive electoral rule, but that still leaves open the question of how they should have intervened. Here, I offer four different possible routes, some of them overlapping. Keeping in mind that politics will constrain the court, I offer the options in order of most to least assertive intervention. First, and most controversially, the court may have unilaterally required that the voting rule be a proportional one. Here, the court would have greatly pushed the boundaries of its role. This may have been difficult without enlisting the help of other actors, such as the Congress.

Second, the court may have required the ballot to provide voters with the opportunity to choose between two different electoral rules. This may have raised awareness of the stakes and importance of the electoral rule in two ways. Voters may not have understood the consequences of the electoral rule for the composition of the Constituent Assembly. The choice between two rules may have forced voters to think about "the nature of the choice they must make and the likely repercussions of their action."[98] It would force them to think about whether they would want an electoral rule that would make the assembly more representative of the nation as a whole. Civil society groups and the media, both of them very active during this period, may have raised awareness and mobilized supporters around the issue. Given Chávez's high level of popularity, it may not have made a difference to the result as his supporters would have likely approved his electoral rule. Even more importantly, voters may have been uncertain what the consequence of voting

---

[98] Jeffrey A. Lenowitz, *Constitutional Ratification without Reason* (New York: Oxford University Press, 2022), 36–37.

"yes" to the first question to approve the Constituent Assembly, but "no" to second question to approve Chávez's FPTP electoral rule. Would the failure to select an electoral rule hinder the process of electing a constitutional assembly? Giving voters the option of two rules would have allowed them to express their preference for a more representative assembly without fearing that it would set back their desire for a new constitution.

Third, the court may have required approval from the legislature or the provinces for the electoral rule. The Organic Law set some guidelines for the process, but it was vague and subject to interpretation. During Chávez's repeated calls for an electoral assembly, many debated what role Congress should have in constructing the framework. Wary of the possibility of congressional intervention, Chávez chose to issue a decree calling for the Constituent Assembly the day of his inauguration, almost two weeks earlier than he originally promised. In his inauguration speech, Chávez rationalized cutting Congress out of the proposal. He lamented that Congress and the other candidates had "demonized the constituent power" rather than debate it with him. He "hoped that Congress calls a referendum, I said it; I hope that Congress takes the baton." However, now the "time was lost" for debate. Due to the "clamor of the people," Chávez had to "accelerate" the process.[99] The court may have disagreed that there was no time for debate and buttressed congressional authority by handing them "the baton."

Lastly, the court may have ruled that approval of the referendum questions required 50 percent of the eligible voters and not just 50 percent of those who voted.[100] The justification is simple: even by Chávez's majoritarian standards, without 50 percent of eligible voters, the people have not spoken. High rates of absenteeism suggest that if the people had any message at all, it is widespread disillusionment or apathy toward the political system. Indeed, this seems to have been the case in the 1999 Venezuelan referendum. While 81.7 percent of those voting approved Chávez's electoral rule, that approval constituted only 30.8 percent of the electorate.[101] If Chávez had been forced to turn out 20 percent more voters, he may have offered a more inclusive electoral rule to gain the assent of the moderates.

---

[99] Hugo Chávez, *Discurso de toma de posesión como Presidente*, 22.

[100] For an example voting requirement concerning eligible voters during Russia's period as a democracy in the 90s, seeMark Clarence Walker, *The Strategic Use of Referendums: Power, Legitimacy, and Democracy*, 1st ed. (New York: Palgrave Macmillan, 2003), 117.

[101] Coppedge, *Venezuela: Liberal Democracy*, 187.

Congress's Failure

I have focused on the shortcomings of the court's doctrine, but perhaps the greatest fault lies with Congress's failure to push for extraordinary adaptation. Congress may have lacked the legitimacy to use its amendment powers to create a new constitution, but this did not exclude it from contributing to the structuring of the process. It possessed both amendment powers and the power under the Organic Law of Suffrage and Participation. It could have used either to call for and structure elections to a constitutional assembly. This newly elected assembly would have possessed the legitimacy that Congress lacked to renew the constitution, but Congress's influence over the electoral rules would have ensured it was plural and diverse, minimizing the risk of it running completely amok.

In fact, Allan R. Brewer-Carías as President of the Academy of Political and Social Sciences and who would go on to be the leader of the opposition in the Constituent Assembly petitioned Congress to hold a debate to amend the constitution to create a constituent assembly. Carías presented his proposal to Congress; Congress debated it, but nothing was passed.[102] Chávez would later argue that since the 1961 constitution lacked a legal route to a constitutional assembly, he had to plunge Venezuela into a legal abyss. If Congress had heeded Carías's plea, that argument would not have held water. Indeed, something similar occurred in Bolivia. As I discuss in Chapter Five, before Evo Morales's election to the presidency in 2005, the Congress illegally amended the constitution to guarantee inclusive electoral rules for and supermajority approval rules within the Constituent Assembly. This was not in response to the prospect of Morales's victory, but a sincere attempt to initiate constitutional reform. Congress's amendment helped the opposition beat back Evo Morales's attempt to consciously mimic the Venezuelan idea of a lawless constituent assembly. The Venezuelan Congress missed the opportunity to initiate a process of extraordinary adaptation.

---

[102] *Gaceta del Congreso*, Período 1998-1999, No. 27 Sesión Conjunta, 30 de julio de 1998, 24-31; *Gaceta del Congreso*, Período 1998-1999, No. 34 Sesión Conjunta, 27 de agosto de 1998, 18-22; Allan R. Brewer-Carias, *Asamblea Constituyente y Proces Constituyente 1999. Coleccion Tratado de Derecho Constitucional, Tomo VI* (Caracas: Fundacion Editorial Juridica Venezolana, 2014), 57-66.

Ecuador's Missing Opposition

Venezuela was a lost opportunity. Law, albeit in an altered form, had some role to play in buttressing the opposition. In the pre-assembly moment, participation from multiple institutions would have likely led to an inclusive electoral rule that would have prevented its sovereign and tyrannical constitutional assembly. We will see how such an inclusive rule redeemed constitution-making efforts in Colombia and Bolivia. Ecuador too had the inclusive electoral rule similar to those in Colombia and Bolivia, the very type of rule that Venezuela lacked. Yet, the Ecuadorian process still followed the Venezuelan one's path: all opposition institutions were purged, and the Constitutional Assembly produced a constitution that concentrated power in the executive branch. Why did the inclusive electoral rule fail in Ecuador? Should this failure cast doubt on the merits of the broader theory of extraordinary adaptation?

Democratic institutions can buttress an opposition, but it cannot create one. In Ecuador, due to the opposition's dismal election results, there was little to no chance for extraordinary adaptation. President Rafael Correa and his allies so overwhelmingly won the election to the Constitutional Assembly that there was no one standing in their way. Ecuador is not damning for the theory of extraordinary adaptation, but it does exemplify its limits and conditions for success.[103] Sometimes, law simply runs out.

Rafael Correa's Radical Constituent Power

Rafael Correa, a former economics professor who had a brief stint as Minister of Finance, decided to run for the presidency in the 2006 presidential elections. Mimicking Hugo Chávez, he made the creation of a new constitution a central plank of his platform. Also like Chávez and other radicals, Correa constructed the people through a friend/enemy relationship and

---

[103] Since inclusion was the crucial issue in the countries of this study and since its failure in Ecuador is so telling, I focus on it in this section. However, while extraordinary adaptation's first principle of legal exhaustion is easily fulfilled in the other three countries, it is more questionable here. Whereas the other countries had older constitutions, Ecuador had made a new one less than nine years before the creation of the 2009 Constitution. If it had succeeded recently, why not again? On the other hand, attempts to legally change the constitution had failed in 2000 and 2001. An illegal, even lawless, attempt also failed in 2005. "La Constituyente no logra apoyo políco," *El Universo*, October 16, 2005; "Candado Constitucional sigue ligado a las propuestas de reforma política," October 8, 2006.

through top-down representation. In Ecuador, the friend group were the urban mestizos, and their embodying institution was a sovereign constitutional assembly.

President Raphael Correa's campaign posited the people, or friends, as composed of "citizens," and this became the unifying theme of his presidential campaign. His political movement was "a revolt of indignant citizens" who would achieve "a citizen's revolution."[104] Citizenship did not stand for a set of formal legal rights, but rather a devotion to the common good of the country. His campaign slogans were "the homeland returns" and "Passion for the homeland."[105] The name of his political party was "Proud and Sovereign Fatherland."[106] In his speech at the opening of the Constitutional Assembly, Correa called for citizens to leave behind their particular interests and identities in order to pursue the common good: "Our vision cannot be other than a national and historical vision. We are no longer the Assembly members from Manabí, Carchi or Zambora, saraguros, montubios or cofanes, workers, professionals or entrepreneurs, we are a national whole."[107]

The enemy of the common good were the political or economic elites, the "pelucones" or "big wigs" who had enriched themselves at the expense of the country as a whole.[108] Although legally citizens, the elites had violated the responsibilities of citizenship and betrayed the country by selling it out to foreign business interests through their neoliberal policies. This "neoliberal globalization," Correa maintained, was unpatriotic because it "turns countries into markets, not nations."[109] Citizens would retake their patrimony from these "mafiosi . . . clowns, vipers, wolves, cadavers, sell-outs, and swindlers."[110]

[104] Rafael Correa, "Rafael Correa, Ecuador's Path, NLR 77, September–October 2012," *New Left Review*, Sept. 2012, https://newleftreview.org/issues/II77/articles/rafael-correa-ecuador-s-path.

[105] Catherine Conaghan, "Rafael Correa and the Citizen's Revolution," in *The Resurgence of the Latin American Left*, eds. Steven Levitsky and Kenneth M. Roberts, 1st ed. (Baltimore: Johns Hopkins University Press, 2011), 266.

[106] Ibid. Carlos De La Torre, *Populist Seduction in Latin America* (Athens: Ohio University Press, 2010), 184.

[107] Rafael Correa, "Speech at the Inauguration Ceremony of the Constituent Assembly" (speech, Montecristi, Sept. 30, 2007), https://www.presidencia.gob.ec/wp-content/uploads/downloads/2012/10/30-09-07DiscursoInauguracionAsambleaNacionalConstituyente.pdf

[108] Conaghan, "Rafael Correa and the Citizen's Revolution," 266.

[109] Rafael Correa, "Speech at the Inauguration Ceremony of the Constituent Assembly" (speech, Montecristi, Sept. 30, 2007), https://www.presidencia.gob.ec/wp-content/uploads/downloads/2012/10/30-09-07DiscursoInauguracionAsambleaNacionalConstituyente.pdf

[110] Catherine M. Conaghan, "Ecuador: Correa's Plebiscitary Presidency," *Journal of Democracy* 19, no. 2 (2008), 54.

Correa's rhetoric is similar to Hugo Chávez's and Evo Morales's as all three condemned the "patriarchy" or ruled by political parties captured by the rich. Where Correa departed is that he also explicitly tagged as enemies left-wing movements, such as unions and the indigenous. Correa loathed their independence that threatened the image of a unified people. A focus on the indigenous is particularly instructive. In Venezuela, Chávez always spoke glowingly about the indigenous population, but they are a tiny part of the population with no real political weight.[111] In Bolivia, the opposite is true: a significant majority of the population consider themselves to be indigenous, and in 2005 indigenous identification and the social movements were at their peak. Drawing from the indigenous' long-standing resentment against homogenizing modernization projects, Evo Morales painted the people as a coalitional project that embraced the variety of social movements and groups that had brought him to power. In Ecuador, the indigenous are not a majority, but a significant and well-organized minority that compose about 25 percent of the population.[112] However, at the time of Correa's rise, they were in poor political shape, having lost public legitimacy for allying with the last discredited president. They were divided and lacked direction. For Correa, they were too large to be ignored but weak enough that he was be able to marginalize, divide, and co-opt them.[113]

Correa shunned the idea of a diverse people. He called for "the return of the state" by "decorporatizing it." Fernando Bustamente, Correa's Minister of Government, laid out the meaning of decorportaizing the most clearly. Both the old corporatist order and the neoliberal one had devolved too much power to civil society organizations, which "weaken[ed] or distort[ed] the proper functional separation between the private interest and the common good." Such groups used their power to pursue their own private interest enervating the state, leaving it "weak" and "corrupt" and ultimately leading to a "sustained crisis for democracy." For Bustamente, civil society organizations were premodern, part of an outmoded system

[111] Donna Lee Van Cott, "Andean Indigenous Movements and Constitutional Transformation: Venezuela in Comparative Perspective," *Latin American Perspectives* 30, no. 1 (Jan. 1, 2003), 49–69.

[112] Donna Lee Van Cott, *From Movements to Parties in Latin America: The Evolution of Ethnic Politics* (New York: Cambridge University Press, 2005), 101. The population of the Indigenous in Ecuador is contested. Cott takes her number from the Inter-American Indigenous Institute and the Ecuadorian government's website in 2005.

[113] For an excellent overview, Marc Becker, "The Stormy Relations between Rafael Correa and Social Movements in Ecuador," *Latin American Perspectives* 40, no. 3 (May 1, 2013), 43–62.

of "urban clientilism" and the "family and patrimonial heritage of the hacienda."[114]

Correa thus made clear that the threat came not only from the right, but from the left as well: "Paradoxically, the main dangers have not come from an opposition...but from our own contradictions...from Trojan Horses." These Trojan Horses were the "leftism, ecologism and infantile indigenism . . . the new reactionaries are precisely those ecological fundamentalists and, I would add, those so-called organization that do not represent anybody but that behave as though they represented everybody."[115] Correa appropriated indigenous rhetoric and recruited a few leaders, but he attacked indigenous social organizations every time they protested against policies.

This examination of the enemy allows us to circle back and reflect more carefully about who are the "citizens" that compose Correa's people. The unions and the indigenous are not the people, but rather self-interested parasites leeching the state for themselves. "Citizens" are the urban middle class and poor who lack a social organization to represent them.[116] This accords with the history of Correa's political movement. In two of the three presidential overthrows, indigenous and social movement organizations had played a crucial role. The next overthrow, the one that is associated with Correa was different: it was a spontaneous uprising by urban citizens residing in the capital of Quito. Indeed, the deposed president has been an ally of the indigenous. As one indigenous leader commented, "Quito threw out" the president that "the countryside had voted for."[117] These urban citizens lacked strong social organizational ties and thus appeared to be a mass, something that Correa believed he could more easily mold and shape.

That mass, consistent with the radical's second step of top-down representation, would be embodied in a lawless constitutional assembly. Correa explained that the first "axis" of his revolution was constitutional. Its central pillar was a "Constitutional Assembly with total power," which he would call for on his first day of office.[118] Correa was insistent that no ordinary assembly

[114] Pablo Ospina Peralta, "Corporativismo, Estado y revolución ciudadana: el Ecuador de Rafael Correa," *Corporativismo, Estado y revolución ciudadana: el Ecuador de Rafael Correa* (2011) 87.

[115] Rafael Correa, "Speech by the President of the Republic, Rafael Correa in the Closing Ceremony of the Constituent National Assembly" (speech, Montecristi, July 25, 2008), https://www.presidencia. gob.ec/wp-content/uploads/downloads/2013/10/2008-07-25-Intervención-Presidencial-Clausura-Asamblea-Constituyente.pdf

[116] Marc Becker, *Pachakutik: Indigenous Movements and Electoral Politics in Ecuador* (Lanham, MD: Rowman & Littlefield Publishers, 2010), 119.

[117] Becker, *Packakutik*, 94.

[118] "Trece propuestas para gobernar al Ecuador," *El Universo*, Oct. 14, 2006, https://www.elunive rso.com/2006/10/14/0001/8/BB6CBE78C66047B2A2E74827E5DBBAEB.html.

would be sufficient; only one with total power could withstand the resistance the oligarchy in government would inevitably pose to change. Indeed, Correa refused to run any candidates in the Congress because it was a viper's nest of corruption, guaranteeing that he would have little support in government for his project.[119] In October, in the second round of voting, Correa won the presidency. While the margin was impressive, it was not the same kind of stunning and surprising victory as Chávez or Morales had achieved in their respective countries. Nonetheless, Correa claimed he had a mandate for revolutionary change, change that would be possible only through revamping the institutions. Correa declared, "We won elections, but not power." Power would have to come through "the mother of all battles," by which Correa meant the battle to establish a sovereign constituent assembly.[120]

The Sovereign Constituent Assembly in Ecuador

The battle for the Constitutional Assembly had two stages. In the first stage of the process, Correa successfully defeated Congress and the courts in order to issue a decree stating that the Constituent Assembly would be sovereign. Mimicking Chávez and under the influence of Chávez's constitutional advisers, on his first day of office, January 15, 2007, Correa issued a decree calling for a referendum on whether to have an assembly with "plenipotentiary powers."[121] In other words, it would be superior to all other governing institutions. On the best reading of the 1998 constitution, the decree was illegal because it violated the constitution's amendment rule. Enforcing that rule, the Electoral Tribunal required the approval of Congress for the refendum to proceed. Congress ultimately agreed to the holding of a referendum by a 57-1 vote, but insisted on inserting text guaranteeing that the assembly would not be sovereign and thus would lack the power to purge the Congress or other elected officeholders.[122]

---

[119] Becker, Pachakutik, 113.Hernán Salgado Pesantes, "El proceso constituyente del Ecuador: Algunas reflexiones," Revista IIDH, no. 47 (2008), 267.

[120] Conaghan, "Rafael Correa and the Citizen's Revolution," 271.

[121] "Decree of the Election, Creation and Operation of the Constituent Assembly," 2 Executive Decrees (2007), available at https://www.eluniverso.com/2007/01/17/0001/8/C47559BD5B5040458 712216F79F4668C.html. The literal translation would be plenary power, which is equivalent to the concept of sovereignty.

[122] For a detailed blow by blow of the process, Allan R. Brewer-Carías, "El Inicio del Proceso Constituyente en Ecuador en 2007 y las Lecciones de la Experiencia Venezolana de 1999," Iuris Dictio 7, no. 11 (Oct. 2007), 73–76. Also see Angélica M. Bernal, "The Meaning and Perils of Presidential Refounding in Latin America," Constellations 21, no. 4 (2014), 452; Pérez Loose, "Ecuador y su

Correa refused to compromise and on February 28th reissued the decree without Congress's changes proclaiming that "once the Constituent Assembly meets, I will ask for the resignation of Congress."[123] The decree once again came before the Electoral Tribunal. Rather than reject it again, this time the chief justice of the tribunal switched his vote, which meant Correa won by a 4-3 vote.[124] From here, the process quickly degenerated, and the different institutions of government turned against each other. Angered by the Electoral Tribunal's authorization of the referendum, in March, Congress lashed out at the tribunal and illegally voted to remove the chief justice. The tribunal retaliated by removing the 57 members of Congress who voted for the removal. Their replacements were Correa's allies. Correa had captured Congress, which became his tool to further dismember government institutions. The constitutional court was next on the chopping block. On April 23, 2007, the constitutional court reversed the Electoral Tribunal and reinstated the 57 deputies. However, with the replacements in Correa's pocket, the Congress voted to replace the members of the constitutional court. Even before the convening of the assembly, Correa had tamed and purged opposition institutions.[125]

The framing of the assembly as sovereign was a victory for Correa, but it was not the key victory. Words are just parchment barriers; what matters is representation or power to enforce those words inside the assembly. Recall that in Venezuela, Chávez lost the battle that Correa won: the Venezuelan Supreme Court successfully struck from Chávez's decree the awarding of sovereign powers to the Constitutional Assembly. Nonetheless, stacked with Chávez's allies, the assembly declared itself sovereign anyway.

What is crucial for limiting the assembly's powers is not the wording of the decree, but the composition of the assembly. Unlike in Venezuela, Ecuador's electoral rule was inclusive. Why did it not lead to a more democratic constitution?

Metamorfosis Constituyente," in *Procesos constituyentes contemporáneos en América Latina*, ed. José María Serna de la Garza, 37, https://archivos.juridicas.unam.mx/www/bjv/libros/6/2728/10.pdf; .

123 "Executive Decree 148," Supplemental Official Registrar § (2007), 148; "Consenso de Correa y Congreso en reglas finales de la consulta," *El Universo*, Feb. 28, 2007, https://www.eluniverso.com/2007/02/28/0001/8/3A251B566B5D41DF881A46F7D8D7EE1F.html.
124 Loose, "Ecuador y su Metamorfosis Constituyente."
125 Allan R. Brewer-Carías, "El Inicio del Proceso Constituyente en Ecuador en 2007 y las Lecciones de la Experiencia Venezolana de 1999," *Iuris Dictio* 7, no. 11 (Oct. 1, 2007), 77–81. Two other helpful accounts: Bernal, "The Meaning and Perils of Presidential Refounding in Latin America"; Loose, "Ecuador y su Metamorfosis Constituyente."

The electoral results for the Constitutional Assembly, specifically the re-sounding victory of Correa's party, explain the inefficacy of the inclusive electoral rule. The assembly would have 130 delegates, 24 from national lists, 100 from districts, and a separate list of immigrants living outside Ecuador.[126] This was roughly similar to the preexisting system and did not unfairly privilege any group. Voters cast their ballots on September 30th, 2007, and the election was free and fair. Correa's party and his allies received a stunning and overwhelming electoral victory and earned 71.5 percent of the assembly's seats with 70.7 percent of the vote, a number that significantly dwarfed even that of Evo Morales and Hugo Chávez whose parties earned 61.6 percent and 65.8 percent respectively in their electoral victories for the Constitutional Assembly.[127] Even if the assembly's voting rule had required two-thirds approval for the constitution, Correa's coalition would have dom-inated the assembly. When discussing Venezuela, I argued that even when the opposition is significantly outnumbered in a constitutional assembly, it still may exert significant influence due to the possibility of defections from moderates in the majority. But the greater the majority, the more defections are necessary. In Ecuador, the number of defections necessary to create a sig-nificant counterweight to Correa was far too high. Extraordinary adaptation can help an opposition buffer and redirect the force of charismatic presi-dents, but in Ecuador that force was so great and the opposition so small that there was little hope.

In the second stage, the Constitutional Assembly put Congress into per-manent recess. All power now centered in the assembly. The unanimously chosen president of the assembly, Alvaro Acosta, was a professor, activist, and public intellectual who had his own independent base of support and was deeply committed to participatory democracy. That commitment proved to be his undoing. His extensive public consultations so slowed down the process that the assembly was unlikely to produce a draft constitution by the deadline. Under pressure from his party's leadership, Acosta resigned. Ultimately, much of the constitution was drafted in a rush by a small editing

---

[126] "European Union Election Observation Ecuador 2007," 19–22.

[127] Consistent with the proportional electoral rule, Correa led an umbrella coalition of which his party was the largest member. I calculate the figures of 70.7 percent of the vote and 71.5 percent of the seats by combining the votes of his coalition. His party, the PAIS Alliance, won 64.5 percent of the vote and 60.8 percent of the seats. The following are the numbers for his coalition partners: the Democratic Popular Movement won 1.9 percent of the vote and 3 percent of the seats; Pachakutik won .9 percent of the vote and 3 percent of the seats; the Ethics and Democracy Network (RED) won 2.7 percent of the vote and 2.3 percent of the seats; and the Democratic Left (ID) won .7 percent of the vote and 2.3 percent of the seats. Figures are from the Consejo Nacional Electoral.

commission whose members were not part of the assembly and were loyal to Correa.[128] Unsurprisingly, their finished product greatly centralized powers in the presidency. The assembly had little power to offer amendments or changes, and had to approve the constitution in an up or down vote. They approved it, and so did the electorate in a referendum.[129] As in Venezuela, a sovereign constituent assembly was the president's tool to consolidate power. What differentiates Ecuador from Venezuela is that Correa's enormous popularity meant that even an inclusive electoral rule was no barrier to the triumph of a sovereign constitutional assembly.

* * *

Ecuador was hopeless, but the Venezuelan story offers lessons for those who want to find a middle path between legalists and radicals. I agree with legalists that it stands as another example of how a charismatic strongman may invoke a lawless vision of the people to seize power. I disagree that the ultimate lesson is that the constituent power is too dangerous a concept to retain in our theoretical vocabulary. In their eagerness to condemn the idea of the people, legalists miss the need and potential for popular sovereignty in Venezuela. Radical proponents of the constituent power are the right that the system was on the verge of collapse and it was incapable of reforming itself. The state of democracy in Venezuela both before and after the creation of the 1999 constitution was problematic; neither the before of a decrepit and dying party system nor the after of a semi-authoritarian regime are satisfactory outcomes. The question then is how to harness the constituent power to empower the people to solve the crisis of legitimacy through the creation of a new constitution while guarding against the dangers of centralizing power.

The Venezuelan Supreme Court confronted this problem directly and attempted to resolve it through the extraordinary adaptation of preexisting statutory law on consultative referendums. This allowed new political forces to circumvent the barriers to change while still giving the court and other constituted institutions an appropriate role in shaping the process. The court lost, and legalists claim this proves that the constituent power overwhelms the capacity of courts and Congress to fight back. Their interesting doctrinal maneuvers are noted in passing, but dismissed as too little and too late.

---

[128] Bernal, "The Meaning and Perils of Presidential Refounding in Latin America," 450–51.
[129] Ibid.

I think the Supreme Court deserves better. Jurists who spent most of their life addressing the day-to-day intricacies of reoccurring issues of doctrinal law were suddenly confronted with the rare phenomenon of the constituent power. Like any good judge, they researched the problem and found only the long Latin American tradition of the original and unified constituent power, a power designed for ruptures and total breaks, for situations in which the old constitution had ceased to apply. Yet, here these judges were adjudicating a case initiated by the actions of an elected president under a still governing constitution. There were no guidelines, no textbooks for their situation. They had to, as Arendt has said, judge "without banisters."[130] They struggled to articulate a new idea of extraordinary adaptation on the fly and understandably fumbled their way through its implications. Under immense time and political pressure and with little theoretical armor, they arrived to the battlefield with poor provisions. Their example nonetheless gives food for thought, and it provides a starting point for rethinking the constituent power. My goal in this book is to arm future political actors so there can be a fair fight. The central weapon is extraordinary adaptation. In the next chapter on Colombia, we'll see how it successfully overcame a crisis of governance to create a new, democratic constitution. Colombia—Venezuela's anti-model, the very country's constitution-making process that Chávez condemned as insufficiently revolutionary—I will argue. is a partially successful effort to construct a plural people to begin anew.

---

[130] "On Hannah Arendt," in *Hannah Arendt: The Recovery of the Public World*, ed. Melvin A. Hill (New York: St. Martin's Press, 1979), 336.

4

A Quarrel Among Friends

Partially Inclusive Extraordinary Adaptation in Colombia

The making of the 1991 Colombian Constitution broke new ground in the history of the Andes. This was South America's first post-Cold War case of popular constitutional creation, and several years later it served as both a model and an anti-model for Venezuela. It was also the country's, the region's, and perhaps the continent's first case of extraordinary adaptation. Since the early nineteenth-century's wars of independence, the proximate cause of constitutional creation in Colombia was a whole-scale rupture with the old order caused by wars, insurrections, and coups.[1] What happened in 1991 was different. This time, the old constitution's institutions were in session. This time, in the name of the people, preexisting institutions—most notably the presidency and the Supreme Court structured the process in odd and unorthodox ways. This opened up the creation of the constitution to new actors. Unlike in Venezuela, the inclusion of multiple actors produced a liberal and democratic constitution, but the process was still far from fully inclusive as the rural guerillas and their peasant constituents remained on the political and constitutional periphery. Colombia, then, is an example of partially inclusive extraordinary adaptation.

The scholarship on the Colombian Constitution has failed to fully recognize the novelty of the process. Nearly all of it, to different degrees, view it as another instantiation of the traditional South American theory of a lawless people or the "original constituent power," which grants all powers to a

---

[1] For a broad overview of Latin American constitutional history between 1978 and 2008, Gabriel L. Negretto, *Making Constitutions: Presidents, Parties, and Institutional Choice in Latin America* (Cambridge: Cambridge University Press, 2013), 17–42. For background on the post-independence constitutions, Gerardo Pisarello, *Procesos constituyentes: Caminos para la ruptura democrática*, 1st ed; 1st imp. ed. (Madrid: Trotta, 2013). On Colombian constitutional history, Arturo Sarabia, *Reformas Políticas En Colombia. Del Plebiscito de 1957 al Referendo de 2003* (Bogotá: Norma, 2003); Hernando Valencia Villa, *Cartas de Batalla. Una Crítica Del Constitucionalismo Colombiano.* (Bogotá: Panaamericana, 2010); Hernando Valencia Villa, *El Anticonstitucional. Introducción a a La Crítica de La Constitución Política.* (Bogotá: Uniandes, 1981).

We, the Mediated People. Joshua Braver, Oxford University Press. © Joshua Braver 2023.
DOI: 10.1093/oso/9780197650639.003.0005

sovereign constitutional assembly. Proponents of the idea of a lawless people, whom I call "radical," celebrate how the all-powerful Colombian sovereign Constituent Assembly attempted to overthrow the old two-party clientelist system and regenerate the state's legitimacy by creating a new constitution.[2] Radicals have few regrets or fears about the use of the original constituent power in Colombia. If anything, they regret that the powers were not used more expansively; they regret that the process was not lawless enough to truly uproot the old political class, which they believe explains the present regime's continued corruption.[3]

"Legalists" have the exact opposite regret. They argue that the multiple invocations of the original constituent power left an unfortunate scar on an otherwise praiseworthy process and product. Law had set out a careful structure to preserve order and avoid conflict, they argue. The dangerous idea of the lawless people led the participants astray and threatened to derail the entire project. This near disaster is testimony to the "corrosive effect of bad theory."[4] Luckily, the persistence of the original legal framework's effects, especially the inclusive electoral rule, managed to rescue the assembly from its own reckless actions. It was the "assimilat[ion]"[5] of legalist or at least non-popular theory into a revolutionary process, or the "eclectic mix"[6] of the two

---

[2] Note that by radicals I refer to those who believe that the people are a lawless unity. This has right- and left-wing variations. Radicals of the left are skeptical of the Colombian process as it did not fulfill their redistributive goals Oscar Mejía Quintana, "El Poder Constituyente En Negri Y Habermas: Aproximaciones Descriptivas Y Perspectivas Críticas," in *Poder Constituyente Y Crisis Política En Colombia* (Bogotá: Universidad de Los Andes (CIJUS), 2005).

[3] Oscar Mejía Quintana, "El Poder Constituyente En Negri y Habermas: Aproximaciones Descriptivas y Perspectivas Críticas," in *Poder Constituyente y Crisis Política En Colombia* (Bogotá: Universidad de Los Andes (CIJUS), 2005); Óscar Mejia Quintana, "A dos décadas de la Constitución Política de 1991," *Araucaria. Revista Iberoamericana de Filosofía, Política y Humanidades* 15, no. 29 (2013), 99–116; July 27th Interview Antonio Navarro Wolf, ex-guerrilla leader of M-19 and co-president of the Constituent Assembly. Interestingly, this analysis of the Colombia process is shared by both Hugo Chávez and his constitutional adviser, Ricardo Combellas, and it influenced their design of the 1999 Venezuelan Constituent Assembly. Hugo Chávez, Marta Harnecker, and Chesa Boudin, *Understanding the Venezuelan Revolution: Hugo Chávez Talks to Marta Harnecker* (New York: Monthly Review Press, 2005), 32. ("We were very aware of what happened in Colombia, in the years of 1990–1991, when there was a constitutional assembly—of course!—it was very limited because in the end it was subordinated to the existing powers. It was the existing powers that designed Colombia's Constitutional Assembly and got it going and, therefore, it could not transform the situation because it was a prisoner of the existing powers."); Ricardo Combellas, *El proceso constituyente: una historia personal*, 2010 (memoirs of Chavez's constitutional advisor comparing the Colombian process to the putting together of the pieces of a broken vase whereas in Venezuela they aimed to break and throw away the vase).

[4] Andrew Arato, *Adventures of the Constituent Power* (New York: Cambridge University Press, 2018), 315.

[5] Ibid., 315.

[6] Nicolás Figueroa, "A Critique of Populist Jurisprudence: Courts, Democracy, and Constitutional Change in Colombia and Venezuela" (Phd diss., New School for Social Research, 2016), 118.

that account for the process' success. These legalists praise the inclusion of multiple parties and its fruition of a liberal and democratic constitution. For legalists, the Colombian process' success occurred despite the influence of a theory of a lawless constituent power that repeatedly threatened to derail a promising legal framework.

Radicals and legalists focus on one or some combination of three key moments to construct their narrative about the role a lawless theory of the constituent power played in the process. In the first, the Supreme Court declares the Constituent Assembly sovereign. In the second, the Constituent Assembly affirms its sovereignty. In the third, the Constituent Assembly exercises its sovereign power by purging the Congress.

In this chapter, I revisit each of these moments to show that the historical record contradicts the present understanding. Scholarship has been filtered through juridical distinctions that have distorted the dominant role of extraordinary adaptation. The problem is that the dichotomy between strict adherence to the rule of law or its total violation, between legalism and lawlessness, has distorted our understanding of the process.

Unlike in Venezuela, at no time did the Colombian Supreme Court or Constituent Assembly declare that the assembly was all-powerful. Nevertheless, the Constituent Assembly did not hesitate to break the law when necessary to break through resistance from the old guard, which was invested in preserving the previous regime. These targeted and narrow illegalities are what legalist critics misconstrue as examples of the lawless or original constituent power. The Supreme Court and the Constituent Assembly stumbled onto and enacted the theory of extraordinary adaptation: it repurposed the institutions of the old constitutional order to create a new one while fulfilling, in haphazard and incomplete ways, the three principles of legal exhaustion, popular vindication, and inclusion.

My argument challenges the radical and legalist narratives of the presence of the original constituent power. Against radicals, I emphasize the process' continuity with preexisting institutions and the limits of the Constituent Assembly's power. Against legalists, I show that illegalities were not a mistake but key to the process' success. Legalists must explain away a "paradox." They argue that sovereign constituent assemblies lead to authoritarianism, but in Colombia that very same model led to a liberal and democratic constitution. Legalists mobilize ostensibly anti-revolutionary features of the process, features drawn from or consistent with their more legalist models, to explain the process' success, especially its inclusionary electoral rule.[7] While legalists explain away the contradiction, I dissolve it. It does not exist. The theory and the practice are internally consistent. Extraordinary adaptation is linked to the proportional electoral rule and the process' irregularities did not mar the process but help us understand its success.

I also argue that the process' success should be contextualized, specifically that the process took great strides toward but failed to fully meet extraordinary adaptation's third principle of inclusion. Although disturbed by its revolutionary features, legalists are still eager to turn the process, properly understood, into a model of how to create a constitution. If Venezuela is the "bad" South American case, Colombia is the one in which constitutional re-founding managed to "go right."[8] Legalists and others laud the pluralism of the process, its spirit of orderly compromise, and the 1991 constitution's checks and balances, especially the Colombian Constitutional Court's expansive powers and its sophisticated doctrines of individual rights.[9] The new constitution greatly restored legitimacy to a broken and closed system.

These are no small achievements. But the inclusion these boosters celebrate was only partial. It was enough to prevent semi-authoritarianism and to significantly chip away at the political system's reputation for exclusion. However, the largest and rural-left guerilla groups were not part of the process. The new constitution accomplished little for these guerillas' constituents, the peasants who remained poor and vulnerable and struggled to survive in the midst of war. The guerillas' most important demand was economic, specifically land redistribution, a demand that threatened the power base of powerful rural landlords who had ruthlessly protected their wealth by creating paramilitary organizations.[10] Would the process have run

---

[7] Arato, *Adventures of the Constituent Power*; Figueroa, "A Critique of Populist Jurisprudence: Courts, Democracy, and Constitutional Change in Colombia and Venezuela."

[8] Arato, *Adventures of the Constituent Power*, 1.

[9] Carlos Bernal, "Unconstitutional Constitutional Amendments in the Case Study of Colombia: An Analysis of the Justification and Meaning of the Constitutional Replacement Doctrine," *International Journal of Constitutional Law* 11, no. 2 (Apr. 1, 2013), 339–57; Martha I. Morgan, "Taking Machismo to Court: The Gender Jurisprudence of the Colombian Constitutional Court," *The University of Miami Inter-American Law Review* 30, no. 2 (1999), 253–342. Indeed, the court and its rich doctrine is widely celebrated in the scholarship of comparative constitutional law.

[10] Julieta Lemaitre, "Peace at Hand: War and Peace in Colombia's 1991 Constituent Assembly,"Paper Presented at Seminar in Latin America on Constitutional and Political Theory, Rio de Janeiro, 2015), https://law.yale.edu/sites/default/files/documents/pdf/sela/SELA12_Lemaitre_CV_Eng_20120511.pdf, p. 9. For a more detailed analysis in Spanish, Julieta Lemaitre Ripoll, *La Paz En Cuestión: La Guerra Y La Paz En La Asamblea Constituyente de 1991*. (Universidad de los Andes, 2014), 271.

so smoothly if the peasants had been included? Would it have been so easy to cabin demands for seizing all power if the assembly had faced resistance from landlords against redistribution? To what extent was the assembly's agreement built and dependent upon the exclusion of a significant portion of the population? These questions may be impossible to answer, but they at least need to be asked before we make Colombia the paradigm of cooperation and consensus. In the next chapter on Bolivia, we will see the great strains full inclusion puts on the process of extraordinary adaptation.

LEGAL EXHAUSTION

Extraordinary adaptation is dangerous. While less reckless than the radical theory of constituent power, extraordinary adaptation's embrace of limited and targeted illegalities still presents significant risks. Without the traditional legal boundaries, the system may spiral out of control. For that reason, the first principle of extraordinary adaptation, "legal exhaustion," requires that revolutionaries first try to achieve their goal legally. In Colombia, the decision to use extraordinary adaptation was not to be made lightly; it did not spring from romantic visions of the people that could seize the common good outside the unpleasant and inevitable negotiations present in any constitutional change. Nor was it the subterfuge of a semi-authoritarian dictator trying to exclude and weaken his opponents. It was a response to the inability of the political class to reform its own institutions to restore order and the government's legitimacy, efficiency, and representativeness. The legal route was exhausted.

In the late 1970s and 1980s, Colombia was in a dire crisis, and its political system was incapable of resolving it. The constitution facilitated the entrenchment in power of the elites of two increasingly indistinguishable political parties. To transition from the brutal and decade-long civil war that ended in 1958, referred to as "the Violence," the Conservative and Liberal Parties pacted together to share power. The pact was called the "National Front," and its central provisions were amended into the constitution. For the period of 1958 to 1974, it guaranteed the two parties alternation of the presidency and equal power in the Congress, the judiciary, as well as state and municipal legislatures and mayoralties. The constitution also permanently required "adequate and equitable participation to the majority party other than the president of the Republic" in "the executive branch and in public administration."[11] This patronage, along with the peculiar electoral rule for the legislature,[12] contributed to a vast clientelist system that prevented the political parties from presenting coherent national platforms. Since presidents were elected in a single nationwide district, they were more programmatic than congressional representatives. Presidents often presented ambitious proposals only to watch the plan wither in Congress as the president's party refused to support him.[13] The pact also effectively excluded radical and peasant parties from participation in government for sixteen years. This exclusion and the military operations against it were key factors that converted the Communist Party from an electoral vehicle seeking political participation to an armed insurgency devoted to violent revolution. The Communist Party became the foundation for the Revolutionary Armed Forces of Colombia (FARC) that became the single largest guerilla group and peasant-based insurgency in South America.[14]

The FARC was only one of many nonstate actors that contributed to the chaos. The country was buffeted by violence from a wide variety of leftist guerillas, drug cartels, and right-wing paramilitary groups. We'll see that the momentum for the new constitution slowly picked up steam beginning with the inauguration of the new Conservative President Virgilia Barco in August of 1986. In the almost four years between that date and the next presidential election in May of 1990, Julia Lemaitre notes that there were "19 car bombs, resulting in around 300 victims; hired killers (sicarios) shot and killed 250 policemen; guerillas blew up the Caño Limón-Coveñas oil pipeline 125 times

---

[11] 1886 Colombian Constitution, Art. 120. For a discussion of the pact's provisions and effects, Ana Maria Bejarano, *Precarious Democracies: Understanding Regime Stability and Change in Colombia and Venezuela*, (Notre Dame, IN: University of Notre Dame Press, 2011), 115–22.

[12] Gabriel Negretto summarizes the electoral rule for the Congress: "Since 1931, deputies had been elected by a Hare PR formula in multi-member districts from multiple closed lists per party. In the absence of a legal threshold, the electoral formula was biased in favor of small parties. As a result of the use of multiple lists per party, however, the potential for multipartism was channeled via intra-party competition among the various factions of the two main parties. The lack of control by party leaders over the use of party labels reinforced this competition. Since 1945, senators had been elected in a direct election by the same formula used to elect deputies." Negretto, *Making Constitutions*, 168.

[13] Negretto, *Making Constitutions*, 171–72.

[14] Bejarano, *Precarious Democracies*, 101–6, 163–75. The two parties, the Liberals and Conservatives, had an upper- and middle-class urban base, and the pact had overthrown a populist dictator who had reached out to the underclasses. Bejarano, 101–4. So neither political party had an interest in giving true electoral choices to the rural peasants who still had substantial control over their own territories. Although excluded from power at the national level, the communist parties still had a strong foothold in certain rural areas and as a legacy of the civil war or "the Violence," Communist Party members remained heavily armed and still independent from the central government. In 1964, at the behest of the Conservatives, the government launched a military operation against them. The peasants lost and immigrated into the Eastern Plains, where two years later some of them formed the Revolutionary Armed Forces of Colombia (FARC).

and death squads murdered thousands of anonymous militants from the left-wing party *Unión Patriótica*."[15] In the 1990 presidential elections, four of the presidential candidates were assassinated, including the front-runner Luis Carlos Galán.[16] Colombia spent thirteen of the sixteen years between 1974 and 1990 under the constitution's state of emergency, giving the president extraordinary powers to legislate by decree.[17]

During this crisis of representation and order, what did the government do to repair the constitution? Recall that "legalists," such as Andrew Arato, William Partlett, and to a lesser extent David Landau, call for lawful amendments to address the need for constitutional change.[18] Colombia repeatedly tried different variations of the legalist route and over and over it failed to surmount the political system's trenchant resistance to change. Serious calls for constitutional change began as early as the 1970s. Seven significant attempts were made to achieve it, once each in 1977, 1979, 1983, and 1986, and three times in 1988 until finally an illegal constituent assembly convened in 1991.[19] Before 1991, almost every attempt had tried to adhere to one of the legalist formulas.[20] All the attempts met the same fate. Each time, a nationally minded president led the reform effort. Each time, either the Supreme Court or the Congress pulled the rug out from under the process, and critics understood these sabotages as efforts to protect current officeholders against change. Only after these failures did the student movement mobilize for an extralegal vote for a constituent assembly that finally allowed the president to circumvent Congress.

---

[15] Lemaitre, "Peace at Hand: War and Peace in Colombia's 1991 Constituent Assembly," 2.

[16] Ibid.

[17] Negretto, *Making Constitutions*, 8. For an account of the state of emergency and its role in the creation of the 1991 constitution, Antonio Barreto Rozo, "La Generación Del Estado de Sitio: El Juicio a La Anormalidad Institucional Colombiana En La Asamblea Nacional Constituyente de 1991," *Precedente* 1, no. 9–48 (2012), 13.

[18] David Landau, "Constitution-Making Gone Wrong," *Alabama Law Review* 64 (2012), 923; William Partlett, "Elite Threat to Constitutional Transitions," *Virginia Journal of International Law* 56 (2016), 407.

[19] The following account of these attempts draws very heavily from chapter 5 of John Dugas, "Explaining Democratic Reform in Colombia: The Origins of the 1991 Constitution" (Unpublished diss., Indiana University, 1997). For an account of the court's jurisprudence on constitutional change during these attempts, Mario Cajas Sarria, *El control judicial a la reforma constitucional: Colombia, 1910–2007* (Cali, Colombia: Universidad Icesi, 2008). For broad overviews of Colombian constitutional change, Arturo Sarabia, *Reformas Políticas En Colombia. Del Plebiscito de 1957 al Referendo de 2003*; Hernando Valencia Villa, *El Anticonstitucional. Introducción a a La Crítica de La Constitución Política*; Hernando Valencia Villa, *Cartas de Batalla. Una Crítica Del Constitucionalismo Colombiano*.

[20] Of the seven failed attempts at constitutional reform, the first two by Barco in 1988 disregarded the legalist route of the traditional amendment method in favor of referendums.

I will review each of the seven attempts, including the three in 1988 under the Colombian president who eventually successfully convoked an assembly in 1991.[21] In 1977, after extensive resistance from Congress and in accordance with the wishes of the president, the Congress amended the constitution to allow for a constituent assembly solely tasked with the project to reform the byzantine system of courts, replace the Supreme Court with a constitutional one, and reform the state and municipal systems. In essence, the route taken was something akin to the round-table model advocated by Andrew Arato that pursues a limited constitutional assembly through a legal and negotiated process of amendment by the political parties and interest groups. The method failed: the Supreme Court struck down the amendment as unconstitutional. Even if it had succeeded, the electoral rule for the assembly would have ensured the dominance of the Liberal and Conservative Parties, perpetuating the problem of exclusion in the political system.[22] The next president again pushed for constitutional reform in 1979. This time, he shifted away from the round-table model and he followed William Partlett's preferred method and the court's advice to follow the straightforward and traditional method of constitutional amendment.[23] Congress passed the amendment, but the court again struck down an amendment, this time on narrow and procedural grounds. The court had foiled the first two attempts at reform, and critics alleged that the court was wary of an attempt to replace and destroy its own base of power. Yet, even if they had passed, the proposed amendments were too shallow to the meet the challenge the Colombian political system faced. The price of getting Congress's consent was the watering down of the reforms and the assurance that the two political parties would completely dominate the process.[24] As John Hartlyn writes, it "was an effort to correct some of the more glaring congressional and judicial institutional flaws . . . without breaking out of the constraints of coalition rule."[25]

While the Supreme Court obstructed the first two attempts, Congress was the spoiler in the third and fourth. Unlike his more cautious predecessors, President Betancur intended to make a series of wide-ranging political

---

[21] My narrative of these failed attempts draws very heavily from chapter 5 of John Dugas, "Explaining Democratic Reform in Colombia: The Origins of the 1991 Constitution."

[22] Ibid., 270–72.

[23] William Partlett, "Elite Threat to Constitutional Transitions."

[24] Dugas, "Explaining Democratic Reform in Colombia," 274–77.

[25] Jonathan Hartlyn, *The Politics of Coalition Rule in Colombia* (Cambridge: Cambridge University Press, 1988), 225, quoted in Dugas, "Explaining Democratic Reform in Colombia," 274. In his study of the 1991 Colombia Constitution, John Dugas agrees that they were "attempt[s] to modify political institutions in Colombia without introducing significant democratic change." Ibid.

reforms to open up the system to outsiders and tied these attempts the-matically together with a separate set of peace talks with the left-wing gue-rilla groups. Soon after his inauguration in 1982, he held a series of summit meetings with the Liberal, Conservative, Communist, Socialist, and Christian Democratic Parties to draft proposals. The two dominant parties who had the most to lose, the Conservatives and the Liberals, walked out. In the wake of the failure, Betancur only submitted two reforms to Congress on the financing of political parties and the reformation of the civil service. Congress passed neither of the reforms.[26] One Colombian analyst at the time remarked that "without a doubt there exists a very considerable sector of rep-resentatives and senators who do not consider expedient a restructuring of the rules of the game of the Colombian political process, given that these transformations will alter their actual political power."[27] Betancur tried again to submit amendments to Congress; Congress again refused to enact them;[28] and critics once again were scathing, with one commenting that "Congress preferred to adopt the attitude of the ostrich: to stick its head in the ground while the storm lasted."[29] On these third and fourth attempts, the president tried the method of congressional amendment and both times Congress thwarted the promising plans for profound constitutional reform.

President Virgilia Barco was responsible for the final attempts—the fifth, sixth, and seventh ones, all in 1988. Since Congress had stymied the last round, in this fifth attempt President Virgilia Barco chose legally question-able methods that would bypass Congress through two referendums. In the first referendum, citizens would vote to amend the constitution to allow for a referendum centered method of constitutional change. In the second ref-erendum, the citizens would use the new method to enact far-reaching re-form. President Barco was open and explicit about the need to circumvent Congress: "I am a friend of the spirit of transaction that the parliamentary

---

[26] Ibid., 280.

[27] Gabriel Silva Luján, "Del Frente Nacional a la apertura democrática: Entre la represión y el reformismo," in *Proceso político en Colombia: Del Frente Nacional a la apertura democrática,* ed. Ricardo Santamaría Salamanca (Bogotá: Fondo Editorial CEREC, 1984), quoted in Dugas, "Explaining Democratic Reform," 280.

[28] Dugas, "Explaining Democratic Reform in Colombia," 281–82.

[29] Socorro Ramirez Vargas and Luis Alberto Restrepo Moreno, *Actores en conflicto por la paz: El proceso de paz durante el gobierno de Belisario Betancur (1982–1986).* (Bogotá: Cinep, 1988), quoted in Dugas, "Explaining Democratic Reform," 281–82. As John Dugas notes, later in the term Congress did pass constitutional measures for the "popular election of municipal mayors . . . and some related local-level reforms." Dugas comments, however, "the reform was still somewhat limited in its dem-ocratic content." For example, "the power to remove mayors from office lay solely in the hands of the president or of the department governor." Ibid., 282.

work of Congress implies. But we must recognize that so many negotiations and so many compromises have only produced some timid and insufficient laws." The plan aroused such ferocious opposition from the mass media, the Conservative Party, and Liberal ex-presidents that Barco withdrew it.[30] He shifted tactics to gain Congress's consent. For the sixth try at reform, Barco proposed that the president and Congress would elect a fifty-member commission, with party representation proportional to the March election of departmental assemblies, to draw up proposals that would then be approved in a referendum. The process would be dominated by political insiders. The highest administrative court, the Council of State, struck it down as unconstitutional because it circumvented the amendment method.[31]

After facing such resistance against legally questionable methods of amendment, Barco tried to follow the traditional Congress-centered route and submitted proposed constitutional amendments to Congress. After Congress whittled out the most significant parts of Barco's proposal, those opposed to the bill amended it so that there would also be a referendum on whether to ban extradition. This was a poison pill, which doomed constitutional reform. Extradition was an explosive issue in Colombia. For proponents of extradition, the Colombian court system had proven too corrupt to prosecute drug lords, such as Pablo Escobar, and extradition was a tool to bring them to justice.[32] To denote their fierce opposition, Escobar and his allies called themselves the "extraditables" with the motto, "Better a grave in Colombia than a prison in the United States."[33]

A referendum posed an immense danger to the safety and order of the country. The minister of government explained:

This is a monstrosity, a shame! If you approve the proposition, you will be inviting the Colombian people, not to an election, but to a slaughter. Because this is a subject that, if brought to a popular consultation, will provoke tremendous violence, it will provoke deaths, intimidation. The drug traffickers will make their terrorist power felt in order that the Colombian people vote in accord with their desires. We will find ourselves before the spectacle of elections carried out under the sign of bombs, of car bombs,

[30] Dugas, "Explaining Democratic Reform," 291–93.
[31] Ibid., 293–96. Indeed, Barco's shots at altering the constitution were of much more questionable constitutionality than his predecessor's efforts.
[32] Ibid., 296–300.
[33] Lemaitre, "Peace at Hand: War and Peace in Colombia's 1991 Constituent Assembly," 22.

of airplanes that don't complete their flights because they are blown up, of every kind of horror that the drug traffickers tend to use to persuade.[34]

To prevent the referendum on extradition, Barco opposed passing what was originally his own reform and after all the squabbling, Congress ran out of time and lacked a quorum to even have a vote on the reform bill. After seven failed attempts in eleven years, there was little hope for constitutional reform.[35]

Extraordinary adaptation's first principle of legal exhaustion was fulfilled: every possible legal route had been tried and failed. It was a stalemate between the president on the one side and the court and Congress on the other. Progress was impossible, and without some dramatic break the system would continue to limp along, hobbled by an archaic and inefficient constitution.

The popular mobilization of the citizenry in the movement for a seventh ballot changed all that. The constituent power gave new life to the project of constitutional reform. On August 18th, 1989, as he gave a speech in front of ten thousand people, Luis Carlos Galán, the leading candidate in the 1990 presidential elections, was gunned down. Galán had been on the liberal ticket but had long led his own separate reformist movement.[36] He was a fiery, inspirational figure believed to be the hope for the "renovation of the political class."[37] Pablo Escobar considered Galán a threat and ordered the hit against him. Galán's death shocked the nation. In response, a week later, between fifteen thousand and twenty-five thousand students marched.[38] In the first of their seven-point proclamation, they "reject[ed] any type of violence regardless of the ideology or interests that seek to justify it." They condemned violence of "the so-called narcotraffickers, guerillas, paramilitary groups and others."[39] They also rejected the idea that the current government, especially

[34] *Semana.* 1989d. "¿Herida de muerte?' 396, December 5, 1989, quoted in Dugas, "Explaining Democratic Reform," 296.

[35] Dugas, "Explaining Democratic Reform," 300–1.

[36] Francisco Gutiérrez Sanín, *Lo que el viento se llevó?: los partidos políticos y la democracia en Colombia, 1958–2002* (Bogotá: Grupo Editorial Norma, 2007).

[37] Julieta Lemaitre Ripoll, *El derecho como conjuro: fetichismo legal, violencia y movimientos sociales* (Bogotá, D.C.: Siglo del Hombre Editores: Universidad de los Andes, 2009).

[38] Julieta Lemaitre Ripoll. For another overview of the student movement, Jaime Buenahora Febres-Cordero, *El proceso constituyente de la propuesta estudiantil a la quiebra del bipartidismo* (Bogotá, Colombia: Cámara de Representantes: Pontificia Universidad Javeriana, Programa de Estudios Políticos, 1991).

[39] Lemaitre Ripoll, *El derecho como conjuro*, 87. In addition, at various points, students held signs with slogans that called "For Peace, now" and "for the right to life, no more violence." Luis

the Congress, could be relied upon to address the violence and corruption. If anything, they were part of the problem.[40] Rather than armed revolution or government action, their official statement pushed for "a convocation of the people to reform the institutions that are blocking the solutions to the crisis."[41]

In the days and weeks that followed the march, student groups began to develop proposals for a constituent assembly. Their efforts, however, received little attention as the nation focused on Barco's plan to propose amendments through Congress. On December 15th, Congress effectively killed the plan by attaching amendments to create a referendum on extradition. That failure was the match that ignited the constituent power. The hopes of the nation now turned to the student movement, which had settled on an ingenious proposal.[42] In the upcoming congressional elections in March of 1990, each voter would deposit one ballot for each of the six candidates. The student movement printed a seventh and extralegal ballot, "la séptima papeleta," to vote for a constituent assembly. The plan received endorsements from the political parties, the trade unions, the guild of industrialists, ex-presidents, and some of the presidential candidates. The news media also signed on and the major national and regional newspaper included a ballot in one of their issues. One of the largest newspapers, *El Tiempo*, printed a million ballots. There is no official count of the ballots, but the student movement and *El Tiempo* estimated that voters deposited one million, three hundred thousand ballots.[43]

President Barco seized the opportunity.[44] Without popular support, he had lost three times in his contests with the Congress over the amendments. The president's newfound ability to invoke the people broke the logjam. Citing the mobilization, the more than one million votes for a constituent assembly, and his emergency powers, President Barco issued a decree calling for a referendum for citizens to vote on whether to hold a constitutional assembly. The

Ángel Arango Library, "Library Display, De Toda La Gente, 25 Años de La Asamblea Nacional Constituyente" (Bogotá, Jan. 2017).

[40] Figueroa, "A Critique of Populist Jurisprudence: Courts, Democracy, and Constitutional Change in Colombia and Venezuela," 106.

[41] Lemaitre Ripoll, *El derecho como conjuro*, 88.

[42] Ibid., 98.

[43] Ibid., 100–3, 107.

[44] Although the student movement was independent and distinct from the government, a few key professors with close ties to government, especially Fernando Carillo and Manuel Jose Cepeda, collaborated with the students on their proposals for a constituent assembly. Ibid., 93, 98, 100.

Supreme Court allowed the vote but only on the basis that it was consultative and not binding. After winning 88.8 percent of the votes in the consultative referendum, Barco issued a second decree calling for a second referendum to vote again on whether to hold a constitutional assembly and to vote on candidates for the assembly.

The decree also set the basic framework for the assembly. There are two features that are of particular import. First, unlike in Venezuela and as in Bolivia, the electoral rule was both inclusive and proportional. Second, the decree forbade the Constituent Assembly from shortening the terms of Congress so as to hold new elections after the creation of the constitution. This was necessary to gain the two traditional parties' acceptance because they wanted to protect their power in the Congress.[45]

The decree enabled Barco to circumvent Congress to hold a referendum on whether to convoke a constitutional assembly, but Congress was only one of the two traditional barriers to constitutional reform. Would the Supreme Court strike down the emergency decree? If not, would it uphold the limitations that the decree would impose on the assembly?

THE SUPREME COURT'S EXTRAORDINARY ADAPTATION

The court upheld the central thrust of the decree: there would a referendum in which citizens could vote both on whether to hold a constitutional assembly and who the members of the assembly would be. However, the court struck down the topical limitations on the assembly, especially the limit on the Constitutional Assembly's ability to immediately hold new elections after the approval of the constitution. Why did the court uphold the referendum on the Constitutional Assembly but strike down the limitation on what the assembly could pass?

In the dominant narrative, the court recognized the lawless constituent power was not only unbound by the amendment rule but could not be bound by any limitation. Nicolas Figueroa states that "the court claimed the Assembly was absolutely sovereign."[46] Hence, "as a completely

---

[45] Decreto 927 del 3 de Mayo de 1990. The limit on calling early elections was one in a long list of limitations on the topics that the assembly could discuss and actions it could take. However, the decree listed so many topics that it would not serve as much of a barrier, except in the case of the revocation of Congress.

[46] Figueroa, "A Critique of Populist Jurisprudence: Courts, Democracy, and Constitutional Change in Colombia and Venezuela," 95. I am deeply in debt to Figueroa's work on Colombia and to our many conversations on Colombia and Venezuela. Figueroa fits somewhat uneasily in the legalist camp

sovereign body it had the power to interfere with the functioning of the legislature and all the other constituted powers."[47] Andrew Arato agrees that the court "declared [that the Constitutional Assembly] possessed the original constituent power" and thus "declared all limits on the constituent assembly to be unconstitutional."[48] These authors argue that the theoretical errors that would plague the Venezuelan experience first occurred in Colombia with the creation of an all-powerful sovereign constituent assembly.

This is a misreading of the Supreme Court's decision. The court never embraces the idea of a sovereign constituent assembly.[49] Instead, the court struggles to articulate a nascent vision of extraordinary adaptation that would allow for the circumvention of the amendment rule while still striking down threats to the integrity of the constitution-making process.

because he expresses some openness to developing an alternative definition of the constituent power. In his case studies, the openness manifests itself in the chapter on Colombia, in which he supports the process up until the Supreme Court strikes down the content limitations on the assembly as a violation of the constituent power. Yet, he never fully acknowledges nor places any emphasis on the illegality of the presidential decree without which the process would have been impossible nor the failure of legal routes to amendment that had continuously plagued previous attempts. Indeed, in his dissertation's conclusion, after conceding some potential for populist jurisprudence, he shifts gears and writes that "the principle of *legality* should take the place of a regulative ideal that courts can try to enforce even during those moments in which it is evident that most sectors of political society feel the need to replace the constitutional regime." Here, Figueroa seems to disavow or at least deemphasize the need for any illegality in the process. Figueroa, 245.

Figueroa's objects to the Colombian Supreme Court striking down the substantive limits placed on the Colombian Constituent Assembly. Extraordinary adaptation is suspicious of such restrictions, and Figueroa notes that they belong to the logic of the Andrew Arato's post-sovereign model, a model that is hostile to illegality and the ideas of the people and revolution. Indeed, Andrew Arato argues that the model is the best lens through which to understand the success of the Colombian process, and Figueroa characterizes the Colombian process as an "eclectic mixture of the two paradigms" of the post-sovereign model and Schmittian original and lawless constituent power commending the former's influence and condemning the latter's. In the Colombia chapter, in particular, Figueroa seems to greatly embrace Arato's round-table model and insofar as he does, Figueroa is a legalist. Figueroa, 118.

[47] Figueroa, "A Critique of Populist Jurisprudence: Courts, Democracy, and Constitutional Change in Colombia and Venezuela," 116.

[48] Andrew, *Adventures of the Constituent Power*, 312, 315.

[49] The court refers to the Constituent Assembly as sovereign only once, in passing, and to make a separate point. Here is the passage: "The issuance of the decree that was reviewed was motivated by the very spacious circumstances that the nation lives in, so that if a similar statute were ever issued in the future, the Court would carefully and prudently examine the national situation prevailing at that time. Such an eventuality will be more remote, insofar as the National Constitutional Assembly, in its sovereignty, in article 218 of the Charter, alongside legislative acts, so cumbersome processing, other mechanisms for reform of the Constitution, as those issued by previous governments or those that govern at the municipal level." Corte Suprema de Justicia [C.S.J.] [Supreme Court], Sala Plena, Sentencia No. 138 del 9 de Octubre de 1990.

Extraordinary Jurisdiction

Scholarship on the constituent power and past doctrine gave the court no pathway for upholding the decree. Indeed, opponents of the decree astutely argued in its filings that since the people existed outside of law, the court had two unpalatable options, either "the Court lacked jurisdiction or the [decree] was unconstitutional."[50] The court resolved this dilemma by recognizing that the constituent power was not lawless but rather manifested itself through the extraordinary adaptation of current institutions. Rather than existing in a legal void, the people would be constructed through the court's and the president's unconventional use of their emergency powers. On the surface, this was a completely legal exercise: despite the ominous name, the emergency powers are regulated, limited, and constitutional. However, the president and the court repurposed this constitutional power beyond its original mandate of making temporary change to protect the status quo. Instead, in the name of the people, the emergency powers gave birth to a whole new and permanent constitution.

Opponents of the decree argued that the court had two options, neither of which the court wished to pursue. The first option was for the court to decline jurisdiction and refuse to rule on the case because it lacks power over the people. It is, in the language of U.S. scholarship, a "political question" unfit for adjudication. The people, through the constitution, granted the court power to hear cases, usually against the government or against individuals based on the government's laws. In other words, the court is following the people's orders, and has no authority over its superior, over those forces that stand above the constitution. The idea of jurisdiction over the people would be logically equivalent to and almost as absurd as asking the court to adjudicate a case against God's injustice. If the court chose this option, it would lose all input into the process, leaving the Constitutional Assembly totally unchecked. Given that constitutional assemblies are difficult to control once they are convoked, the court and all political actors have an important role to play in structuring the assembly in accordance with the three principles of extraordinary adaptation, especially the third principle of inclusion.

The second and alternative option is that the court may strike down the measure as unconstitutional because it violates the constitution's amendment method. The court must uphold its oath to the constitution even if that

---

[50] Argument of the Procurador General as quoted by the Supreme Court.

constitution no longer can claim to represent the people. Here, the court would again be the spoiler, but unlike other times the court would not be checking just the president but a massive social movement that had taken to the streets demanding change. Not only did the court likely agree with such movements, the court might lose its legitimacy or prove to be ineffective if it tried to stop the whirlwind that was the people. In other words, current scholarship asked the court to either abstain or to doom Colombia to continued political stagnation.

The court refused to gore itself on either horn of this dilemma. Instead, the court turned to the 1886 constitution's emergency powers but in an extraordinary way. We saw in the previous chapter how the Venezuelan Supreme Court repurposed that country's statute on referendums. About nine years earlier, the Colombian court tried a similar tactic, reinterpreting the president's emergency powers in a novel way.

To understand the novelty, we must first understand the standard understanding in which the emergency powers existed within the 1886 constitution. We often think of emergency powers as a "state of exception" that resides in a legal vacuum. For example, Carl Schmitt argued that in Rome, during a crisis, a commissarial dictator was given a limited time to restore order and during it, he was "not bound by the law; he was a kind of king with absolute power over life and death."[51] That is not how it worked in practice or in design in Colombia. While it greatly enhances the powers of the presidency, the state of emergency was carefully regulated by the constitution.

Per the constitution, in cases of external war or internal commotion, the president, with the consent of his ministers, may declare a state of siege in which the president has the power to initiate extraordinary decrees tailored to address the threat. These decrees have the temporary force of law but are invalid as soon as the emergency ceases. Among other limits, the constitution forbids the president from disbanding Congress, from interfering with the social rights of workers, and holds that the presidents and ministers will be held responsible for any abuse of their emergency powers.[52]

Most importantly, the president cannot issue decrees unilaterally. He has only the power of initiation. For each decree, he must obtain the approval

---

[51] Carl Schmitt, *Dictatorship* (Cambridge: Polity, 2013), 2. To be clear, Schmitt acknowledged that the dictator was, in some sense, regulated by the constitution because the dictatorship could not last longer than the duration of the emergency and for a maximum of six months. Within that time span, however, the dictator has all power.

[52] 1886 Colombian Constitution, art. 121.

of his ministers and the approval of the Supreme Court. The day after its issuance, the president must send the decree to the Supreme Court, and the
Supreme Court must decide the case in twenty days. Failure to hear the case
"is a cause of misconduct that will be sanctioned under the law." The constitution is clear about the broad scope and mission of the court in these cases,
stating that the court must "decide definitively about [the decree's] constitutionality."[53] The court itself, in the first of the two referendum cases I will
discuss, specifically rejects Schmittian approaches that place the emergency
decree power outside law:

> [The power to issue emergency decrees] is, therefore, a normalized power,
> with express powers, that does not suspend the Constitution. Emergency
> power does not grant the ruler absolute powers. This Court does not ac-
> cept the theory of the state of necessity which implies powers implicit in the
> function of government. We rejects Carl Schmitt's claim that "sovereign is
> the one who decides the State of Exception."[54]

Under his emergency powers, on two separate and back-to-back occasions,
the president issued a decree for a referendum to create a constitutional assembly. Per the 1886 constitution, for each of the two decrees, the court had
to decide whether they were legal.

But the traditional legal understanding of the president's decree powers
would not be a sufficient justification for upholding this kind of sweeping
constitutional change. Legalists could not have their cake and eat it too.
Emergency decrees have the temporary force of a statute. As soon as the
emergency powers are lifted, the decrees are invalid, and the old laws are
restored. Hence, this method of a temporary change in statutory law was
ill-suited for achieving permanent change for the constitution. The correct
method for that, as the court had ruled many times, was the constitution's
amendment method.[55] In summary, it was impossible to justify legally the

---

[53] Ibid.

[54] Corte Suprema de Justicia [C.S.J.] [Supreme Court], Sala. Plena, Sentencia No. 59 del 24 Mayo de
1990. Note here that the court is rebutting Schmitt's argument about sovereign dictatorship, not the
commissarial one I mentioned before. But the court could have said the same thing about the idea of
commissarial dictatorship as well. See Schmitt, *Dictatorship*, 2.

[55] These arguments are laid out in the second Supreme Court decision. Corte Suprema de Justicia
[C.S.J.] [Supreme Court], Sala Plena, Sentencia No. 138 del 9 de Octubre de 1990. Additionally, statutes and constitutional history also weighed against constitutional change through a referendum.
On one previous extraordinary occasion, in 1957, the constitution had been reformed through a
referendum. Colombia had just ended its most violent civil war, called "La Violencia" or the Violence,

president's use of emergency powers to create a new constitution through referendums.

Instead, the emergency powers, unconventionally adapted, were a means for the people to express themselves. The court recognized that as the ultimate authority, the people had the right to circumvent the constitution's amendment rule and the doctrine on the state of emergency. The court states, "As the Colombian nation is the constituent power, it can at whatsoever time give itself a new constitution distinct from the one in force and in a manner not subject to the requirements of the old constitution. Otherwise, there would be many absurdities: the constitutional reforms of 1957 and the whole constitution of 1886 would be invalid."[56] Yet, it refuses to abide by the additional premise that the need for this illegality implies that the people are completely lawless, that is, are outside all institutions. The court notes that the people are manifesting themselves through the government institutions, through the constitutional emergency power. Therefore, the court affirms its right to hear the case: "[I]t is . . . certain that the mechanism utilized to permit the popular manifestation that convoked the assembly is a decree of the state of siege, whose control corresponds to the court according to the cited norms."[57] It denies, however, that it is the decree that is making these permanent changes. The decree is "not reforming the Constitution, the reform will come from the votes of the 9th of December" when the referendum will be held. Indeed, the court asserts that "The president is being used . . . to permit the registration of the expression of the popular will about the possibility of the creation of a constituent assembly."[58] The court might have added that it too is participating in the process of constructing the people by legitimizing parts of the decree while striking down others.

and was transitioning from military to civilian rule. The referendum approved the power-sharing arrangements for the two sides of the civil war.

But this is poor precedent for a referendum in 1991 for two reasons. First, the statute authorizing the 1957 referendum forbade ever repeating that act stating that "[f]rom now on, the reforms of Congress can only be made, in the form established by the Constitution's amendment method." To get around this statute, one would have to resort to the constituent power.

Second, and as the dissent pointed out, that plebiscite was necessary because a dictator had purged the Congress and so there was no body to set up the foundations of government. Corte Suprema de Justicia [C.S.J.] [Supreme Court] [Dissent], Sala. Plena, Sentencia No. 59 del 24 Mayo de 1990. That was no longer the case in 1991 after the transition to democracy. Consistent with this reasoning, courts had struck down previous referendums. *Infra* text accompanying notes 21–25, 31.

[56] Corte Suprema de Justicia [C.S.J.] [Supreme Court], Sala Plena, Sentencia No. 138 del 9 de Octubre de 1990.

[57] Ibid.

[58] Ibid.

Through and alongside the constitution, the people are expressing themselves. The court concludes in the next sentence that "the situation is not diminished but increased by the extraordinary circumstances of the State of Siege to look, before all, the reestablishment of the public order."[59] In other words, under traditional emergencies the state of siege powers could never be used this way. However, under these "extraordinary circumstances" of popular mobilization, the power is a medium for the people to speak. The people's judgment ultimately does not manifest itself outside all institutions but through them, through the constitutional state of siege as enacted by the president, and even through the court. This odd illegality conducted through current institutions is the essence of extraordinary adaptation.

The continuity of institutions is what permits the court to make these novel interpretations of its jurisdiction and of the state of siege. In past Colombian history, new constitutions or substantial overhauls to old ones were prompted by total ruptures with the old order in which invaders or caudillos had overthrown the old regime. For example, as I discussed earlier, the excruciating civil war, called "the Violence," was the immediate cause of addition of the National Front power-sharing provisions. In 1953, Gustavo Rojas Pinilla led a peaceful coup of the government and established a military junta, and a year later the Liberal and Conservative Parties collaborated to overthrow him. At that time, in its decision to approve the plebiscite on the new constitution, the Supreme Court fittingly called upon the lawless constituent power. However, in 1990, there was no rupture of the constitutional thread. The dissent in the second 1990 Supreme Court decision recognizes this event's novelty in Colombian constitutional history:

Only the victors in war (1863, General Tomas Cipriano de Mosquera, and in 1886 President Nunez) appealed to an extraconstitutional route to justify the constitutions then promulgated. The rupture of the legal order was obvious, as in 1957 given the inexistence of Congress and the illegitimacy of the President, General Gustavo Rojas and the members of the Military Junta. The plebisicite, without a doubt, the first time, gave a mandate to the military junta and the second time, it established the national front. Presently, the branches of the public order has a regular origin and

---

[59] Ibid. (citing the court's decision on the firs decree, Corte Suprema de Justicia [C.S.J.] [Supreme Court], Sala. Plena, Sentencia No. 59 del 24 Mayo de 1990).

those who represent them have been elected in conformity with the current order.[60]

While the dissenting opinion is correct that the solution is novel, it mistakenly marshals this continuity to argue that no illegality is necessary. In fact, the old rules had continually proven unable to reform the political regime. A breaking and bending of the rules was necessary to initiate a new beginning, but the continuity by the president, the Supreme Court, and the political parties allowed for a collaboration to extraordinarily adapt old institutions to inclusively structure the creation of the new constitution.

The Supreme Court and Legal Exhaustion

After establishing jurisdiction and that the emergency powers would be the means of extraordinary adaptation, the rest of the court's decision is best interpreted as a grappling with the three principles of extraordinary adaptation. The first principle is legal exhaustion, a topic I covered extensively earlier in the chapter, but I return to it briefly to show that the court effectively used the principle as justification for the authorization of the vote to hold a constitutional assembly. The state of emergency doctrine requires that there be "sufficient connection" between the decree and the emergency. In discussing this connection, the court lays out the case for legal exhaustion.

The emergency resulted from a guerilla war against the central government. The FARC was only one of many nonstate actors that contributed to the chaos. The country was buffeted by violence from a wide variety of leftist guerillas, drug cartels, and right-wing paramilitary groups. The Supreme Court summarizes,

> Everyone in Colombia knows that the causes that have generated the disturbances, far from having been extinguished, have increase[d]. . . . [T]he country has witnessed multiple acts of violence that have horrified

[60] Corte Suprema de Justicia [C.S.J.] [Supreme Court] [Dissent], Sala. Plena, Sentencia No. 59 del 24 Mayo de 1990.

it; the taking of the Palace of Justice and the immolation of 11 magistrates of this Corporation, the death of three presidential candidates, the explosion of an airplane loaded with passengers, the massacres, the mass graves, the attacks on the newspapers, the bombs that indiscriminately charge innocent victims, are examples of a situation not only attributable to the guerrillas and drug trafficking, but to other manifestations of organized crime. . . . Multiple forms of violence threaten not only a possible insurrectionary crisis, but also a generalized anarchism of the political life of the country.[61]

The problem goes deeper than even violence to "the inefficiency of the institutions to face these situations."[62] Crises are recurrent features of democratic politics and can often be overcome by either normal or emergency measures. But here, more far-reaching and permanent measures are necessary because current institutions "are not sufficient to confront the various forms of violence that they have to face. . . . [T]hey have lost effectiveness and have become inadequate, they are unable to combat intimidation and attack methods not imagined even a few years ago, so their redesign is an obviously necessary measure so that the causes of the disturbance do not continue to worsen. . . ."[63]

Institutional redesign was necessary, but the question was how to achieve it. Recall that "legalists" call for lawful amendments to address the need for constitutional change. For the court, the repeated failure of this legal route justifies the illegal establishment of a constitutional assembly. It states, "The country has been demanding institutional change . . . and since state bodies responsible for the change have failed to enact it, the country has been calling for a Constitutional Assembly that can carry it out."[64] Here, the court is alluding to the seven previous attempts at constitutional reform, which is more than enough to show that the illegality was necessary.

---

[61] Corte Suprema de Justicia [C.S.J.] [Supreme Court], Sala. Plena, Sentencia No. 59 del 24 Mayo de 1990. While this section on the Supreme Court has been dealing with the court's second of two decisions on the president's decree powers, this quote is from the first decision. Nonetheless, the second decision so extensively cites from the first that I think the use of the quote is justified.

[62] Ibid.

[63] Corte Suprema de Justicia [C.S.J.] [Supreme Court], Sala Plena, Sentencia No. 138 del 9 de Octubre de 1990.

[64] Ibid.

Popular Vindication

The second principle of extraordinary adaptation holds that the violator must openly acknowledge the illegality and throw himself upon the mercy of the public for popular vindication. But there is little incentive for politicians to take this road and concede the illegality of their action. For politicians, the safer route is to take advantage of extraordinary adaptation's legal ambiguity, to argue that they are acting in accordance with the law. They may even argue in the alternative: they are following the law, but even if they were not their illegalities would be legitimate because of popular support. Courts lack these escape hatches because their reasoning must be internally consistent to provide clear precedent for themselves and for other courts. Hence, for extraordinary adaptation they are uniquely suited to place the burden on politicians to seek popular support for their illegality. How well did the Colombian Supreme Court perform here?

It took a step in the right direction, but it was unwilling to fully acknowledge the decree's illegality. The court rightly asserted that the constituent power "can at any time give a new constitution . . . without being subject to the one in force" and cites previous examples from Colombian history. Indeed, the constituent power "knows how to open obstructed channels of expression, or establish those that have been denied to it" for it is "a moral and political power of last resort, capable, even in the darkest hours, of fixing the historical course of the State, insisting as such with all its creative essence and vigor."[65]

The court has provided the right rule: as the highest authority, the people's approbation may, as James Madison puts it, "blot out all antecedent errors and irregularities." Yet, it refuses to apply the rule to the case at hand. It only comes close once. It highlights the decree's legal inconsistencies and acknowledges its "special characteristics" but then suggests that the conflict is illusory. The court alludes to arguments that the decree violates the doctrine on the State of Emergency, "The permanent nature of the norms issued by the National Constitutional Assembly may lead to the *mistake* that the Legislative Decree under review violates [the State of Emergency provisions] according to which the legislative decrees cease to be in force when the law is lifted."[66]

---

[65] Corte Suprema de Justicia [C.S.J.] [Supreme Court], Sala Plena, Sentencia No. 138 del 9 de Octubre de 1990.
[66] Ibid. (emphasis added).

The court notes that state of emergency decrees are meant to enact tem-porary change to restore the status quo, not create an entirely new and permanent constitution. However, the court believes the conflict is in ap-pearance only, that the assertion of a conflict is a "mistake." Why? The court explains, "The Decree has its special characteristics, since it is not reforming the Constitution, the reform will arise from the votes of December 9 when the constituent power is manifested and proceeds to form the National Constitutional Assembly."[67] According to the court, the decree itself is not enacting the constitutional change, but rather the permanent change comes from the separate source of constituent power or the people who will vote in the referendum on whether to hold an assembly. The court creates a false di-vision of labor in which the president legally issues a decree at the edge of his authority, and the people pick up the baton to authorize the creation of the new constitution. Hence, the decree is completely legal!

Extraordinary adaptation denies this neat dividing line between con-stituent and constituted powers. Yes, in normal times a government only represents the people. But in extraordinary moments, this representation has a role to play as well. What is different in extraordinary adaptation is that those institutions bend and break their rules, in accordance with three prin-ciples, to give voice to the people. As the court acknowledges, "The President is clearly and legitimately used in the present case to register the expression of the popular will."[68] It might have added that not only the president, but the court too, was a vehicle for the construction of the popular sovereign. Yet, the court failed to play its role and acknowledge the legal violations necessary to open space for popular sovereignty.

The court's role is not only to throw the illegality into stark relief but also to examine whether there is true, deep, and enduring popular support for the Constitutional Assembly. Here again, the court heads in the right direc-tion but stops short of fully realizing its goal. The court rightly substantiates the claim of constituent power through multiple empirical examples: "The popular claim for the institutional strengthening to occur is a public and well-known fact that in law does not require proof." Nonetheless, the court offers that proof: "The political parties, the media, the university bodies and the people in general" all have called for a referendum on a constitutional

---

[67] Ibid.
[68] Ibid.

assembly.[69] There are three moments relevant to the court's claim concerning the "people in general." First, the court cites the so-called seventh ballot, which was "spontaneously recorded on March 11th, 1990." Second, the court invokes the first referendum in which 89 percent of voters approved the calling of a constitutional assembly. These two moments are in the past whereas the third concerns the future. The court notes that the decree concerns the calling of a second referendum; the court must decide whether to "open[] the roads to register [the people's will]."[70] Perhaps the first time a citizen voted for the assembly, but upon further education, conversation, and reflection, she changed her mind. The second referendum then gives voters an opportunity to express their deeper judgment about a constitutional assembly.

So far, so good. Yet, the court should have pushed further. The decree has no requirement for a referendum on the assembly's draft constitution. Whatever the assembly decides on a constitution would be final. Without accountability, drafters lack a crucial incentive to design a constitution that accords with the preferences of the general public. Furthermore, it undermines the legitimacy of the constitution by feeding into a narrative that it was crafted by elites. Indeed, this narrative has plagued the 1991 Colombian Constitution and Chávez used this narrative to justify his own lawless method.[71] Final referendums on the constitutional draft were required in Colombia's sister countries of Venezuela, Ecuador, and Bolivia and are common worldwide. I do not want to overstate this issue's importance. There is not much evidence that a final referendum would have made a difference to the content of the constitution. Even more importantly, it is not popular vindication but inclusion that is the key dividing line between legitimate and illegitimate constitution-making in post-Cold War South America. Whereas Venezuela's lack of inclusion is a fatal flaw, Colombia's absence of a final referendum is by comparison a small defect. Still, unless there were prudential reasons to suggest otherwise, the court should have pushed for the decree to give citizens a vote on the completed draft of the constitution. Despite these shortcomings, the court played an important role in verifying there was popular support that justified violating the old constitution's amendment method.

---

[69] Corte Suprema de Justicia [C.S.J.] [Supreme Court], Sala. Plena, Sentencia No. 59 del 24 Mayo de 1990.

[70] Ibid.

[71] Hugo Chávez, Marta Harnecker, and Chesa Boudin, *Understanding the Venezuelan Revolution: Hugo Chávez Talks to Marta Harnecker*, 32.

An Autonomous and Inclusive Assembly

So far I have discussed why the court upholds the president's decree for a referendum on a constitutional assembly but still leaves open the question of why the court decided to strike down certain limitations of the assembly. It is this act that forms the backbone of the dominant academic narrative in which the court declares the Constituent Assembly to be sovereign. By contrast, I will argue that the courts struck down the limitations to protect the independence of the Constitutional Assembly as a fourth branch of government whose primary power is to propose a draft of the constitution.

The standard interpretation of the court giving the Constitutional Assembly sovereignty has two snags. First, while the court states that the people are a sovereign and unlimited power, it never says the same for the Constituent Assembly and never attributes to it the power to purge other institutions at will. Sovereignty in the people does not imply sovereignty in the assembly. In making this point, the Colombian Supreme Court quotes and explains at length Article 2 of the constitution that states, "The sovereignty resides essentially and exclusively in the nation, and from it emanate the public powers, that will be exercised in terms that this Constitution establishes."[72]

Second and most importantly, the court explicitly upholds several of Congress's limitations to the Constituent Assembly. It is not subtle about this move: under the headings, "Limits imposed by the primary constituent power" and "other limits imposed by the decree," it repeatedly and openly validates the principle of limiting the assembly's powers and upholds several provisions that do so. It holds these limitations to be consistent with invocations of the people.[73] The court's upholding of these limitations on the assembly is inconsistent with the prevailing narrative that the court declared the assembly to be sovereign.

The key question for the court then is not whether limitations per se are legitimate, but which ones? And what principles will distinguish between them? So far scholarship has not sufficiently parsed the court's rulings. I argue that ultimately the court's concerns are with the autonomy and inclusiveness

---

[72] Corte Suprema de Justicia [C.S.J.] [Supreme Court], Sala. Plena, Sentencia No. 59 del 24 Mayo de 1990. To be clear, the quote and the court's explanation of it concerns the relationship between the normal institutions of government and the people. It does not draw the parallel between this relationship and that of a constitutional assembly and the people.
[73] Ibid.

of the Constitutional Assembly. I discuss both of these at much greater length later in the chapter, but here I focus on the court's role. By addressing these concerns, the court is not actually upholding limits on the people but ensuring that their voice is actually heard.[74]

The first concern is the autonomy of the assembly. A new constitution poses a threat to the current officeholders as it may alter the rules in a way that threatens the foundations of the government's power. Hence, when calling the assembly into being, the government may unduly limit the assembly to protect its power.

On that basis, the court strikes down the prohibition on a constitutional provision requiring new elections after the approval of the constitution.[75] Such a provision would force the end of the Congress before members' terms have expired. The court offers very little reasoning to support the point. Nonetheless, it is not difficult to see why the court may have been concerned. The new constitution was an effort to purge Congress of corruption and to open it up to long-excluded social actors. It threatened the political power of the clientelist political class and of the two long dominant political parties. Without new elections, excluded actors would still remain outside of the government for another 2.5 years, undermining the purpose of the constitution.[76] Furthermore, it would entrust the implementation of the constitution to its enemies, to the very actors most opposed to it. This is not to say that the traditional political elites have no role to play in this new beginning, but that their representation should be proportionate to their actual support in the country.

But using the same logic, the court also upholds some limitations on the assembly stating that "not all the decree's limits unduly limit the primary constituent power, but the contrary tends to assure the independence and

---

[74] For similar examples of limitations in democratic and constitutional theory, Jean-Jacques Rousseau, *The Social Contract: And Other Later Political Writings*, ed. Victor Gourevitch (New York: Cambridge University Press, 1996), 58. N.W. Barber, "The Afterlife of Parliamentary Sovereignty," *International Journal of Constitutional Law* 9, no. 1 (Jan. 1, 2011), 145–49. For an in-depth study, see Jeffrey Goldsworthy, *The Sovereignty of Parliament: History and Philosophy*, 1st ed. (Oxford: Oxford University Press, 2001).

[75] This limitation and the other discussed are part of a broader enumeration of the sole topics that the assembly could consider, but those topics are defined so broadly as to be almost meaningless. Only these specific provisions have any real bite.

[76] I calculated this number based on the following. The Congress's original term was from July 1990 to July 1994. According to the transitional provisions of the constitution, the new Congress would take office on October 27th, 1991. The figures for the term of the 1990 Congress can be found at the Inter-Parliamentary Union website, http://www.ipu.org/parline-e/reports/arc/2068_94.htm (accessed Feb. 23, 2017).

dedication of the members of the Constitutional Assembly." After this sentence, the court upholds the limitations on who can qualify for office and particularly lauds the requirement that no member of the assembly could hold political office because that requirement assures that the assembly "could exercise its functions with autonomy, disinterest, and responsibility." It also upholds the right of the electoral section of the administrative court to enforce these provisions. Constitutional theory recommends a constitutional assembly separate from the constituted powers because the latter's members would seek to increase their own powers in the constitution. If a political officeholder could be elected to the Constituent Assembly, it would undermine the division between the Constituent Assembly and the government.[77] Hence, the court upholds this limitation to ensure the independence of the Constituent Assembly.

The court's next concern is inclusion, which is the third principle of extraordinary adaptation. On that basis, the court strikes down as undemocratic a provision that would allow an individual to get his or her name on the ballot by posting a bond of five million pesos that can only be recovered if the list of which the candidate is a part receives at least 20 percent of the vote. This is an alternative to the normal means of qualifying by collecting ten thousand signatures. Democracy gives each citizen equal political power, and thus the bond provision is undemocratic and exclusive because it unfairly privileges the rich over the poor. For the court then, the process must be open to and include all concerned parties.[78]

The court does not endorse a lawless constituent assembly. The assembly's sovereignty is neither in the text of the opinion nor is it consistent with its upholding of many limitations on the assembly. Granted, it is easier to say what the court is against than what it is for. The decision is not a model for clarity. This is not surprising, and the fault does not lie completely with the court. Under immense political pressure and with little time for deliberation, it confronted a novel situation with few theoretical resources. Extraordinary adaptation provides a lens for understanding its decisions without distorting them. The court opened up the road for the people to be mediated through the president's unorthodox use of the emergency powers. It then protected the autonomy of the assembly and the implementation of the constitution from the old guard that had the motive to undermine it.

[77] Ibid.
[78] Ibid.

A Sovereign or Autonomous Constituent Assembly?

Elections for the Constituent Assembly proceeded on December 9th, 1990. Each of the three main parties—the liberals, the conservatives, and M-19—earned about one-third of the seats.[79] In the traditional narrative, which foreshadows Venezuela eight years later, three months into their deliberations, the Colombian Constituent Assembly declared itself sovereign and used this all-powerful status to revoke Congress's mandate. Both Andrew Arato and Nicolas Figueroa condemn this power grab as indulging "an authoritarian temptation."[80] I argue that both authors misunderstand the Constituent Assembly's actions, and I contextualize and revisit them to show that they claimed a limited power as a defensive maneuver to protect the assembly's independence. While scholars can reasonably disagree about the appropriateness of some of the assembly's actions, they are part and parcel of the process of extraordinary adaptation and were emblematic of inherent tensions between constitutional assemblies and the governments that convoke them.

Conflicts between constitutional assemblies and governments are almost inevitable. When institutions are functioning smoothly, no assembly is necessary or wanted. Governments convoke the assemblies in response to crises in which the public has lost faith in the constitution. As its creator, the government structures and shapes the assembly, and it has every incentive to do so in a manner that protects its own power. Hence, the assembly's rules will often systematically privilege the status quo. Yet, the assembly's purpose is to upend the present. Often, a sizable number of assembly members will try to

---

[79] Liberals earned 34.3 percent of the seats. M-19 earned 27.1 percent of the seats. The Conservative Party splintered into three with significant differences, but their combined total of seats was 28.5 percent. Segura and Bejarano, "¡Ni Una Asamblea Más Sin Nosotros! Exclusion, Inclusion, and the Politics of Constitution-Making in the Andes, 220."

Abstention was high with only 26 percent of eligible voters participating, the lowest turnout in thirty years. This reflects the Colombian system's reliance for turnout on clientelist networks that had little invested in these elections since they offered few opportunities for patronage and their basic message was anti-corruption. David Rampf and Diana Chavarro, "The 1991 Colombian National Constituent-Assembly" (Berghof Foundation, 2014), http://www.berghof-foundation. org/fileadmin/redaktion/Publications/Other_Resources/IPS/The-1991-Colombian-National-Constituent-Assembly.pdf. Indeed, recently, a referendum on the peace deal with the FARC, the single most important decision in at least fifty years in Colombia, also had low turnout for similar reasons. "Colombia Referendum: Voters Reject Peace Deal with Farc Guerrillas | World News | The Guardian," accessed Feb. 23, 2017, https://www.theguardian.com/world/2016/oct/02/colombia-ref erendum-rejects-peace-deal-with-farc.

[80] Figueroa, "A Critique of Populist Jurisprudence: Courts, Democracy, and Constitutional Change in Colombia and Venezuela," 121, 123.

ride and mobilize the popular discontent to restructure the assembly so that it may enact the revolution. They will argue that the assembly itself should set its own rules, and that the rules restricting its discretion are relics of the old regime that cannot bind the people. The government will respond that the assembly is violating the rule of law and creating the risk of chaos or even dictatorship.[81]

Constitutional theory should be wary of immediately siding with either the assembly or the government. In recent years, legalists have sided with Congress in order to ward off the danger that the constitutional process will destroy liberal democracy by producing an authoritarian constitution.[82] Indeed, both Arato and Figueroa analyze the Colombian case as an example of an assembly usurping Congress's powers.[83] We must, however, be aware of the other possible danger, the danger to the assembly's autonomy. The assembly's mission and legitimacy require it to stand apart from and in some ways even above a constitution whose legitimacy is rapidly spiraling downward. After all, the reason the Colombian assembly was necessary in the first place was that the government's institutions lacked the will and legitimacy to reform themselves. If the assembly became a pawn of the government, or even if it was perceived as such, then it would be unable to produce a constitution that satisfies the thirst for change and commands its citizens' confidence.

Which was at greater risk in Colombia: The possibility of an authoritarian assembly or the assembly's autonomy and legitimacy? I, along with many others, have argued that one of the most important elements to prevent a constituent assembly from overstepping its bounds is the assembly's internal diversity.[84] Colombia achieved that requirement. Indeed, Arato, Figueroa, and others argue that the different levels of inclusion in the electoral rule is the key factor that accounts for the divergent results of

---

[81] Jon Elster, "Constitutional Bootstrapping in Philadelphia and Paris," *Cardozo Law Review* 14 (1994), 558–60.

[82] David Landau, "Abusive Constitutionalism," *U.C. Davis Law Review* 47 (2013), 189–260.

[83] It should be noted that Arato is also very wary of government overreach and disempowerment of the Constitutional Assembly and blames just this for the legitimacy crisis of the Hungarian Constitution. Andrew Arato, *Post Sovereign Constitutional Making: Learning and Legitimacy* (Oxford: Oxford University Press, 2016), 161–223.

[84] Joshua Braver, "Hannah Arendt in Venezuela: The Supreme Court Battles Hugo Chávez over the Creation of the 1999 Constitution," *International Journal of Constitutional Law* 14, no. 3 (July 1, 2016), 571–73; Arato, "Adventures of the Constituent Power"; Segura and Bejarano, "¡Ni Una Asamblea Más Sin Nosotros! Exclusion, Inclusion, and the Politics of Constitution-Making in the Andes"; Figueroa, "A Critique of Populist Jurisprudence: Courts, Democracy, and Constitutional Change in Colombia and Venezuela"; Landau, "Constitution-Making Gone Wrong," 962–64.

the Colombian and Venezuelan processes.[85] Furthermore, no actor in Colombia had the presidential charisma or semi-authoritarian impulses that would later rear their heads in the sister countries of Ecuador, Venezuela, or Bolivia.[86]

The greatest threat to the process was not that the assembly would dominate the government, but that the government might dominate the assembly. The Congress and the courts had thwarted reform attempts seven times in less than thirty years, and the last three failures had occurred only two years prior. The public believed that clientelist, unprincipled, cross-party pacts and drug cartel money had prevented needed constitutional change.[87] To enact it, the assembly needed to stand apart from the taint of the current system. I analyze the assembly's attempts to maintain its independence in two moments: (1) The assembly's Declaration of Autonomy, and (2) The assembly's Two Acts of Immediate Validity.

Declaring Sovereignty or Autonomy?

The Constituent Assembly and the constituted powers fought over who had the right to decide the voting threshold or how many of the assembly members' votes were necessary to approve the new constitution's provisions on the electoral rule. In its internal rules, the Colombian Constituent Assembly had unanimously decided that a majority would be the threshold for all changes. This clashed with the presidential decree which, citing the current constitution, required that changes to the constitution's rule for how Congress and the president would be elected would require the favorable vote of two-thirds of the attendees.[88] The issue boiled over when the highest

---

[85] Arato, *Adventures of the Constituent Power*, Figueroa, "A Critique of Populist Jurisprudence: Courts, Democracy, and Constitutional Change in Colombia and Venezuela," 118; Segura and Bejarano, "¡Ni Una Asamblea Más Sin Nosotros! Exclusion, Inclusion, and the Politics of Constitution-Making in the Andes."

[86] Although Colombian President César Gaviria had run as a reform candidate and heir to the assassinated martyr of reform, Luis Galán, Gaviria lacked the charisma of both his former boss and the future generation of radical leftist presidents such as Hugo Chávez. Chávez idolized Fidel Castro and sought to channel a similar form of anti-imperial and nationalist charisma, and the new presidents of Bolivia and Ecuador followed Chávez's lead. William I. Robinson, *Latin America's Radical Left: Challenges and Complexities of Political Power in the Twenty-First Century*, ed. Steve Ellner (Lanham, MD: Rowman & Littlefield Publishers, 2014).

[87] Lemaitre, "Peace at Hand: War and Peace in Colombia's 1991 Constituent Assembly."

[88] Decreto 927 del 3 de Mayo de 1990.

administrative court ruled that the decree's provision was binding, and the constituent assembly quickly rebelled against the ruling.[89]

In what way did the assembly rebel? What power precisely did it claim? On May 1st, 1991, the Constituent Assembly passed its response to the decision of the court. The next day, El Tiempo, perhaps the most widely circulated newspaper in Colombia at the time, ran the headline, "The Constituent Assembly Declares Itself Sovereign."[90] Likewise, Arato and Figueroa portray the assembly as lashing out, asserting itself to be unlimited and all-powerful so that it could choose to conduct a total assault on the constituted powers. To them, the assembly's decision was grossly disproportionate to the threat. I disagree. The assembly did not assert itself to be all-powerful but to be independent from the constituted powers so that it could accomplish the sole task of writing a new constitution. Its declaration was defensive and meant to protect itself while leaving the rest of the juridical system intact. The text of the measure, the measures that were rejected, the assembly speeches, and even the aforementioned article in El Tiempo all support this interpretation.[91]

I begin with the text of the assembly's assertion of autonomy. The measure states, "Constituent Acts of Immediate Validity: The Assembly can pass those constitutional norms that are considered necessary to guarantee the process and application of the reformatory acts of the Constitution."[92] The assembly's statement gives it a targeted power and limits the purposes to which it may be used. It was the power to pass "constitutional norms" or individual provisions of the constitution that take immediate effect rather than waiting

---

[89] Ricardo Zuluaga Gil, *De La Expectativa Al Desconcierto.* (n.p.: Editorial Acad Mica Espa, 2011), 123–25.

[90] Edulfo Peña, Carlos Obregon, and Jesus Ortiz, "Constituyente Se Declara Soberana," *El Tiempo*, May 2, 1991, accessed Feb. 24, 2017, http://www.eltiempo.com/archivo/documento/MAM-75497.

[91] A caveat is in order. In principle, there is nothing particularly wrong with supermajority voting requirements within assemblies, and, in the next chapter, I document the role they played in protecting smaller parties during the creation of the Bolivian Constitution. The Bolivian Constitutional Assembly, at least at the beginning, was roughly split between two blocks with the majority commanding nearly two-thirds of the seats and the minority possessing the remaining one-third. Without some supermajority provision, the threat was very real that the larger party would run roughshod over the smaller ones. Minorities within the assembly agitated and protested to protect and even enlarge the supermajority rule. The situation was very different in Colombia. No party had a majority. The three main parties each had about one-third of the seats. Party discipline was weak, and no group had aspirations to achieve hegemonic rule. There was no preexisting controversy within the assembly over the voting rule, which had been approved by consensus. The assembly was functioning smoothly when the court decided to crash the party. Once it ruled, the court's defenders within the assembly sided with it based on the principle of the rule of law, not on the basis of the voting threshold. The fight was over the powers of the assembly and did not concern the already well-established and enforced principle of inclusion. A supermajority rule may then be context dependent, and this book takes no strong position on it one way or another.

[92] Asamblea Nacional Constituyente, Actos Constituyentes de Vigencia Inmediata.

until the entire project is completed. Whereas normally, a provision of the draft constitution is nothing but a flimsy piece of paper until after the entire project is approved, the Colombian Constituent Assembly claimed the right to give individual provisions "immediate validity." This might seem problematic because often the people approve the constitution in a referendum, but popular ratification was never seriously on the table in the Colombian case. The last step of the process would be the assembly's approval of the constitution. The controversy over the provisions of "immediate validity" concerned only whether certain provisions should wait until the whole constitution was approved by the assembly or whether such provisions could be applied earlier.

The power to pass constitutional provisions of immediate validity follows the intertwined logic of the separation of powers and law, not that of the radical idea of a sovereign assembly. Drawing from the model of an unlimited god, sovereignty is the claim to concentrate all power is a single site. As an unmediated act of will, it stands in no need of justification or principle. By contrast, the separation of powers divides power between separate sites, and its justification is to not only prevent tyranny but to protect law's generality. Generality is protected, at least in theory, by ensuring that those who create the law and those who apply it are different bodies within the government.[93] Properly conceived, a constitutional assembly fits squarely within this model. Just as each body of government has primarily a singular power— legislative, executive, or judicial—so too the constitutional assembly is limited to passing a constitution, which it itself cannot execute.[94]

Hence, the Colombian Constituent Assembly does not claim the same sovereignty as that claimed by the 1793 Jacobin French Constituent Assembly or the 1999 Venezuelan one. The Colombian Constituent Assembly could never exercise any of the legislative, judicial, or executive powers. It could not empower a Robespierre to act as a judge to determine who should be imprisoned or executed. It could not follow the Venezuelan example and create a temporary body to pass statutes and replace old officeholders with new ones. None of these would be exercises of the power the Constituent Assembly claimed, which was only the power to create a general and durable

---

[93] Jeremy Waldron, "Separation of Powers in Thought and Practice," *Boston College Law Review* 54 (2013), 433.

[94] Fitting this logic, the Colombian process forbade members of the Congress from participating in the assembly. In other countries, most notably in nineteenth-century Revolutionary France, members of the Constituent Assembly could not run in the first elections to the new government.

constitutional provision. Jaime Castro, one of the key authors of the measure, in an extended speech on the powers of the assembly, summarized these limits well:

> It is clear that the [Constituent Assembly] cannot exercise administrative, legislative, or jurisdictional powers. It cannot, therefore, appoint the holders of determined public powers. Even less may it substitute or replace the government in managing public or other authorities in the exercise of its attributions such as deciding pending lawsuits or granting pardons.[95]

Furthermore, the assembly's newfound power was not only limited to constitutional measures but was also bound by the assembly's purpose: it could only pass new norms toward the end of creating the new constitution. The assembly could not, for example, pass an immediately applicable provision to create a new Congress because the assembly disagreed with recently passed environmental legislation. Such legislation would be deemed irrelevant to the Constituent Assembly's mission. The Constituent Assembly could only pass constituent acts of immediate validity if necessary to their sole task of creating a constitution.

The text's carefully tailored and narrow wording becomes even clearer when we compare it to the alternative and rejected measures. The first read, "At any time, the Assembly may issue immediately effective legislative acts, which will come into force once they are announced by the Presidency. The violation or disregard of the provisions of this constituent act is a cause of misconduct that leads to the loss of the position for the public servant that committed the violation, regardless of the organ of the State to which it belongs."[96] Let us focus on the second sentence. This clause's threat to strip and purge individuals from the institutions that interfered with the assembly's work is a step in the direction of Venezuelan-style sovereignty. Yet this measure is still less radical than the Venezuelan one because it is reactive and defensive. No power is exercised unless the assembly is targeted. If the assembly disagrees with the government or court's decision on other matters it has no right to interfere. Furthermore, only the public servant loses the position. The institution as a whole continues to function, and most likely that

---

[95] "Constancia" of Jaime Castro, May 6th, 1991, printed in *Gaceta Constitucional* No. 69, May 7th, 1991. Constancias are officially submitted printed versions of a speech that sometimes are more detailed than the oral version.

[96] National Constituent Assembly, Report of the Plenary Session of May 1st, 1991, 22.

servant will be replaced through the normal procedures. Still, this rejected draft would have been a significant and ominous step toward an all-powerful constituent assembly. For that reason, the proposal caused an uproar, and the assembly went into recess so that the different parties could deliberate privately. One assembly member responded that it was an attempt "to replace the constitution with a bad joke."[97] Soon after returning, the measure's sponsor withdrew it, and speakers expressed their gratitude that the most egregious proposal to aggrandize power had been filed away.[98] One member quipped that he was relieved that the proposal to strip public officers of their positions had not passed because it would have inevitably been used to kick him out of the assembly.[99]

The second rejected and radical proposal was a truncated and more moderate version of the first one. It cut the original draft's provision empowering the assembly to remove individuals from their public offices but left intact the provision giving the assembly the power to "at any time . . . issue immediately effective legislative acts."[100] "At any time" is the key clause and would have still left a far more expansive grant of power than was ultimately settled on in the final text. Whereas the final text limited the assembly to passing those constituent acts immediately "necessary to guarantee the process" of creating a new constitution, the rejected measure would permit the assembly to exercise legislative power for any purpose or any reason.[101] No justification would have been required.

Many assembly members commented on the differences, and the assembly ultimately rejected both radical proposals in favor of the more moderate final text. Jaime Castro, the lead drafter of the final measure, argued that the rejected and radical proposal "would have no limit in regards to its material, in regards to its content, any matter could be dealt with." By contrast, in his proposal, which became the final text, the assembly could only pass those "acts that are necessary to the current circumstances, to the situation in which the assembly has been confronted." Those future acts passed under the measure "ought to refer precisely to the procedural norms related to the process and approval of the distinct proposals that are being studied by

---

97 Ibid., 41.
98 Ibid., 34.
99 Ibid., 15, 34.
100 Ibid., 28–30.
101 The second draft also dropped the language of "constitutional norms" for that of "legislative acts," though that may be interpreted in a variety of ways. I do not discuss it as it was not an issue in the debates and it is unclear what this change meant if anything to the assembly.

the assembly." Lastly, Castro justifies the assembly's newly claimed power as a regrettable necessity because "what is at stake are the attributions, the *autonomy* of the Constituent Assembly."[102]

Subsequent speakers agreed that what was at stake was the assembly's autonomy and independence. They specifically distinguished the idea of autonomy from the rival one of an all-powerful assembly. Horacio Serpa's speech is noteworthy, as he was one of the three presidents of the assembly and the leader of the Liberal Party, one of the two main parties that wrote the final text:

> I have never believed in the omnipotence of the National Constituent Assembly . . . It is difficult to accept, almost impossible, that such powers exist . . . I have made statements about our limits, such as the July 4th deadline, on our powers which in my opinion cannot dismantle the national juridical order . . . The liberal party shares the criteria of the independence of the Constituent Assembly, it defends it.[103]

Among the advocates of the final text, Serpa's and Castro's are the most insightful, clear, and influential speeches.

So why did the newspaper *El Tiempo* mistakenly declare in a headline that the assembly was sovereign? Partly the confusion is likely related to a lack of an alternative vocabulary from a dominant radical intellectual frame and experience through which Colombia had experienced all past constitutional assemblies. Part of the confusion also lies in many members' uses of the word, "sovereignty," as it was often used in inconsistent or ambiguous ways.[104]

Rather than use sovereignty to refer to an all-powerful entity, almost all the members used the term to refer to the assembly's autonomy and independence. In turn, they understood that independence to entail the assembly's right to enact its own rules and to create a completely new constitution with a different spirit than the old one. This assertion of the right to start writing a constitution from scratch was an important issue because the original

---

[102] Ibid. (emphasis added).

[103] Ibid., 69.

[104] The word "sovereignty" is ambiguous in other contexts as well. Sometimes, it means that an individual, group, or institution is all-powerful. This describes the 1793 Jacobin and 1999 Venezuelan Constituent Assembly. It is the nightmare scenario to which this book is devoted to avoiding. In other contexts, the term "popular sovereignty" refers to the people's power to create a constitution. The people are sovereign in the sense that they have the final word over the foundational structure and framework to which all government bodies owe their power. In this second sense of sovereignty, no institution or body is all-powerful.

presidential decree convening the assembly had limited the range of topics the assembly could consider, a limit that the court had struck down.

August Ramirez's speech is particularly interesting because it acknowledges this dual use of the term sovereignty. After attacking the more radical proposal to strip power from those officials who interfered with the assembly's work, Ramirez clarified his limited definition of sovereignty:

> I feel that we have the juridical, institutional and sovereign capacity to reform the Constitution of 1986. Of this, I have no doubt and I have no doubt that we have no boundaries in that regard. In this fact lies our sovereignty, but this is distinct from the sovereignty of being all powerful, to exit from the rule of law, to have the inadmissible claim that the Colombian Constitution, the Colombian laws, the Colombian authorities, stop at the door of this compound . . . that we are in some extraterritorial realm or exceptional nirvana in which we do not apply any legal rule.[105]

Ramirez distinguishes between two types of sovereignty, one that is synonymous with the right to draw up a new constitution and the other of being "all powerful." Ramirez opts for the former, more restrictive definition.[106]

This limited understanding of sovereignty is consistent with the newspaper *El Tiempo*'s understanding of the events as well. As I stated at the beginning of this section, the headline was "The Constituent Assembly Declares Itself Sovereign." However, the body of the article clarifies what that sovereignty consists of:

> In an energetic reaction to the Council of State ruling that limited the reform process, the National Constituent Assembly decided last night to grant the power to issue immediately applicable constitutional rules granting full sovereignty. That is to say, *autonomy* was given through the regulation to issue rules of immediate compliance that are considered necessary to prevent the failures of the constitutional reforms in the event that the courts declare them to be unconstitutional . . . The step taken, according to the agreement of the majority of the delegates, seeks to defend the sovereignty of the acts of before all juridical litigation.[107]

---

[105] National Constituent Assembly, Report of the Plenary Session of May 1st, 1991, 36–37.
[106] Ibid.
[107] Peña, Obregon, and Ortiz, "Constituyente Se Declara Soberana" (emphasis added).

In this quote, after again stating that the assembly arrogated sovereignty, the article immediately qualifies and defines the term as autonomy. That autonomy is in turn defined as an act of self-defense directed against court decisions that targeted the assembly. The goal is not to aggrandize power but to defend the assembly's power to draft a new constitution that breaks from the old one. The Constituent Assembly never goes on the offense against the government; rather, as one member of the Constituent Assembly told *El Tiempo*, the power to pass immediately effective constitutional provisions was a defensive "survival formula."[108]

Two Acts of Immediate Validity

A week after declaring its power to pass measures of immediate constitutional validity, the Constituent Assembly exercised this power for the first time. The assembly was still dwelling on how to best handle the administrative court's incursion into the assembly's rules and was worried about future rulings. It passed an act in which the first part declared that "the rules of the National Constituent Assembly have constitutional character."[109] Since the rules had the status of a constitutional provision, the rules were outside the jurisdiction of the administrative court, whose main purview is regulation. This would ward off future attacks from the court in this specific area.

Yet the assembly went even further. It also asserted, "the Acts that are sanctioned and promulgated by the National Constituent Assembly are not subject to any jurisdictional control."[110] No court could review any decision of the assembly under this clause. Here, the assembly crossed the line. Whereas the first part of the act's constitutional enshrining of its own rules was a defensive maneuver about a specific area provoked by the administrative court, this second and additional power could have set the stage for an offensive one. It is a step away from the logic of protecting the assembly's autonomy to asserting its sovereignty. If the Constituent Assembly stepped outside its boundaries by exercising other branches' powers, the court had every right to declare such acts as invalid and outside the rights of the constituent power.

---

[108] Ibid.
[109] First Legislative Act of Immediate Validity, National Constituent Assembly, Report of the Plenary Session of May 1st, 1991, 54.
[110] Ibid.

However, the gravity of the offense should not be exaggerated. It is not a statement that the assembly has no limits, only that it believes the courts are not the right body to enforce them.[111] This acknowledgment of the assembly's limits was even made by those who pushed for the most radical interpretations of the First Act. In the debates over the act, the demobilized guerillas' party of M-19 were the most strident in their assertions of the assembly's power, particularly member Alvaro Echevery, who in his thunderous speech on the floor claimed that the assembly is "plenary and absolutely sovereign." In the debate, the Liberal Party, which was the largest in the assembly, repeatedly denied that the assembly was all-powerful. In the midst of Echeverry's speech, the leader of the Liberal Party and co-president of the assembly, Horacio Serpa, intervened to ask whether Echeverry really embraced the sinister implications of his position. In response, Echeverry backed down:

I would say to you that undoubtedly we cannot designate, that is to say, it would be improbable, no impossible, that we could choose who holds various offices . . . We do not have the capacity to issue judicial opinions, no. We have the capacity to institute, to reform the political institutions and establish all the measures that make possible the functioning of the institutions that we create.[112]

When pushed, Echeverry refused to truly own up to the meaning of his words and abandoned his push for the assembly to claim plenary power. Although in this moment there was some bluster about sovereignty in the assembly, neither the text of the First Act nor the vast majority of the delegates truly welcomed the concept.

Of the two acts, the Second Act of Immediate Validity, often characterized as the revocation of the Congress, is the most controversial. On June 15th, 1991, the Constituent Assembly closed down the current Congress and

---

[111] This has some similarity to the idea in U.S. constitutional law scholarship that often certain constitutional norms are judicially "under-enforced" because courts are not suited to review them. For example, the Supreme Court seems to have no jurisdiction over the specifics of impeachment proceedings or over Congress's power to expel a member by two-thirds. Lawrence Gene Sager, "Fair Measure: The Legal Status of Underenforced Constitutional Norms," *Harvard Law Review* 91 (1978), 1212–64. For years, the dominant position in academia was that federalism was primarily protected through political means, such as the state's equal representation in the Senate, rather than through court decisions. See Jesse H. Choper, *Judicial Review and the National Political Process* (Chicago: University of Chicago Press, 1983). So too we might argue just as federalism would not be judicially enforce, the doctrine over the assembly might not be enforced.

[112] National Constituent Assembly, Report of the Plenary Session of May 3rd, 34.

called for new congressional elections that would take place shortly after the ratification of the new constitution. The Constituent Assembly also elected a thirty-six-member Little Congress or *El Congresito* that would meet for the five and a half months between the declaration and the seating of the new Congress. In the previous chapter, I condemned the Venezuelan Constituent Assembly for usurping the constituted powers, including the creation of its own *El Congresito*. Is there any difference between these two countries' Congresitos? Andrew Arato and Nicholas Figueroa argue that the differences are that ultimately both the Colombian and Venezuelan *Congresitos* embody the same Schmittian logic and that the Colombian version "made evident the authoritarian potential of an all-powerful constituent assembly."[113] I take a different tack and argue that the two actions are not equivalent. While the Venezuelan *Congresito* seized all the powers of the government for an indefinite period, the Colombian one wielded a limited and enumerated sets of transitory powers necessary to set up a new government for a specific duration.

It is not unusual for new elections to occur after the creation of the new constitution. Recall that the Colombian Supreme Court specifically struck down an effort to prevent the Constituent Assembly from setting a date for new elections. Part of the justification for new elections harken back to the inherent conflict between a constitutional assembly's desire to institute a new order and the old government's desire to protect its power. Likewise in Colombia, the Constituent Assembly's goal in creating a new constitution was to reduce corruption and clientelism in government, especially in Congress. But whether the constitution realized those goals would depend not only on its contents but its implementation. Without new elections, the old government, viewed by many as the constitution's enemy, would be its executor. The fear was the government would undermine it at every turn. Nor would this Congress be representative. The country was in the middle of a political realignment that threatened the dominance of the Liberal and Conservative Parties and aimed to reincorporate former guerilla groups like M-19 into the political system. Indeed, M-19 had won the most votes in the 1991 elections to the Constitutional Assembly, even more than the liberals

---

[113] The quote is from Figuera, "A Critique of Populist Jurisprudence: Courts, Democracy, and Constitutional Change in Colombia and Venezuela," 122. See also Arato, *Adventures of the Constituent Power*, 312 (noting that Colombia had a sovereign constituent assembly because "the Constituent Assembly did dissolve the elected legislature, and for a transitional period . . . put a body chosen from itself, the little Congress (Congresillo) in its own place." Andrew Arato does note that the Venezuelan Congresito wielded more power than its Colombian counterpart. Ibid., 316, 320–21, 324.

who had dominated elections for more than three decades.[114] A splinter group from the Conservative Party, MSN, won more votes than the traditional party. Yet, M-19 had no seats in the Congress and MSN had few.[115] For that reason, M-19 repeatedly pushed for new elections.[116] Such elections would ensure that new forces as well as the old would be involved in the realization of the new constitution.

Nonetheless, there was no Congress in place for the five and a half months from June 15th, 1991, until the seating of the new Congress on December 1st, 1991. Might Colombia share with its sister country of Venezuela the usurpation of legislative powers by "El Congresito?" There are four key differences to note. First, the duration of effective congressional suspension was more than twice as long in Venezuela than in Colombia.[117] Sometimes, unusual measures are necessary to implement a new constitution, but their duration should be as limited as possible so as to quickly restore the normal functioning of government. Colombia more faithfully complied with this guideline than did Venezuela. Second, in Venezuela, the purge included every conceivable power, down to labor unions and municipalities, while in Colombia it focused solely on the Congress. The Supreme Court, for example, continued to meet.[118] Third, the Venezuelan Congresito was an extension of the Constituent Assembly's sovereignty. The assembly authorized the body and wielded a veto power over its actions. The legitimacy of the Colombian Congresito comes not from the assembly but from the constitution itself, which outlined how it functioned.[119]

The narrow range of the Colombian Congresito's powers is the last mark that distinguishes it from its Venezuelan counterpart. The Venezuelan Little Congress had full legislative power.[120] By contrast, per the transitory

[114] However, the liberals gained more seats through electoral strategy, but it came at a cost to their coherence. On the strategy, see Gil, *De La Expectativa Al Desconcierto.* For an analysis of the voting records of the parties, Cepeda Espinosa et al., *La constituyente por dentro.*

[115] "Colombia: Elecciones Legislativas de 1990 (Senado)," accessed Mar. 10, 2017, http://pdba.geo rgetown.edu/Elecdata/Col/Elesenado90.html.

[116] Gil, *De La Expectativa Al Desconcierto,* 139–51. Ultimately, these efforts were successful, though in return M-19 unfortunately agreed to disqualify all current members of the Constitutional Assembly from being candidates in the upcoming elections. This was a concession to the liberals and the conservatives. Many of the most able and popular members of the new parties as well as the reform-minded members of the traditional parties were barred from running, giving the traditional parties an unfair advantage. Ibid.

[117] Colombian Constitution, Transitory Articles 1, 3, 4. In Venezuela, the suspension of Congress lasted about eleven and a half months while in Colombia it was about five and a half months.

[118] Figueroa, "A Critique of Populist Jurisprudence: Courts, Democracy, and Constitutional Change in Colombia and Venezuela," 122–23.

[119] Colombian Constitution, Transitory Articles 1, 3, 4.

[120] The Constituent Assembly, however, could veto legislation by the Congresito.

provisions of the Colombian Constitution, the Colombian Congresito had the limited role of collaborating in the initial setup of a few offices created under the new constitution. Under Transitory Article 5 of the constitution, the president could issue regulations to organize the Office of the Attorney General, the Superior Council of the Judicature, and the Constitutional Court. It could also issue regulations to relieve the judicial agencies and to temporarily set the general national budget to go into effect in 1992. The Congresito wielded a veto power over all these measures and could prepare bills for the next Congress. Simply put, the Congresito had no power to legislate or create any kind of binding measure. While the Venezuelan assembly declared itself to have total and plenary power, the Colombian revocation of Congress was a constitutionally authorized and carefully limited move to protect the constitution's implementation.

INCLUSION AND REVOLUTION

The Colombian process partially fulfilled the third principle of inclusion. Importantly, the process was more inclusive than its Venezuelan counterpart, preventing the establishment of a semi-authoritarian constitution. However, it was still not fully inclusive because the rural guerillas did not participate. Today, the Colombian public holds the Revolutionary Armed Forces of Colombia (FARC), the largest rural guerilla group, and other left guerillas in contempt as thugs, drug dealers, and murderers. Their communist ideology is nothing but a thinly veiled attempt to disguise their own pursuit of wealth and power. In the 1980s, the common understanding was different. Whether it was delivered by taxi drivers, teenagers, or intellectuals, the most common line was that guerillas represented rural peasant interests and had armed themselves in response to a corrupt political and social system that was of no aid to rural communities. Peace would require addressing their grievances.[121]

In the 1980s, the three largest guerilla groups—the M-19, the FARC, and the EPL—had all called for constituent assemblies, and its key intellectuals believed the assembly to be capable of addressing the root causes of their insurgency. Its promise incentivized the M-19 to demobilize in order to

[121] Lemaitre Ripoll, *El derecho como conjuro*," 11. I draw heavily from Julieta Lemaitre's work for this section on inclusion.

participate, and indeed it became one of the most powerful parties in the assembly. As the assembly was conducting business, three other insurgency groups also agreed to disarmament and were given four honorary, non-voting seats in the assembly. In the assembly, they became allies and caucused with the M-19. This was an incredible achievement for peace. The symbolism cannot be overstated. Despite having been kidnapped by M-19, conservative Alvarez Gomez Hurtado shared the assembly's presidency with M-19 member Antonio Navarro Wolff.[122]

M-19 was an urban-based group with heavy recruiting from the country's best public universities. Its goals were primarily political, not economic. M-19 saw its mission as opening up the closed political system dominated by the Conservative and Liberal parties. Consistent with this ideological commitment, they, like the liberals in the Constituent Assembly, sought a constitutional revolution to create an open and participatory democracy that robustly protected human rights.[123] As liberal president Horacio Serpa commented in his speech on the floor, "Our homeland is afflicted with all types of violence, but [violence] carried out under political pretexts is the one that warrants the special attention of this Assembly."[124] The M-19's demands were met. The 1991 constitution provided an extensive list of rights and the means to enforce them through a new constitutional court and through the innovation of the *tutela*, a simplified procedure that made it easy for the average citizen to file constitutional claims against the government. It reined in presidential discretion under the state of emergency and provided new venues for citizen participation. These measures were perhaps less radical than what the M-19 had originally fought for, but they nonetheless satisfied them. The M-19's ranks had been greatly reduced, if not decimated, in combat and the army had killed the M-19's ideological leader. In need of new blood and in a bid to become more mainstream, the party recruited from all walks of life for its list of candidates in the assembly. In so doing, they reduced the intensity and radicalness of their understanding of what a true political revolution would look like. As David Ramp writes, paraphrasing a member of the M-19, "All participating former guerilla groups primarily sought political reforms and neglected reforms of the economic system."[125]

---

[122] Lemaitre, "Peace"; Rampf and Chavarro, "The 1991 Colombian National Constituent-Assembly."

[123] Lemaitre, "Peace," 13.

[124] Lemaitre, "Peace," 11.

[125] David Rampf & Diana Chavarro, "Entering the Political Stage: An Analysis of Former Guerillas' Experiences in Colombian Politics" (Berghof Foundation, 2014), 13.

The rural guerillas who hoped for not just a political but also an economic revolution did not participate in the assembly. While the M-19's goals were always primarily political, the FARC and the ELN were peasant-based, Marxist movements that sought redistribution, especially of land. The vestiges of the colonial era had long left land highly concentrated with a few owning large estates and the peasants struggling to make ends meet.[126] Since the peasants lacked effective representation in the assembly, their economic concerns were left largely unaddressed.[127]

There were many attempts to incorporate the FARC and the ELN into the assembly, but none were successful. Arguments abound about why these efforts failed and who is at fault. While the M-19 had been crippled by several military defeats, the FARC and ELN had far less incentive to demobilize because they had continued to prosper and grow larger. Additionally, the FARC's intellectual leader and greatest supporter of the Constituent Assembly, Jacobo Arenas, died in 1990 of natural causes. The government argued that the FARC rejected many reasonable offers to join the assembly and that the FARC only negotiated to buy time to regroup for further battles. The FARC points to the government decision to bomb the hideout of the FARC secretariat on the very day of the elections for the Constituent Assembly. Indeed, apparently the FARC leaders had been listening to the incoming results when the attack commenced. In response, the FARC escalated their attacks and the frequency and lethalness of combat significantly increased. As Julia Lemaitre remarks, "While the Constitution was presented as the national peace pact, the war raced along."[128]

No doubt, the constitution was a political revolution. It successfully rid the constitution and political system of the old National Front's limits on political competition. Its openness delegitimized armed struggle. How could guerillas thunder on about exclusion from the political system when M-19 and three other former guerilla groups participated alongside the very politicians they had violently targeted for years?[129] Although they never managed to achieve their goal of becoming a new political party, several members of M-19 went on to achieve successful political careers. Antonio Navarro Wolff, the leader of M-19 in the assembly, ran for the presidency; served as the minister of

---

[126] León Zamosc, *The Agrarian Question and the Peasant Movement in Colombia: Struggles of the National Peasant Association, 1967–1981* (New York: Cambridge University Press, 2006), 9.

[127] Lemaitre, "Peace," 19.

[128] Ibid.

[129] Bejarano, *Precarious Democracies*.

health; was governor of Nariño, and is currently a senator. He is widely respected throughout Colombia. In the years after the assembly, sympathy for the FARC dropped precipitously. The public no longer understood the FARC as a political group but rather as just another drug trafficking organization dressed up in communist paraphernalia. In the subsequent years, the country also managed to reduce the levels of violence to manageable levels. In 1993, police officers killed Pablo Escobar and by 1997 the drug cartels had been dismantled.[130] The new constitution restored a great deal of stability and legitimacy to the political system.

But the benefits of the new system were unevenly distributed. While cities enjoyed the freedoms of the new constitution, the peasants in the periphery remained mired in poverty and civil war. The Constitutional Court protected the freedom of speech and association, but in rural zones thousands of journalists and unionists were gunned down by right-wing paramilitary organizations.[131] Peasant concerns rarely made it onto the national political agenda. In August of 2016, President Manuel Santos managed to negotiate a peace agreement with the FARC. Yet the agreement contained little to address the plight of peasants, especially not on issues of land redistribution, and it lost in a national referendum.[132] Rural voters, both the constituency of the FARC and the greatest victims of the civil war, overwhelmingly voted for the agreement, but it lost due to the opposition of urban voters. Once again, the center's concerns triumphed over the periphery's.[133] Eventually, a new deal was reached, partially through sacrificing measures intended to help the peasants, and approved through Congress.[134] The agreement is fragile but so far endures.

The achievements of extraordinary adaptation and the constitution-making process in Colombia are considerable but should not be romanticized. The process included new sectors in society but left others out in the cold. The parties negotiated and compromised in good faith, but the path to agreement was easier to pave because of the absence of more radical parties with redistributive concerns. The danger is that the relative ease of the

---

[130] Lemaitre Ripoll, "Peace," 31.

[131] Lemaitre Ripoll.

[132] For an analysis of the final accord, see "Los Cambios En El Acuerdo Final, Uno a Uno," *La Silla Vacía*, accessed Mar. 11, 2017, http://lasillavacia.com/hagame-el-cruce/los-cambios-en-el-acuerdo-final-uno-uno-58739.

[133] Kirk Semple, "With Colombia's Peace Deal in Doubt, a Battered Town Fears a Return to War," *The New York Times*, Oct. 10, 2016, https://www.nytimes.com/2016/10/11/world/americas/colombia-peace-deal.html.

[134] "Los Cambios En El Acuerdo Final, Uno a Uno."

process will lull us into complacency about the lurking explosive dangers and conflict that accompany extraordinary adaptation.

* * *

For legalists, the Colombian process was a messy compromise between two models of constitution-making. It was a matter of luck that the enlightened round-table model ultimately beat back the "corrosive effects" of the competing radical theory of lawless constituent assemblies.[135] Rather than an "assimilation" or "eclectic mix,"[136] I have argued that the Colombian process exemplifies a sophisticated set of higher-level principles called "extraordinary adaptation." This theory fits both the practice as well as the understanding of relevant participants who believed that, in the words of key Constituent Assembly member Jaime Castro, "constitutional theory does not recognize claims of omnipotence."[137] Onlookers have misinterpreted Colombia because the idea of extraordinary adaptation has not previously been fully explored or elaborated. Key parts of speeches and court opinions that have been overlooked now come into focus as perceptive attempts to articulate the method. With the theory, we can now understand the Colombian experience, not only in its best but also in its most accurate light.

Seven times in a span of nine years, to protect their own power, Congress or the Supreme Court thwarted presidents' plans to enact badly needed constitutional reform. There was little hope of disrupting the pattern. The extraordinary mobilization of citizens to deposit an extralegal seventh ballot changed the equation. The president and the Supreme Court extraordinarily adapted the doctrine of the legalized state of emergency to give life to the protesters' demands. In so doing, the president was able to include multiple parties—traditional ones, new splinter parties, and guerilla groups— to give birth to the Constituent Assembly. Both the Supreme Court and the Constituent Assembly fought to preserve the process's integrity, particularly the independence of the assembly and the implementation of the constitution. The inclusion of multiple parties served the foundation for the creation of a liberal and democratic constitution. However, multiple parties are not all parties. The peasants were left by the wayside and their absence

---

[135] Arato, *Adventures of the Constituent Power*, 315.

[136] Ibid., 315; Figueroa, "A Critique of Populist Jurisprudence: Courts, Democracy, and Constitutional Change in Colombia and Venezuela," 118.

[137] "Constancia" of Jaime Castro, May 6th, 1991, printed in *Gaceta Constittucional* No. 69, May 7, 1991.

should significantly temper praise for the process as one of openness and compromise.

The closest analog to the Colombian case is the United States. Both are examples of partially inclusive extraordinary adaptation. Both irregularly drew upon the powers of preexisting democratic institutions, specifically the states in the United States and the presidency and Supreme Court in Colombia, to achieve a liberal democratic constitution. Both limited participation in the process and left already marginalized groups outside of its benefits. I have already spoken about the rural peasants in Colombia whose exclusion facilitated a smoother route to a new constitution. In the United States, women, Native Americans, and African Americans were the relevant excluded groups. Indeed, the constitution fortified and perpetuated the peculiar institution of slavery.[138] In Colombia and the United States, the participants to the assembly agreed on fundamental values, easing the way to establishing their constitutions. These were lover's quarrels. The constitutional revolutions restored the state's legitimacy but achieved little for the most vulnerable. Only in Bolivia, which I discuss in the next chapter, do we see how extraordinary adaptation unfolds when initiated by and achieved in the name of the subordinated. Only there do we see the deep difficulties of compromise when all participants strain and bend the very law that is supposed to shape and constrain the fight between radically different parties.

---

[138] Akhil Reed Amar, *America's Constitution: A Biography* (New York: Random House Trade Paperbacks, 2006), 20–21, 89–120.

5

The Enemies' Truce

Inclusive Extraordinary Adaptation in Bolivia

Both radical proponents and legalist critics of constituent power were bitterly disappointed by the Bolivian constitution-making process. Radicals condemned the excess of law that restrained the people from enacting their true revolution.[1] Raul Prada, one of Bolivia's most important radical intellectuals and key player in the early stages of the assembly, lamented that "[law] deformed the constituent power . . . trapping the constituent assembly in the spider webs of the constituted power diminishing it to nothing . . . into the scaffolding for the constituted power."[2] The process "supplanted the constituent spirit with the spirit of Congressmen." It reduced a radical constitution to a "conservative, restrictive, and destructive" one.[3] Legalists had the exact opposite assessment: they bemoaned the lack of law that unleashed the people to wreak havoc. David Landau called the Bolivian process an example of "constitutional breakdown" and lops Bolivia in the same category as Venezuela, the category of "Constitution-making Gone Wrong."[4] Jorge Lazarte, a member of the assembly and key figure in the reform of the old constitution asserted that "[the] dysfunctionalities, inconsistencies, and instability" of the Bolivian Constitution can be traced back to the constitution-making process's repeated violations of the law. He meticulously documents, categorizes, and lists the sixteen most egregious ones.[5]

---

[1] See Ruben Martínez Dalmau, "El inventor de los 2/3 y la cuadratura del círculo," *Rebellion* (2008); Luis Tapia "Consideraciones Sobre el Estado Plurinacional," in *Descolonización en Bolivia, Cuatro Ejes para Comprender el Cambio*, ed. Vice Presidencia del Estado (La Paz: Bolivia, Vice Presidencia del Estado 2010), 135–69; Luis Tapia, "Constitution and Constitutional Reform in Bolivia," in John Crabtree and Laurence Whitehead, *Unresolved Tensions: Bolivia Past and Present* (Pittsburg, PA: University of Pittsburgh Press, 2008), 160–71. See also Jeffery R. Webber, *From Rebellion to Reform in Bolivia: Class Struggle, Indigenous Liberation, and the Politics of Evo Morales* (Chicago: Haymarket Books, 2011), 84–98.

[2] Raul Prada, *Horizonte Político de La Asamblea Constituyente* (Santa Cruz: Repac, 2006), 73

[3] Raul Prada, *Paradojas de la Rebelión* (La Paz: Comuna, 2015), 7

[4] David Landau, "Constitution-Making Gone Wrong," *Alabama Law Review* 64 (2012), 949–59.

[5] Jorge Lazarte, *Reforma del "Experimento" Constitucional en Bolivia: Claves de un Nuevo Modelo Estatal y Societal de Derecho* (2016), 16.

We, the Mediated People. Joshua Braver, Oxford University Press. © Joshua Braver 2023.
DOI: 10.1093/oso/9780197650639.003.0006

I argue that Bolivia is the most inclusive example of extraordinary adaptation, its test by fire. Its sister cases are the constitution-making processes that birthed the 1789 U.S. and the 1991 Colombian Constitutions. In all three, the extraordinary adaptation of old institutions prevented any one party from dominating the process. The presence of multiple parties, however, does not necessarily entail the presence of all of them. In the United States and Colombia, inclusion was partial, which helped the processes run smoothly. For the white U.S. men of the North and the South, the path to agreement was relatively clear because British Loyalists had immigrated to Canada, women were second-class citizens, and African Americans were slaves. Likewise in Colombia, negotiations between the reformist, urban classes were undisturbed by the demands for land redistribution by the rural peasants represented by guerilla groups of the FARC and the ELN. In Bolivia the path to a new constitution was considerably more difficult because it was highly inclusive. All the major groups—the traditional centrist and mestizo elite class of La Paz, the radical indigenous-peasant coalition of the highlands and lowlands, and the neoliberal leaders of the hydrocarbon rich Media Luna region—were represented in the assembly and ready to fight.

Bolivia's inclusive path of extraordinary adaptation is particularly striking given that its initial path to a new constitution was so similar to the Venezuelan one. In both countries, Congress had tried to enact a consensus about the need for constitutional change legally, and in both those efforts repeatedly failed. In both Venezuela and Bolivia, the old constitutions lacked a provision to call for a constitutional assembly. Lacking a legal path, the governments decided to violate the old amendment rule to create a new constitution. But at this point, their paths diverged. Although initially intent on mimicking Venezuela, Evo Morales and the Bolivian government decided on a different path. The type of illegality and its relationship to inclusion was ultimately very different in these two countries.

Citing the need for a constituent assembly and that Congress had ignored his repeated calls to action, Hugo Chávez plunged the country into the legal abyss in order to effectively exclude the opposition from participating in the writing of the constitution. Even if Chávez's lament on congressional action was an insincere ploy, it contained an important grain of truth. In the months before the election, the future de facto opposition leader of the Constituent Assembly, Allan Brewer-Carías, repeatedly petitioned Congress to amend the constitution to set the ground rules for a constituent assembly.[6] But after

[6] *Gaceta del Congreso*, Período 1998–1999, No. 27 Sesión Conjunta, 30 de julio de 1998, 24–31; *Gaceta del Congreso*, Período 1998–1999, No. 34 Sesión Conjunta, 27 de agosto de 1998, 18–22; Allan

a perfunctory debate, Congress took no action. What if Congress had heeded Carías's plea? What if this institution of the old constitution had participated alongside Chávez in the illegal but not lawless construction of the people?

Venezuela may then have followed the same path as Bolivia. Whereas Chávez successfully denounced the old Venezuelan Constitution as "moribund,"[7] in Bolivia the Congress extraordinarily adapted the old constitution by illegally amending it to create an inclusive framework for the Constitutional Assembly. I call this stage the initial structuring of the assembly. In the next and second stage of "subsequent adjustments," in response to the opposition's obstructionist and narrow reading of the framework for the Constituent Assembly, the Movement to Socialism (MAS) Party interpreted, bent, or broke individual parts of the framework to rescue the process and preserve its general legality. This process vindicated the principles of extraordinary adaptation, that of legal exhaustion, popular vindication, and inclusion.

No one would call the process pretty. It was chaotic, agonizing, and even bloody. But ultimately it was a success. The majority and radical MAS Parties achieved a revolutionary constitution and prevented the minority and the more conservative Media Luna region from declaring independence. To the very end, the opposition waged a fierce fight against ratification, but they ultimately agreed to accept the results. Through the process of creating the constitution, the Media Luna became a loyal opposition. The process was turbulent, but such messiness might be the necessary price of change and of success in popular and inclusive constitution-making.

But succeed in what way? The process gave birth to a new constitution and prevented civil war, but at what cost to the indigenous and peasant classes' dream of a true economic revolution? I address the degree of change extraordinary adaptation can deliver by focusing on the Bolivian Constitution's compromise on land redistribution. At stake is the question of whether extraordinary adaptation is too conservative to redress economic injustices. I ultimately concede that the method's inclusion may place limits on the scale

R. Brewer-Carias, *Asamblea Constituyente y Proces Constituyente 1999. Coleccion Tratado de Derecho Constitucional, Tomo VI* (Caracas: Fundacion Editorial Juridica Venezolana, 2014), 57–66.

[7] Hugo Chávez Frîas, "Juramento en el acto de toma de posesiòn de la Presidencia 1999," in *Hugo Chávez: La construcción del socialismo del siglo XXI: discursos del comandante supremo ante la Asamblea Nacional 1999–2012*, ed. Carlos Escarrà Malave (2013), 144.

of change; many revolutionaries will feel betrayed. Nonetheless, it is still capable of delivering significant cultural, political, and economic change. I note that the alternative of radical constitution-making may also be unable to deliver on its promise of total change and that it risks centralization and violence.

The chapter proceeds in five parts. Part I focuses on legal exhaustion, or the failure of the Bolivian constitutional system to reform itself legally. Next, Part II elaborates the political party MAS's radical vision of the people and its relationship to its push for a first-past-the-post election rule for the Constitutional Assembly. Parts III and IV detail the two-stage process of extraordinary adaptation that created the Bolivian Constitution and how it fulfilled the principles of popular vindication and inclusion. Lastly, Part V discusses the constitution's compromise on land distribution to show the limits on the type of change that inclusive constitution-making can deliver.

Before beginning the narrative, a little background will be helpful. Bolivia is the smallest and poorest country in South America but holds out an outsized place in the region's political and revolutionary imagination, probably because it has the largest indigenous population in the continent. However, a white and mestizo elite has long dominated the country. Society discouraged and disparaged indigenous self-identification. That only began to change in the year 2000. In response to waves of neoliberal privatization, grass-roots Bolivian social and political movements organized themselves on the basis of a pan-Bolivian indigenous identity. In 2005, Bolivia elected its first indigenous president, Evo Morales of the MAS Party. He pledged to realize the social movement's desire for a new constitution. He stood opposed by four of the nine states of the country located in the Northeast. That region is often referred to as the Media Luna and was represented by the new political party Podemos. Its citizens are whiter, richer, and friendlier to capitalist policies.[8] This chapter will analyze the almost twelve-year process of creating the new constitution from its earliest efforts at amendment in 1997 until the ratification of the Bolivian Constitution on January 25th, 2009.

---

[8] For an excellent review of this history, see Linda Farthing and Benjamin H. Kohl, *Evo's Bolivia: Continuity and CHANGE* (Austin: University of Texas Press, 2014).

LEGAL EXHAUSTION

I will laud the illegal process to amend the old Bolivian Constitution to permit the calling of a constitutional assembly. But was this illegality necessary? The first principle of extraordinary adaptation, legal exhaustion, requires that there be a consensus about the need for a constitutional change and that conventional and legal routes be unable to achieve it. This principle acknowledges legalists' worry that violating law in the creation of a new constitution is an inherently risky endeavor. Once the people's will has been called upon to replace one rule, it becomes easy to go on a path that abandons all law so that the ostensibly unmediated will of the people may rule directly.[9]

Legalists have argued that to avoid these risks, the process of making a constitution should adhere to the formal requirements of the amendment process. For Andrew Arato, the constitution should be amended to provide procedures for the calling of a constitutional assembly.[10] William Partlett goes even further, arguing that assemblies should be dispensed with altogether so that legislatures may create the new constitution through using the prescribed amendment method.[11] Both of these prescriptions failed in Bolivia. Neither way of preserving legality was viable because of the deep legitimacy deficit of the Bolivian Congress.

The illegal 2004 Amendments were not Congress's first try. In 1982, the country transitioned from a military dictatorship to democracy, but retained the old 1967 constitution. Much of it had been reformed in 1995. Yet, even after that, "practically all the political forces of the country had expressed their agreement that a new constitutional reform was necessary to complete the work begun in 1995."[12] There were many problems of governance to solve, but there was a basic agreement that the system as a whole had to be democratized to reduce the hold of the political parties on government.

At first, Bolivia tried Partlett's method of legal amendment by Congress, but it failed because in this time of crisis Congress lacked the legitimacy necessary to directly change the constitution. In 1997, the president announced

---

[9] William Partlett, "The Dangers of Popular Constitution-Making," *Brooklyn Journal of International Law* 38 (2012), 193–238.

[10] Andrew Arato, *Post Sovereign Constitutional Making: Learning and Legitimacy* (Oxford: Oxford University Press, 2016), 107–61. It should be noted that the legal amendment for an assembly is only one part of Arato's elaborate round-table model of constitution-making.

[11] William Partlett, "Elite Threat to Constitutional Transitions," *Virginia Journal of International Law* 56 (2016), 407.

[12] Ricardo Paz Ballivián, "Reformas Constitucionales Y Asamblea Constituyente En La Democracia Boliviana 1982–2007," *Opiniones Y Análisis*, no. 88 (2007), 53.

a package of "Constitutional Amendments for Citizen Participation," and on May 9th, 2002, the lower house of Congress approved them.[13] The denunciations arrived swiftly. In between the 1997 announcement for new constitutional amendments and the 2002 approval, new indigenous and peasant-social movements had risen up to demand radical constitutional and political change. They had no faith in the "corrupt oligarchs" that ran the country. The elite politicians believed they were generously bestowing power on the people, but for the social movements the amendments, in the words of their top legal intellectual, "reinforced the dependence of the public powers on the political citizen, restricted the means of citizen participation to the will of the parliament, and excluded the national majority from the definition of the Constitution."[14] In 2002, the highland indigenous social movements began the "March for Popular Sovereignty, Territory, and Natural Resources" to protest the proposed "neoliberal" amendments to the constitution. Their march continued for five weeks and picked up new participants and organizations around the country from a diverse array of groups.

The marchers demanded that instead of the amendment package, Congress should limit itself to one amendment that would convene a constituent assembly to rewrite the constitution completely. For the protesters and for the general public, the congressional amendments could not quell the country's crisis of legitimacy and representation. Only a constituent assembly could re-found the state.[15] But no such assembly was legal under the constitution, so they demanded that the government implement something akin to Arato's preferred method of constitutional change in which a constitution is legally amended to permit a constitutional assembly.[16]

This method nearly succeeded. Congress agreed to protesters' demands, but shortly before the vote the coalition of political parties fell apart due to an unrelated matter of internal politics, and a new president was then elected in March who had opposed a constituent assembly.[17] The prospects for a constituent assembly were dim. At this point, Bolivia fulfills the criteria of

[13] Ibid., 51.

[14] Carlos Romero Bonifaz, *El Proceso Constituyente Boliviano: El Hito de la Cuarta Marcha de Tierras Bajas* (Santa Cruz de la Sierra: Centro de Estudios Jurídicos e Investigación Social-CEJIS, 2005), 155.

[15] Ibid.

[16] Ibid.

[17] Romero Bonifaz, *El Proceso Constituyente Boliviano*, 155–237; Gustavo Rodríguez Ostria, "Marco Histórico: La Larga Marcha a la Asamblea Constiuyente," in *Enciclopedia Histórica Documental del Proceso Constituyente Boliviano*, ed. Juan Carlos Pinto Quintanilla, vol. 1 (La Paz: Estado Plurinacional de Bolivia, 2009), 108–23.

legal exhaustion. Despite the widespread agreement that significant constitutional change was necessary, the political system was incapable of delivering it. The political system would have to be contorted to create space for a new beginning.

THE MAS'S PLURAL AND EXCLUSIONARY PEOPLE

In popular constitution-making, illegalities are justified on the basis that the people approve them. But there are always multiple visions of the people with different implications for inclusion and for how and to what extent law should be violated. Consistent with the radical tradition of constituent power, Evo Morales envisioned the people as lawless and that such lawlessness would justify the creation of a sovereign and all-powerful constitutional assembly. Yet, unlike other radicals and befitting the demographics of Bolivia, the MAS Party thought of the people as plural, as encompassing a variety of oppressed classes. Nonetheless Morales excluded from this diverse people the enemy of the "Camba," or the mestizo class in the "Media Luna" region of the country who should have very little influence in the Constitutional Assembly. Hence, at its root, the MAS's plural people were pretty close to the traditional vision in which law was abandoned and the enemy excluded from the process of creating a new constitution.

Drawing on the Venezuelan example and key legal advisers to Hugo Chávez, Evo Morales and the MAS Party held that since the people were superior to the constitution, the people were outside all law.[18] Hence, Evo's election was a declaration by the people that the constitution was dead. MAS believed that the next step would be the election of a sovereign constitutional assembly by a first-past-the-post voting rule that would have effectively minimized the participation of the opposition. Morales explained that the goal was a constituent assembly with "unlimited power, neither subordinated to the Parliament, nor to the executive power."[19]

But by creating a lawless space, MAS created the same dilemma that all radicals must resolve. With no law, there needs to be some method to identify

---

[18] The two legal advisors were Rubén Martínez Dalma and Roberto Viciano. For an overview of their thought and influence, see Javier Cousco, "Radical Democracy and the "New Latin American Constitutionalism" (unpublished manuscript), available at https://law.yale.edu/sites/default/files/documents/pdf/sela/SELA13_Couso_CV_Eng_20130516.pdf

[19] Ibid., 40.

when and how the people speak. To solve this problem, radical theorists of popular sovereignty divide the people into friends and enemies, with the former usually consisting of one particular social group. This oneness creates a unity that gives the people agency, and it is this group that should dominate the constituent assembly.

At times, Evo Morales followed this path of focusing on a single unified group by using racial divisions with the two largest indigenous groups, the Aymara and Quechuas, being the true people and the mestizos, or "Cambas," as the enemy. Felip Quispe, Morales's greatest rival for power among the indigenous base of the MAS, famously described the country as really being composed of "two Bolivias" in which the mestizo and white enemy had long oppressed the poor indigenous. Quispe sums up the difference between the two groups, "Only that which is native is good; the rest is rubbish."[20] Quispe is more extreme than Morales and his MAS Party, but they share the same basic themes.[21] Evo Morales chose as his 2005 inauguration site the ancient indigenous site of Tiwanaku, and crowned himself "Apu Mallku" or "supreme leader" of the Aymaras, the largest indigenous group in Bolivia.[22] The second largest group are the Quechuas. Throughout his speeches and interviews, Evo Morales celebrates the two tribes and the indigenous at large as the true Bolivian people: "After more than five hundred years, we, the Quechuas and Aymaras, are still the rightful owners of this land. We, the indigenous people, after five hundred years of resistance, are retaking the power."[23]

But the strategy of designating one group as the true people rings a little hollow in Bolivia. The Aymaras and the Quechuas are two groups, not one. Even though they are the largest indigenous groups, there are many more. Indeed, the current Bolivian Constitution recognizes 36 different indigenous groups and languages.[24] And while a majority of Bolivians identify as indigenous, the category fails to fully speak to a large urban population who have long been disconnected from their ancestral lands and languages.[25]

[20] James Dunkerley, "Evo Morales, the 'Two Bolivias' and the Third Bolivian Revolution," *Journal of Latin American Studies* 39, no. 1 (2007), 136.

[21] For a good and brief comparison of the ideologies of Evo Morales and Felip Quispe, see Andrew Canessa, "Todos Somos Indígenas: Towards a New Language of National Political Identity," *Bulletin of Latin American Research* 25, no. 2 (Apr. 1, 2006), 249–55.

[22] Linda C. Farthing and Benjamin H. Kohl, *Evo's Bolivia: Continuity and Change* (Austin: University of Texas Press, 2014), 35.

[23] Benjamin Dangl, "Interview with Evo Morales on the Colonization of the Americas," *CounterPunch.org*, Dec. 2, 2003, https://www.counterpunch.org/2003/12/02/an-interview-with-evo-morales-on-the-colonization-of-the-americas/.

[24] Andrew Canessa, "Conflict, Claim and Contradiction in the New 'Indigenous' State of Bolivia," *Critique of Anthropology* 34, no. 2 (June 2014), 160.

[25] Ibid., 160–64.

Indeed, radical political theorists in Bolivia have often struggled to find one group that could embody the people, leading Bolivian political theorist Rene Zavaleta to coin the concept of "a motley society" and to argue that there was no revolutionary subject or "people" in Bolivia, only a "multitude."[26] In the early 2000s, a group of political theorists in Bolivia called the "Grupo Communa," or Communal Group, adopted Zavaleta's categories but transvaluated them. These theorists proved enormously influential in Bolivia with one member, Raul Prada, becoming a key member and designer of the Constitutional Assembly and another, Alvaro Garcia Linera, becoming Evo Morales's vice president. While Zavaleta had believed a motley society explained the lack of a unified revolutionary subject, the new generation of Bolivian political theorists believed it explained the rise and potential of a new, diverse, deliberative, and decentralized idea of the people. Bolivia's diversity was no longer a liability but a virtue.

It was not only that Bolivia was especially diverse, but that this diversity was politically organized into separate effective, mobilized, and self-directed social movements. The MAS Party is an umbrella organization that has its origins in the decision of five large social movements to join together in a "unity pact."[27] Thus, MAS and Evo Morales argued that MAS was "not a political party" and instead called it "a movement of social movements" or "a political instrument of the social movements."[28] Unlike in Venezuela, where Chávez almost single-handedly formed his own party and organized its ideology, the MAS is composed of grass-roots organizations that long predate it. The president, Evo Morales, is the product, not the creator, of these social movements.

This new idea of the people embraced that Bolivia had dozens of indigenous groups with their own languages alongside Afro-Bolivians, the middle-class and urban citizens. As the political theorist, member of the Grupo Communa, and future vice president to Evo Morales, Alvaro Garcia Linera stated, the new idea of the a diverse people "unite[s] peasants, full-time workers, part-time workers, small business, sweatshop workers,

---

[26] René Zavaleta Mercado, *Lo nacional-popular en Bolivia* (La Paz, Bolivia: Plural Editores, 2008).

[27] Fernando Garcés, "Domestication of Indigenous Autonomies in Bolivia: From the Pact of Unity to the New Constitution," in *Remapping Bolivia: Resources, Territory, and Indigeneity in a Plurinational State*, eds. Nicole Fabricant and Bret Gustafson, 1st ed. (Santa Fe, NM: School for Advanced Research Press, 2011). For an overview of the organizations that were a part of the Unity Pact and their role laying the groundwork for MAS, Raquel Gutiérrez Aguilar, *Rhythms of the Pachakuti: Indigenous Uprising and State Power in Bolivia*, trans. Stacey Alba D. Skar (Durham: Duke University Press, 2014).

[28] Sven Harten, *The Rise of Evo Morales and the MAS* (London: Zed Books, 2011), 89–90.

artisans, unemployed workers, students, housewives, and so forth."[29] The sheer breadth of the MAS coalition was evident in its early draft of the constitution's definition of the people, "The Bolivian people are made up of all the Bolivians, women and men, the urban of different social classes, the original indigenous peasant nations and peoples, and the intercultural and Afro-Bolivian communities."

And yet, the MAS's draft constitution's definition of the people still didn't reflect the true diversity of Bolivia. Although the constitution referred to all Bolivians, in the subsequent list of groups, it did mention the opposition who are often referred to as the Camba. These are the mestizo or white citizens who compose the majority in the four lowland states or departments, departments that have since independence often clashed with the central government in the highlands. These departments are often referred to as the Media Luna because of their crescent-like shape. The popular understanding is that Cambas are more conservative and friendlier to capitalist policies than the groups supporting MAS.[30]

None of the categories in MAS's draft constitution's definition of the people refers in any way to the Camba. This exclusion was by design and reflected the theoretical underpinnings of the MAS project. Take the work of Raul Prada, at the time considered the leading MAS thinker of constituent power and a key member of the Constituent Assembly. In his book on the idea of a constituent assembly, released shortly after the election of Evo Morales, Prada celebrates a society that is a "hybrid crammed with mixtures," but he still ridicules the term "Camba" as outmoded, as the "pretentious of a regional oligarchy" and argued that it lacks a "collective imagination."[31] Prada concedes that the concerns of the Media Luna should be addressed in the assembly but refuses to grant any legitimacy to Camba identity.[32] As an invention of the oligarchy, the Media Luna cannot be part of the people. The political movements in the Media Luna mirrored the radical strategy,

[29] Alvaro Garcia Linera, "Union, Multitude and Community: Social Movements and Forms of Political Autonomy in Bolivia," in *Plebeian Power: Collective Action and Indigenous, Working-Class and Popular Identities in Bolivia* (2015).

[30] Claudia Peña Claros, "Un Pueblo Eminente: Autonomist Populism in Santa Cruz," *Latin American Perspectives* 37, no. 4 (July 1, 2010), 125–39; Nicole Fabricant and Nancy Postero, "Contested Bodies, Contested States: Performance, Emotions, and New Forms of Regional Governance in Santa Cruz, Bolivia," *The Journal of Latin American and Caribbean Anthropology* 18, no. 2 (July 1, 2013), 187–211; Gabriela Valdivia, "Agrarian Capitalism and Struggles over Hegemony in the Bolivian Lowlands," *Latin American Perspectives* 37, no. 4 (July 1, 2010), 67–87.

[31] Raul Prada, *Horizonte Politico de la Asamblea Constituyente* (La Paz: Yachaywasi 2006), 64.

[32] Ibid.

declaring themselves or the Camba as the true people of what they envisioned would be a new nation-state that would break away from Bolivia's indigenous majority provinces.[33]

Neither the MAS nor the opposition party achieved their goal of creating a constitution based on their exclusionary visions of the people. The creation of the Bolivian Constitution is a story of how these opposed groups through extraordinary adaptation managed to forge a compromise so that the "plural people" would truly include all Bolivians. The process happened in two stages, the first of which was the initial structuring of the assembly.

THE INITIAL STRUCTURING OF THE ASSEMBLY

The old constitutional system had to be contorted but not destroyed in order to create a new one. The political system had been a liberal and pacted democracy that worked through achieving consensus among a number of elite political parties. In the 1990s, reforms opened up the system to new political forces. The creation of direct municipal elections, changes in the electoral rule for Congress, and massive government voter registrations created a more permissive institutional environment for new political parties that would represent the indigenous and peasant-social movements that claimed to represent the majority of the country.[34] The system may have been too rigid for a legal path to a constitutional assembly, but with reforms it was open enough to create space for political actors to enter into government. Rather than overthrowing the government by force to achieve a new constitution, with their hands on the lever of change, new political movements could pull these levers almost to their breaking point to enact revolutionary change through the extraordinary adaptation of the reformed institutions.

This hard lever pulling began much earlier than most accounts of the constitution-making process appreciate. Most of these narratives practically dive right into the tumultuous debates within and the riots outside the Constituent Assembly. But the paths of these later events were all structured by the illegal and inclusive 2004 Amendment that created a new provision for calling a constitutional assembly. To truly understand the relationship

---

[33] Peña Claros, "Un Pueblo Eminente."

[34] Donna Lee Van Cott, *Radical Democracy in the Andes* (Cambridge: Cambridge University Press, 2008), 34–58, 175, 210; Donna Lee Van Cott, *From Movements to Parties in Latin America* (Cambridge: Cambridge University Press, 2005), 49–99.

between law and inclusion in the Bolivian process, we must start with and center the effects of the 2004 Amendment. I show that even as the approval of the amendment violated the law in order to initiate the creation of a new constitution, the continuities in creating the amendment created an inclusionary chain reaction that persisted into the rest of the process, facilitating inclusion in the provisions of the 2004 Amendment, the electoral rule for the Constituent Assembly, and finally the Constituent Assembly's approval rule for the constitution itself. Each of these moments will be discussed in turn.

The Illegal and Inclusive 2004 Amendment Permitting a Constituent Assembly

In the 2004 Amendment lies the foundations for Bolivia's extraordinary adaptation. Its illegality facilitated a break with the past, but its continuity ensured that the new amendment rule would be inclusive. The 2002 marches had failed to force Congress to amend the constitution to provide for a constituent assembly. But the demand flared again in October of 2003, when Bolivia erupted in a historic protest called the "gas wars." Demanding a constituent assembly and the nationalization of hydrocarbons, the protesters shut down Bolivia for months. The president declared a state of siege but ultimately resigned on October 17th, 2003. In his speech upon taking office, the new president, Carlos Mesa, pledged to fulfill the protester's agenda by "find[ing] a road adequate to have a constituent assembly."[35] Congress complied and approved by a two-thirds vote an amendment to provide a method for calling a constituent assembly.[36]

Yet, the 2004 Amendment for a new constituent assembly was illegal. To amend the constitution, each house of Congress had to twice approve the proposed change by a two-thirds vote of the present members. In between these two votes, there had to be an intervening congressional election, which occurs every four years. To amend the constitution, a proposal had to be twice approved by a supermajority vote by two different Congresses separated by an intervening election.[37] To become part of the constitution, a

---

[35] Carlos Mesa, "Discurso de Posesión como Presidente el 17 de Octubre de 2003," available at https://carlosdmesa.com/2013/10/17/mi-discurso-de-posesion-como-presidente-el-17-de-octu bre-de-2003/

[36] Ostria, *Marco Historico*, 125.

[37] 1967 Bolivian Constitution, Arts. 230–35.

new Congress should have approved the constituent assembly provision, the 2004 Amendment, again after the 2007 elections.[38] But the country could not wait. It was on the verge of a political collapse. It was better to cut into a limb of the tree than uproot it completely. The old constitution bent so that the protesters would not break it.

This illegality, under the extraordinary adaptation's second principle of popular vindication, can be excused by multiple popular and widespread mobilizations. So far in our narrative, we have seen two of such moments attesting to popular vindication: (1) the 2002 March for Popular Sovereignty and (2) the 2003 Gas Wars leading to the president's resignation. Both demanded the amendment for a constitutional assembly. These alone, however, would not be sufficient. Citizens are fickle. True expressions of their will must be enduring, broad, and deep. By the end of this chapter, however, we'll see a total of six moments that attest to a true popular approbation of the creation of a new constitution.

Along with this illegal break, there were crucial sites of legal continuity that inclusively structured the constitution-making process. In creating the 2004 Amendment, Congress still complied with the requirement that all amendments be passed by two-thirds of Congress.[39] Since the approval of minority parties would be necessary to pass the amendment, they had leverage in negotiations. Unsurprisingly, to gain their consent, the new procedure for calling a constituent assembly would have to be supermajoritarian and also would have to give the opposition a voice in the process.

Hence, under the new illegal amendment, a two-thirds approval of the total members of Congress was necessary to call a constituent assembly. Unlike the traditional amendment procedure, the new one permitted not just an amendment, but a total reform of the new constitution. The Congress, by a two-thirds vote, could pass a "Special Law of Convocation" to call for and provide rules for the elections to a constituent assembly.[40] The requirement of a two-thirds approval virtually ensured that the "Special Law of Convocation" would have to be approved by multiple parties.

---

[38] Jorge Lazarte, *Hacia un País Moderno y Democrático: la Asamblea Constituyente: Un Nuevo Comienzo* (La Paz: Plural, 2006), 38.

[39] Ibid.; see Ricardo Paz Ballivián, "Reformas Constitucionales Y Asamblea Constituyente En La Democracia Boliviana 1982-2007," Opiniones Y Análisis 88, no. 53 (2007).

[40] Bolivian Constitution 1967 as amended in 2004, Art. 232.

Inclusive Electoral Rule for and Approval Rule Inside
the Constituent Assembly

The continuity and inclusion of the 2004 Amendments spurred inclusive electoral rules for the Constituent Assembly and an inclusive approval rule inside of it. Recall that in response to the protests and the resignation of the president, Vice President Carlos Mesa had assumed office and facilitated the passage of the 2004 Amendments, which created a method to call for a constituent assembly. A year and a half later, in response to massive protests against Mesa's economic policies, Mesa called for early elections to take place in December of 2005. The social movements coalesced around the candidacy of Evo Morales, a congressman, leader of the coca farmer's movement and of many of the protests. His campaign pledged to convene a constituent assembly to write a new constitution. On December 18th, 2005, Evo Morales became the first indigenous president of Bolivia with 53.74 percent of the vote, the highest percentage and the first absolute majority since Bolivia's transition to democracy in 1978. Morales's party, the MAS, also won an absolute majority in the lower house of Congress with about 55 percent of the seats. However, the opposition won a slim plurality of the twenty-seven seats in the Senate, gaining 48 percent, or thirteen seats, while MAS gained twelve.[41] Since MAS lacked two-thirds in the House and lacked a majority in the Senate, it would have to negotiate with the opposition to pass the Special Law of Convocation to create a constituent assembly.

Similar to Hugo Chávez's chosen electoral rule in Venezuela, MAS preferred a first-past-the-post method in district elections so that its likely majority vote would result in the nearly complete capture of all the seats in the assembly.[42] Evo Morales explained that the goal was a constituent assembly with "unlimited power, neither subordinated to the Parliament, nor to the executive power."[43] Unlike in Venezuela, however, a preexisting structure, the 2004 Amendments, existed to regulate the creation of the assembly, and it required a two-thirds vote for approval. Morales did not have Chávez's excuse that he lacked a provision in the constitution to convoke an assembly.

---

[41] For the results of the Chamber of Deputies, http://www.electionguide.org/results.php?ID=184. For the results of the Chamber of Senators, http://www.electionguide.org/elections/id/874/.

[42] Gamboa, *Dilemas y conflictos sobre la Constitución en Bolivia* (La Paz: Konrad Adenauer Stifunge, 2009), 41.

[43] Ibid., 40.

Without this excuse, Morales could not as easily justify plunging the country into a legal abyss.

To gain the approval of the opposition on both the electoral and approval rule, MAS greatly gave up on its majoritarian goals.[44] On March 6, Congress passed the Special Law of Convocation that set the location, deadline, and other important logistics of the assembly. For our purposes, two parts of the law are of importance. First, the law required the Constituent Assembly to pass the constitution by a two-thirds vote of the present members.[45] I will refer to this as the internal approval rule, and we'll see that it became the subject of a great deal of contention. Second, the Special Law of Convocation set down an inclusive electoral rule for the Constituent Assembly. Whereas Venezuela's electoral first-past-the-post electoral rule greatly exaggerated Chávez's majority, the Bolivian Law of Convocation rule guaranteed sufficient seats to minority parties so that they could block the passage of the constitution. The rule specified that voters would elect 255 members to the Constituent Assembly. The law split the country into two different sets of electoral districts that mapped the preexisting ones from the last general election.

The first set was composed of seventy uninominal districts. In each district, voters would select three individual candidates for a total of 210 representatives. While the first two seats would go to the candidates with the most votes, the third had to go to a candidate who was not of the dominant party. The second set of electoral districts was plurinominal and corresponded with the nine regional departments of the country. In each of the nine departments, voters would elect five candidates from party lists for a total of forty-five representatives. The rule allotted the first two seats to the party with the most votes. It then gave one seat each to the party with the second, third, and fourth most votes. In total, no party could possess more than 62 percent of the total 255 seats of the Constituent Assembly, less than the two-thirds majority required to approve the constitution.[46]

On July 2nd, 2006, Bolivia elected its members to the Constituent Assembly. The rules worked as expected. MAS and its allies won an impressive majority, 157 seats of 255, but not a sufficient number to reach the two-thirds threshold or the 170 members necessary to pass the constitution. The

---

[44] Ibid., 54.

[45] Art. 25, Ley 3364, Mar. 6, 2006, available at http://www.lexivox.org/norms/BO-L-3364.xhtml.

[46] See Ley 3364, Art. 14, Mar. 6, 2006, available at http://www.lexivox.org/norms/BO-L-3364.xhtml.

right-wing opposition, Podemos, was the party with the second-greatest number of votes and gained sixty-six seats. Both Podemos and MAS needed approximately the same number of votes, nineteen or twenty of the twenty-six available from centrist parties to achieve their goal.[47] The inclusionary structure of the 2004 Amendments had ricocheted all the way into the composition of the Constituent Assembly. This inclusion would force MAS to compromise with centrists to maintain the legitimacy of the assembly and would force Podemos to begrudgingly accept these compromises to rebut charges that it sought to sabotage the entire process.

Centrists and the Compromise over Internal Approval Rules

In Venezuela, Chávez's overwhelming majority in the assembly prevented it from becoming a true space for deliberation. By contrast, the Bolivian Assembly was inclusive and pluralistic. It became a deep site of contestation between a variety of political parties over the constitutional future and identity of Bolivia. The most well-represented parties in the assembly, MAS and Podemos, were radical and often stubborn and inflexible. However, both softened their positions to gain the support of moderate parties necessary to either pass or block the constitution. Furthermore, since MAS and Podemos themselves were heterogeneous, moderates within both groups could rally against the radicals within their own party by threatening to defect to or by citing the need for support of more moderate parties.[48] The first significant manifestation of this pattern was the protracted fight over the internal rules of the assembly.

On August 6, 2006, the Constituent Assembly met for the first time. For almost six months, they viciously fought over the voting rule for the assembly. The Special Law of Convocation stated that the Constituent Assembly would approve the text by two-thirds of the present members.[49] But that still left substantial ambiguity about exactly which votes the rule covered. The assembly would vote on the internal rules and the committee reports. It would

---

[47] For the election results, see Gamboa, *Dilemas*, 64–73, 78–80.

[48] For social science analyses showing that inclusion correlates with positive outcomes, Todd A. Eisenstadt and Tofigh Maboudi, "Being There Is Half the Battle: Group Inclusion, Constitution-Writing, and Democracy," Comparative Political Studies 52, no. 13–14 (November 1, 2019), 2135–70,. Gabriel L. Negretto and Mariano Sánchez-Talanquer, "Constitutional Origins and Liberal Democracy: A Global Analysis, 1900–2015," *American Political Science Review* (2021).

[49] See Ley 3728, Aug. 4, 2007, art. 25.

also vote on the text on the constitution three times: first as a whole document; second votes on each and every individual line; and last a final approval on the whole constitution again. Did the two-thirds rule cover all of these votes or only some of them? The largest opposition party, Podemos, argued that each of these steps required a two-thirds approval. MAS asserted that the absolute majority was the proper threshold for every step, except for the final approval of the whole constitution.

MAS repeatedly tried to approve its own proposed majoritarian rules by majority vote. Shortly after one such attempt, Doria Medina, the president of the most important center party, the United National Front (UN), began a hunger strike with seven other members.[50] The vice president of the UN began to support Podemos's calls for autonomy for the department of Santa Cruz. On December 15th, 2006, the centrist parties joined with Podemos to hold a huge demonstration of one million people in the opposition stronghold city of Santa Cruz. In effect, the center parties allied with Podemos against MAS. Faced with the loss of the necessary votes to reach a supermajority requirement for the final approval of the constitution, MAS entered into negotiations with the centrist parties and with the occasional participation of Podemos. Some accounts suggest Podemos refused to budge from its own demands of two-thirds for every step. After all, if independence of the Media Luna States was their goal, they had little to gain from compromise, from legitimizing the Constitutional Assembly. However, MAS and the center parties managed to strike an agreement. On February 14th, 2007, the assembly passed the new voting rule by an overwhelming supermajority of 81 percent of the new vote. The leader of Podemos and many of its members abstained.[51] However, the majority of Podemos voted in favor out of fear that a no vote would substantiate MAS's accusation that Podemos aimed to defeat any proposed constitution regardless of its content.[52]

The final approved voting rule is complex, but it can be broken down into three parts and one concession. First, the Constituent Assembly would approve the constitution as a whole by majority vote. Second, the assembly would seek, repeatedly if necessary, to pass each line of the constitution by a two-thirds vote. Those lines that could not reach the two-thirds threshold would go on to a referendum so that they may be decided by the people.

---

[50] Gamboa, *Dilemas*, 144.
[51] Gamboa, *Dilemas*, 182.
[52] Article 70 of Assembly rules, available in Gamboa, *Dilemas*, 181–82.

Third, after reconciling the referendum results, the assembly would approve the final result by two-thirds. The concession was that the final constitution would incorporate the results of the opposition's referendum of July 2nd, 2006, which granted new powers to the departments.

But the content of this complex rule should not distract from the main point. What is important is that inclusion of the centrist parties created swing votes that managed to wring a compromise tolerable to the leading majority and opposition parties. This compromise set a framework that all parties could agree on, and the assembly hoped to move forward with the creation of a new constitution.

SUBSEQUENT ADJUSTMENTS TO THE FRAMEWORK: CONGRESS VS. THE CONSTITUENT ASSEMBLY

In the second stage of the process, new challenges required changes to the Congress's Special Law of Convocation that structured the Constituent Assembly. Who had the right to enact these changes? Who wields superior authority: the Constituent Assembly or the constituted powers that called them into being? May the government set rules for the assembly, or is the assembly sovereign over its own affairs?

The potential for conflict between a government and a constituent assembly is always present. Since the old constituted powers calls into being the constitutional assembly, it also tends to greatly structure it. That structure in turn will likely greatly determine the content of the constitution. The constituted powers then indirectly impinge on the assembly's prerogative to create the constitution. Indeed, the entire purpose of making the new constitution is often to overthrow the old personnel and create space for the election of new ones. The tension between the constituted powers and the constitutional assembly is inherent and structural.[53]

The Bolivian constitution-making process finessed this tension between the creature and its creator through "extraordinary adaptation." Congress had set the basic framework for the assembly, but would the majority MAS Party abide by it? Time and again, fearsome and unexpected events challenged the viability of Congress's framework. Through a narrow reading of

---

[53] Jon Elster, "Constitutional Bootstrapping in Philadelphia and Paris," *Cardozo Law Review* 14 (1993), 549.

the congressional statute, the Podemos opposition sought to take advantage of these challenges to disrupt and end the process. On the majority MAS side, each challenge renewed calls within it to declare the assembly sovereign in order to set new internal rules. But MAS feared that flagrant violations of the congressional statute would discredit the assembly. MAS repeatedly faced the same dilemma: to protect the legitimacy of the assembly, it had to comply with the statute. However, to overcome threats to the process, it had to violate it.

Why didn't MAS follow the Venezuelan example and declare the assembly sovereign? Bright-line rules and inclusion made the difference. In Bolivia fairly clear rules had been set down to regulate the assembly. Blatant violations of these rules would make MAS susceptible to charges of violating the law they had constructed. Additionally, inclusion created actors within the assembly to enforce these rules. If MAS declared itself sovereign it would induce a boycott from both Podemos and the centrist parties, which in turn would greatly damage the legitimacy of the assembly. In Venezuela, the opposition lacked both congressional regulations to cite against Chávez, and a presence within the assembly to publicize its objections.

Lawlessness was not an option in Bolivia. But the opposite extreme possibility also threatened the process. If MAS adhered to a stringent reading of the statute, Podemos would succeed in shutting down the assembly. MAS neither adhered to narrow legality nor lawlessness. Instead, it "extraordinarily adapted" the Law of Convocation by reinterpreting, bending, and amending it. It pushed the law to its brink, but it never declared itself free of it and never acted against its spirit. By contrast, Podemos's total break from law and turn to violence discredited it, giving MAS the momentum necessary to finish the project. I demonstrate this complicated dynamic through four key moments: (a) Extraordinary Reinterpretation of the Assembly's Location; (b) Extraordinary Amendment of the Assembly's Location; (c) Congress's Lawless Attempt to Approve the Referendum; and (d) Podemos's Lawless Autonomy Statutes and the Massacre at Pando.

Extraordinary Reinterpretation of the Assembly's Location

In the first moment, MAS reinterpreted the Special Law of Convocation to move the assembly from the center of Sucre to a nearby military base. The congressional statute, the Special Law, set the location of the assembly in

Sucre, a carefully preserved and treasured colonial city. After a flagrant violation of the voting rule to evade debate on the historically sensitive issue on whether the new constitution should locate the capital in Sucre, the city exploded in protest and shut down the assembly. La Paz, the rival site for the capital, responded with its own demonstrations. Clashes between MAS and Sucre supporters left a few dead and many injured.[54]

Members of MAS began to consider violating the law and relocating the assembly to Oruro, a stronghold of the MAS Party. They would justify the move on the basis that the assembly was sovereign, and hence could violate the statute. The move would set the assembly free from all external rules and would likely empower the MAS to impose a constitution by majority vote.[55]

Ultimately, MAS resisted the temptation to break with all legality. They knew that if they violated the Law of Convocation and declared themselves above all law, the assembly would lose all legitimacy. Not only would the centrists and the opposition refuse to attend the assembly, but they would be able to justify this boycott on the basis that MAS refused to abide by the rules. It would inflame the four Media Luna departments into declaring autonomy. Instead of declaring themselves sovereign, MAS moved the assembly to the nearby military base in the periphery of Sucre. Technically, this may have complied with the statute's location, although they all knew that the intention of the law was for them to meet in the historical heart of the city. On the outskirts, a combination of the military and social movements could better guarantee the safety of the members of the assembly.[56] Reinterpretation was the tool of extraordinary adaptation used to prevent a complete legal break.

Although the base was safer, it was not safe. In the middle of the debate and with centrists on their way,[57] assembly members learned that protesters had crossed the river and were clashing with the police. The protesters would soon break through. The military was the next line of defense. As defenders of the base, they had orders to shoot if the protesters tried to cross their perimeter. The assembly feared a bloodbath, and they evacuated.[58]

[54] Landau, "Constitution-Making Gone Wrong," 955–56.

[55] Salvador Schavelzon, *El nacimiento del estado plurinacional de Bolivia: etnografía de una Asamblea Constituyente* (Buenos Aires, Argentina: CLASCO, 2012), 250.

[56] Ibid., 318–22.

[57] Although the assembly had quorum, it was twenty-five members short of two-thirds of the *total* needed to circumvent congressional approval of the referendum under the amended statute. Podemos boycotted the assembly and hoped that the centrist parties would do the same. Yet, there were signs that the centrist parties were planning to participate. Schalvezon, *supra* note 60, 347, 351.

[58] Ibid., 340–42.

Extraordinary Amendment of the Assembly's Location

Few believed it was possible or safe to meet anywhere in or near Sucre, but this was what the statute commanded. Again, MAS feared that violating the statute would damage the legitimacy of the assembly. But they knew that the Conservative Senate would refuse to amend it. The dilemma then was how to overcome or evade opposition in the Conservative Senate in order to change the location of the Constitutional Assembly. MAS's solution of extraordinary amendment again pushed the boundaries of one legal rule while preserving the framework for the process as a whole.

In coordination with the MAS administration, the social movements formed a fence around the Congress and blocked the opposition from entering. In their absence, MAS amended the Law of Convocation to permit the president of the assembly to unilaterally set the assembly's location with forty-eight hours' notice.[59] The blocking of the opposition puts the amendment on questionable legal footing. But let's understand the choices MAS faced. Violent protests threatened the safety of the assembly's members and prevented the renewal of sessions. The intransigent opposition had little interest negotiating in good faith. By blocking an amendment to the statute, the opposition was supporting and empowering efforts to shut down the assembly by force.

MAS refused to be cowed by physical intimidation. It refused to embolden regional movements' efforts to declare independence. For MAS, the most direct method of solving the problem was to break with legality completely by violating the statute and unilaterally moving the assembly to a new location. However, to maintain its legitimacy, MAS chose instead a process that still maintained a strong semblance of and attachment to legality by ensuring that the statute still regulated the assembly. Even if the rules were bent to change the location, the rest of the statute and its voting rules would still bind and limit the assembly. An ethnographer to the assembly characterized it as a "liminal space between institutional respect and the advance of the social movements confronting the law of a colonial state."[60] Each time MAS stayed within the liminal space, it set a new precedent for MAS to continue to adhere to the statute. And it is this legality that distinguished Bolivia from

---

[59] Ibid., 349–50.
[60] Ibid., 350.

Venezuela by preventing the exclusion of the opposition and centralization of power in the office of the presidency.

The MAS Congress's Lawless Attempt to Approve the Referendum Statute

From the standpoint of extraordinary adaptation, the Venezuelan process is easy to condemn: Chávez openly argued that no law or institution could control the sovereign Constituent Assembly. By contrast, even though the MAS repeatedly violated the law in creating the new Bolivian Constitution, they never took that ultimate step of claiming the old constitution had no binding power whatsoever. Still, that does not mean every step of the process was justified.

Extraordinary adaptation does not excuse any and all illegalities; such breaches must be consistent with the three principles of legal exhaustion, popular vindication, and inclusion. Thus far, the unorthodox maneuvers of the MAS fit those principles. But that was not the case with MAS's attempt to pass the referendum statute by blockading the opposition out of Congress. Unlike the MAS's previous blockade, this one violated the principle of inclusion.

When we last left off, Congress had amended the Law of Convocation so that the president of the Constituent Assembly could choose a new location. She chose the mining city of Oruro, a stronghold of the MAS Party. In Oruro, with the presence of some of the opposition and centrist parties, MAS passed the constitution line by line. Lacking two-thirds of the total, MAS anticipated that the draft constitution would have to also be approved by Congress, so it dialogued and compromised with the centrist parties.[61] Still, the so-called Oruro Constitution was heavily titled toward the radical factions of the MAS. With opposition control of the Senate and its substantial representation in the House, would two-thirds of the members of Congress approve a referendum on a radically left constitution?

The opposition denounced the "Oruro Constitution" as "a text stained with blood, a flawed nullity plagued by jurisdictional aberrations to destroy the rule of law."[62] The states of the Media Luna began to pass autonomy

---

[61] Perhaps the most important concession was limiting the president to two terms. Ibid., 366–67.
[62] Ibid., 385.

statutes usurping great power from the central government in violation of the constitution. They seized government buildings and airports, bringing the country to the brink. In response, the MAS marshaled the social movements to form a fence around Congress to block out the opposition so that it could reach the two-thirds necessary to call a referendum on the draft constitution. The Electoral Court struck down, on technical grounds, both the region's autonomy's statutes and Congress's statute approving the referendum.

The court was right: MAS had gone too far. Recall that I had defended MAS's use of a congressional blockade to amend the statute of convocation so that it might meet in a different location. Why was that initial blockage legitimate and this latter one illegitimate?

The latter violated the principle of inclusion. Law may not be violated to exclude minorities from having a meaningful voice in the construction of a new constitution. Insurgent majorities must violate law to break with the past regime. But the goal of such violation is to move the process forward, not to shut out the opposition. The doors must always remain open to them.

The first blockade's purpose was to pass to a minor change in the Statute of Convocation so that the assembly could meet in a safer location. Either that amendment passed or the opposition's intransigence doomed the process. Nothing about the amendment closed the doors to the opposition's participation in the creation of the new constitution. Indeed, the centrist-right party of the UN attended the meeting in Oruro, and it was Podemos's choice to boycott it.[63] Now, MAS used this same technique to violate one of the key steps in the process to exclude opposition from participation at a time when there was ample space for compromise. The vice president was in the midst of opening up negotiations with the opposition, and this action was taken before they had run their course. There was potential for Congress to become a new site of negotiation. Unlike the members of Podemos in the Constituent Assembly and in local government members, the Podemos congressmen were more nationally minded and more amenable to compromise. Negotiation in Congress had the potential to incorporate enough of Podemos's positions into the constitution so that they may become a loyal opposition and take some of the oxygen out of the independence movement in the region. By contrast, passage without any attempt at negotiation only further polarized the nation, driving it closer to civil war. Even if Podemos

[63] Ibid., 362–63.

was still intransigent, the Electoral Court decision at least bought time for events to try to sway Podemos to the negotiating table.

The Electoral Court's action is an example of extraordinary adaptation of old institutions to prevent any one party from dominating the assembly. If radicals, such as Carl Schmitt, are correct that the people, in any one of their many embodiments, is sovereign, then the old institutions of government have no authority to regulate it. In Bolivia, radicals would argue that the peasant and indigenous social movements are sovereign, and the MAS is their instrument.[64] Logically then, the Electoral Court had no jurisdiction to even hear the case.

By contrast, extraordinary adaptation denies that the people may ever appear outside of all institutions or create new ones from scratch. They must adapt, in odd and jarring ways, old institutions to create new ones. Here, extraordinary adaptation empowered the Electoral Court to intervene to dissolve the impasses so that new negotiations may begin. At this moment, extraordinary adaptation saved the Bolivian constitution-making process or at least bought it some borrowed time. The extraordinary adaptation of the court trumped MAS's lawlessness.

Podemos's Lawlessness: The Autonomy Statutes and the Massacre at Pando

The process again was gridlocked. The assembly had passed a radically left constitution that could not reach a two-thirds approval in Congress. MAS had treaded carefully, resisting time and again the temptation to take the Venezuelan path and break entirely with the old constitution. The same cannot be said of the main opposition, Podemos. In every advance, MAS incorporated a bit more of the opposition's priorities, hoping to induce it to collaborate in the next round. Now, the final round had arrived. Rather than join the negotiations and in response to their loss in the revocatory referendum, Podemos stepped outside the framework of the old constitution and resorted to force and violence. Previously, in condemning MAS for illegal actions, Podemos had positioned itself as a principled adherent to legal rules. But now the party of the rule of law had embraced lawlessness. In so doing, Podemos turned the tide against them, not only bringing international

---

[64] See, e.g., Raúl Prada Alcoreza, *Horizontes*.

condemnation, but fracturing their coalition and opening up a path through Congress to the passage of the constitution.

In accordance with a bipartisan statute passed in the midst of the crisis, in May of 2008, Bolivia held a revocatory referendum putting before the voters the option to revoke the terms of the president, the vice president, and the governors.[65] While MAS came out ahead, the results did little to resolve the gridlock. The president and vice president won a stunning 67.41 percent of the vote, and MAS increased its share of governorships from two to four out of the total of nine.[66] But now the governorships aligned almost perfectly with the regional split between the Media Luna and the rest of the country. The media interpreted the referendum as a tie that ratified that there were two irreconcilable Bolivias. The process remained gridlocked.[67]

From December 2007 to September 2008, the opposition steadily escalated its illegal attacks against the government. Without any statutory or constitutional basis and in defiance of the rulings of both the national and Electoral Courts, in May and June the four Media Luna provinces drew up "autonomy" statutes that greatly increased the power of the departments and then approved them through referendum. Next, in September after the opposition's uneven results in the revocatory referendum, the opposition began seizing airports, gas pipelines, and a variety of national government offices. They prevented Evo Morales's plane from landing in Sucre, blocking him from attending the celebrations of the anniversary of independence, and threatened to shut off the flow of gas and meat to the other half of Bolivia and to neighboring countries.[68]

This lawless escalation culminated in the September 11th Massacre at Pando. Truckloads of armed opposition supporters ambushed indigenous protesters. Estimates of the casualties vary, but most likely twenty indigenous protesters died and between fifty and eighty were injured. The massacre shocked Bolivia and all of South America. It cemented the emerging image

---

[65] Since December, MAS had pushed a law calling for a recall referendum for the president, vice president, and governors. Their hope had been that a new election would consolidate the party's power. But the Senate, in which Podemos had ample representation, had killed the bill. In a surprise turn, in May, the Senate changed its mind and approved the bill. The reasons for this turn remain unclear, but perhaps the recent defeat in a Venezuelan referendum of Chávez's proposed constitutional amendments for indefinite reelection of the presidency played a role. MAS at first hesitated but ultimately agreed to the revocatory referendum. Schalvezon, *Nacimiento*, 401.

[66] MAS gained in the departments of Cochabamba and La Paz. Chuqisaca, the location of Sucre, was not on the ballot. Ibid., 404–6.

[67] Ibid., 401–6.

[68] Ibid., 406–7.

of the opposition as recklessly abandoning all attempts to work within the current institutional framework and to follow the basic principles of democracy. Months before the violence in the midst of the autonomy statutes, the Organization of American States had already expressed concern that the "regional leaders were launching referendums outside the rule of law."[69] Now, the Union of South American Nations called an emergency meeting. Their statement emphasized that Morales had earned a mandate in the recent recall referendum. Even more strikingly, the statement returned again and again to the need to follow the rule of law. They warned that they would not accept "any situation that . . . ruptures institution order" and would not tolerate "disrespect to established democratic institutions."[70]

Within Bolivia, the massacre permanently split centrist parties from the regional leaders of Podemos. Salvador Schalvezon, an ethnographer of the assembly, summarizes the different valuations between the centrist parties and regional Podemos on the rule of law: "the difference between the two sectors of the opposition was that while the [centrist] mestizo liberals elected in the Altiplano emphasized the defense of the rule of law and legality, [Podemos's] regional leaders pushed a road of imposition of reforms outside of institutions, with popular measures imposed by force."[71] The centrist parties were disgusted at Podemos's seizing of national institutions; its incendiary, racist rhetoric; and its possible involvement with the massacre. Podemos's willingness to depart from the law completed the rupture between them and the centrist parties and pushed the latter back into negotiations with MAS.

The issue of the rule of law also created a split within Podemos between its congressional and regional wings. The congressmen had been members of the older political parties that had reorganized after the backlash against their neoliberal policies. As players of a previously pacted democracy, they had a long history of and a devotion to negotiation. They were more nationally minded, more willing to compromise, and less interested in independence for their regions. The regional referendums and the Massacre at Pando convinced Podemos's congressmen that a new constitution was needed to save the country and they should negotiate with MAS.[72]

[69] Ibid.
[70] Unasur Declaration of Sept. 15th, 2008.
[71] Schalvezon, *Nacimiento*, 486.
[72] GAMBOA, *Dilemas*, 225.

The popular and self-understanding of the parties had reversed. The process had begun with MAS flirting with sovereign power and Podemos claiming to protect the rule of law. Yet, MAS turned toward and put one foot in legality in order to save the assembly. Since it was unable to sabotage the assembly, in acts of desperation, Podemos had decided to discard the rule of law and in the process lost all legitimacy. Podemos had become lawless, and the MAS became relatively law-abiding. Later, when radical miners who supported MAS gathered in front of Congress, exploded dynamite, and called to seize the building, President Morales dissuaded them by referring to Podemos. He reminded them that only "oligarchs" take buildings by force.[73]

In response to the widespread condemnation, the opposition de-escalated the protests. MAS opened up a new and more promising line of negotiations with the congressional wing of the Podemos and centrist parties. After the autonomy statutes, the seizure of government buildings, and the massacre, members of Congress felt it necessary to negotiate with MAS to save the country. After veering toward lawlessness and civil war, the process was once again back on track.

FINAL RATIFICATION AND CONTENT OF THE CONSTITUTION

The process ultimately produced a constitution that commanded the loyalty of the opposition. After a long night and morning of debate, Congress barely passed the referendum law by 106 votes, one more vote than was necessary to reach the two-thirds threshold. MAS possessed eighty votes and needed twenty-five of the centrist and opposition votes to reach two-thirds. The law garnered seventeen votes from the centrist parties of UN and MNR and nine from Podemos. Significantly, Tuto Quiroga, a former vice president and the Podemos candidate for the presidency in 2005, supported the compromise. When Evo Morales, waiting outside the steps to Congress, heard that Congress had passed the constitution, he began to weep.

Extremists of both the left and the right condemned the constitution. Felip Quispe, a radical rival to President Evo Morales, released a document titled "TRAITORS TO THE POPULAR, INDIGENOUS MOVEMENT." The Santa Cruz newspapers denounced the new draft of the constitution as an

---

[73] Schalvezon, *Nacimiento*, 512.

agreement between the old political leaders and MAS. But one of the most prominent right-wing newspapers also recognized that the "absolutist project with the indigenous as a shield to perpetuate power has been abandoned or at least postponed." In the upcoming referendum, right-wing parties would oppose the passage of the new constitution, but they also seemed to signal that they would accept the results. The Media Luna stopped pushing for total independence. They had become a loyal opposition.[74]

The broad outlines of the constitution reflected the MAS's priorities, but the compromise reined in the MAS's goals of centralizing power in the national government and in the presidency. As MAS desired, the constitution created a plurinational democracy that would offer more power to the indigenous and average citizen. Indeed, it changed the official name of the country to "The Plurinational State of Bolivia."[75] In plurinationalism, rather than have one juridical system based on what were perceived as liberal and Western values, several different systems would respectfully coexist alongside each other so that regional departments, municipalities, and autonomous indigenous zones would all be equal. The indigenous would be able to form autonomous regions and would have their own separate juridical system and some control over their territory's natural resources. Not only was the plurinational vision opposed by the opposition, but it also encountered significant resistance from the national MAS Party interested in exploiting natural resources and strengthening the national government for redistribution. While the final constitution recognized the constitutional equality of the departments, municipalities, and rural native indigenous territories,[76] it undermined their independence by requiring that they be "in harmony with the Constitution and the law." Indeed, plans for indigenous autonomy must be approved by the central government. Furthermore, the indigenous juridical system is placed under the supervision of the national government and indigenous zones have the right to consultation only before the exploitation of their territory's natural resources.[77]

[74] Ibid.

[75] This discussion of the plurinational features of the constitution draw heavily from Fernando Garces, "The Domesticaiton of Indigenous Autonomies in Bolivia," in *Remapping Bolivia: Resources, Territory, and Indigeneity in a Plurinational State*, eds. Nicole Fabricant and Bret Gustafson (2011). Many have criticized the MAS for watering down its plurinational visions, Nancy Postero, *The Indigenous State: Race, Politics, and Performance in Plurinational Bolivia*, (2017), 41–64.

[76] Bolivian Const, Art. 269, 276.

[77] Bolivian Const. Art. 30 § 15.

In the name of democracy, citizens were granted rights to initiate various referendums. The signatures of 15 percent of a public official's constituents initiates a recall referendum. The signatures of 20 percent of the electorate initiates the process to amend a constitution and that same 20 percent threshold can also initiate a binding referendum on whether to call a constitutional assembly to create a new constitution.

There were important concessions to the opposition. Rather than new elections for members of Congress after the passage of the constitution as in Venezuela, Ecuador, and Colombia, the agreement extended their term for a year. Moderates of Podemos knew that after the passage of the constitution, the MAS would be at the height of their popularity and the Podemos Party might fracture and need a year to try to reorganize. Another concession was the addition of bicameralism. Whereas the Oruro Constitution favored by MAS had only one house in the legislature, the new one restored the Senate with its more inclusive proportional representation system for elections. The new constitution also increased the number of exclusive rights of the departments from twelve to thirty-five and decreased the number of central government competencies from forty-three to twenty-two compared to the previous constitution. The provinces gained the right to tax, to participate and share in the profits from the industrialization of hydrocarbons, and to administer their own royalties received within the framework of the general budget of the nation. Each department also had the right to draw up its own autonomy statute, within the boundaries of the constitution, to delineate its powers.[78] Radical thinker and Constituent Assembly member Raul Prada was deeply disappointed with these changes but conceded that it "did not change the spirit of the constituent power, the constituent will, expressed in the very structure of the constitution, in the vision of the country and in the model of the state; manifesting its will principally in the declarative parts of the constitution and deriving important consequences in its distribution of powers."[79]

Lastly, Evo Morales pledged to serve only one additional term. The 1967 constitution limited the president to two nonconsecutive, five-year terms. The new one kept the five-year term and limit of two terms in office, but now allowed the president to run consecutively. As part of the compromise,

[78] Schalvezon, *Nacimiento*, 429.

[79] Raul Prada, "Crisis Y Cambio. Umbrales Y Horizontes de La Descolonización," 107 quoted in Schalvezon, *Nacimiento*, 431.

Morales agreed and the new constitution's transitory provisions seemed to state that Morales's previous service of four years would count toward the ten-year limit.[80] Effectively, Morales would run only one more time for election after the ratification of the constitution.

Morales flagrantly and repeatedly broke the pledge. He did not run once more as was permitted, but three more times. In response to Morales's appeal, in 2013 the Constitutional Tribunal ruled that the term limit began only with the ratification of the constitution, granting Morales the ability to run and be elected for a third time. When Morales again began to draw close to the limit, Congress legally initiated a process to amend the constitution to allow an additional term, setting the official limit to three, but giving Morales the chance to run for a fourth time. That measure lost in a referendum. That should have been the end of the matter. Nonetheless, Morales persisted, and he again turned to the courts. The Constitutional Tribunal not only permitted an additional term, but took the more radical step of scrapping the term limits altogether on the basis that it violated the president's political rights "to elect and be elected" under the American Convention of Human Rights. The election results became so mired in controversy that Morales fled the country, and a right-wing interim government took power and used it to brutally repress MAS supporters.[81] Nonetheless, MAS and the opposition reached agreement for new elections, the MAS candidate won, and the opposition quickly and uncontroversial accepted the results.[82] Under crisis, ultimately the constitution held firm.

In general, the Bolivian Constitution has significant checks and balances and decentralization of power. Venezuela is a helpful benchmark, and on each measure Bolivia comes out ahead. Let us briefly examine the coding of the texts of the two constitutions by Tom Ginsburg, Zachary Elkins, and James Melton.[83] On executive power, the difference is modest but significant with Bolivia scoring a four and Venezuela scoring a five out of seven. To put in larger perspective, among the Andean countries, Bolivia is tied with Colombia for having the lowest levels of executive power. On judicial

[80] Schalvezon, Nacimiento, 429. Bolivian Constitution, Transitory Provision.

[81] Hetland, Gabriel, "Understanding Bolivia's Nightmare," NACLA (blog), accessed June 16, 2021, https://nacla.org/news/2019/11/19/bolivia-morales-coup.

[82] Julie Turkewitz, "How Bolivia Overcame a Crisis and Held a Clean Election," The New York Times, Oct. 23, 2020, sec. World, https://www.nytimes.com/2020/10/23/world/americas/boliva-elect ion-result.html.

[83] "Comparative Constitutions Project," Constitution Rankings, available at http://comparativec onstitutionsproject.org/ccp-rankings/.

independence, the difference is quite large, with Bolivia earning a four and Venezuela earning a one. Bolivia is second only to Peru among the Andean countries for high levels of judicial independence. MAS's compromises on bicameralism, federalism, the electoral method, and limited presidential terms prevented the constitution from falling into the classic Latin American pattern of excessively centralized power in the executive. Recent developments have thrown the political system of Bolivia into disarray, but the complicity of the constitution in these developments is hardly clear and should not distract from its design that successfully separated and checked powers.

REVOLUTION, INCLUSION, AND LAND REDISTRIBUTION IN BOLIVIA

The process was inclusive, but at what cost? At what cost to the indigenous and peasant classes' dream of an economic revolution? I bite the bullet and accept that because of its inclusion, extraordinary adaptation will not achieve a true revolution in this sense of a radical restructuring of a country's apportionment of wealth. In the Bolivian context this meant that to garner the consent of the opposition to the new constitution, the indigenous and peasants had to greatly compromise on the redistribution of land.

In Chapter Two, I clarified the stakes of economic revolution. I argued that Hannah Arendt, Bruce Ackerman, and Gary Jacobsohn too quickly dismiss the quest for economic and social revolutions as utopian.[84] While some Marxists foolishly prophesize the end of scarcity and history, they are not representative of the majority of radical revolutionaries on the street or in politics who seek a redress for economic inequalities founded on historical injustice and the very political system that is about to be overthrown. The slogan from the French Revolution, Russian, and the recent Egyptian revolutions were all variations of "Peace, Land, and Bread."[85]

---

[84] Hannah Arendt, *On Revolution* (New York: Penguin Books, 1963), 90; Bruce A Ackerman, *The Future of Liberal Revolution* (New Haven, CT: Yale University Press, 1992); Gary Jeffrey Jacobsohn, "Making Sense of the Constitutional Revolution," *Constellations* 19, no. 2 (June 1, 2012), 164–81; Gary Jeffrey Jacobsohn, "After the Revolution," *Israel Law Review* 34, no. 2 (July 2000).

[85] This variation is from the Russian Revolution. In Egypt, it was "bread, dignity, and social justice." Although the French Revolution is most famous for "Liberty, Equality, and Fraternity," the San-Culottes in March and May of 1795 printed on their caps the slogan, "Bread and the Constitution of 1793." Thanassis Cambanis, *Once Upon A Revolution: An Egyptian Story* (New York: Simon & Schuster, 2016), 51; George Rude, *The French Revolution: Its Causes, Its History and Its Legacy After 200 Years*, 116 (New York: Grove Press, 1994), 116; John J. Vail, *"Peace, Land, Bread!": A History of the Russian Revolution* (New York: Facts on File, 1995).

Extraordinary adaptation is unlikely to rectify these social injustices to the satisfaction of the traditional revolutionary. In contrast to the exclusion of the enemy in "true" revolutions, extraordinary adaptation incorporates enough of the opposition's demands so that they may begrudgingly accept the new constitution. That inclusion will obstruct the reach and extent of economic redistribution.

The Bolivian Revolution was certainly political, constitutional, and cultural. I have discussed at length the political and constitutional revolution, but the other dimensions deserve attention too. Culturally, the constitution was part of a larger movement by the social movements to remove the stigma of being indigenous. In the midst of Morales's revolution, indigenous self-identification jumped from its 1970s low of 20 percent to a high of 62 percent in the early 2000s.[86] Indigeneity became a source of pride. Whereas parents formerly neglected to pass their indigenous languages on to their children, the constitution's requirement that government officials be proficient in an indigenous language has pushed almost all schools to have an indigenous language class. It was once common for high-end restaurants and clubs to discriminate against indigenous clients, but now all must post signs vowing to treat all patrons equally.[87]

These are important leaps forward. Yet in one of the poorest and most unequal countries in South America, economic concerns were central in the constitution-making process. Of these economic concerns, the redistribution of land was among the most prominent. A brief history of the Bolivian land situation will help put the demand for its redistribution in context. After Bolivia successfully declared independence from Spain in the early nineteenth century, the new government, dominated by the minority mestizo and criolla classes, outlawed communal land, the most common form of ownership for the indigenous and peasants. Then in the late nineteenth century, the government, still controlled by mestizos and criollos, expropriated indigenous land, ostensibly to put it to more productive uses. This created the system of the semi-feudal ranches, or "latifundias." In this system of

[86] Andrew Canessa, "Who Is Indigenous? Self-Identification, Indigeneity and Claims to Justice in Contemporary Bolivia," *Urban Anthropology and Studies of Cultural Systems and World Economic Development* 36, no. 3 (2007), 195. This 62 percent figure is from the 2001 census and is controversial. Since there was no option to identify as mestizo, the figure may be artificially high. The figure dropped by 18 percent in the 2012 census. "Bolivian Census Highlights How Changes in Bolivian Demographics Might Affect President Evo Morales' Power Base," *International Business Times*, Aug. 7, 2013.

[87] Linda C. Farthing and Benjamin H. Kohl, *Evo's Bolivia: Continuity and Change* (Austin: University of Texas Press, 2014), 58.

servitude and semi-slavery, peasants and the indigenous worked for a master in return for provisional and precarious possession of a family parcel on the hacienda.[88] Policy since then had not redressed, and in some ways had exacerbated the injustice, leaving land in the hands of a small group of the wealthy, and to a limited but shocking extent a system of semi-servitude continued to exist in some large estates.[89] The MAS Party had campaigned on the topic of redistribution, and since being elected, it had begun enacting some of these policies, which whipped up the agro-industrial business elite's resistance to the new constitution and their support for Podemos's independence movement.[90]

In their original proposals for the Constituent Assembly, MAS and the social movements proposed a maximum ownership of 5,000 hectares of land, a figure with immense redistributive implications for the agro-industrialists of the Media Luna region.[91] To diminish the opposition's resistance, the new constitution applied this figure only prospectively, neutering its redistributive implications. The constitution also prohibits latifundio, defined as "the exploitation of land that applies a system of servitude, quasi-slavery and slavery in labor relations." Although the constitution held open the possibility that a future law could seize these lands, the constitution itself posed no immediate threat to their ownership by a handful of wealthy families.[92]

The constitution's effects on land redistribution were mixed. On the positive side, it ended systems of quasi-slavery that had persisted into the

---

[88] The 1952 popular revolution gave peasants ownership of these small parcels in the West, but the results of the revolution in the East, in the most productive areas of the country such as Santa Cruz in the Media Luna, were uneven. In fact, the revolution also gave new grants of land in the East to the latifundio class. The new military dictatorships of the 1970s distributed even more land and fiscal incentives to the eastern barons. Nicole Fabricant, *Mobilizing Bolivia's Displaced: Indigenous Politics and the Struggle over Land* (Chapel Hill: University of North Carolina Press, 2012); Gabriela Valdivia, "Agrarian Capitalism and Struggles over Hegemony in the Bolivian Lowlands," *Latin American Perspectives* 37, no. 4 (July 1, 2010), 67–87.

[89] Nicole Fabricant, *Mobilizing Bolivia's Displaced: Indigenous Politics and the Struggle over Land* (Chapel Hill: University of North Carolina Press, 2012); Gabriela Valdivia, "Agrarian Capitalism and Struggles over Hegemony in the Bolivian Lowlands," *Latin American Perspectives* 37, no. 4 (July 1, 2010), 67–87.

[90] Gonzalo Colque, Efrain Tinta, and Esteban Sanjines, *Segunda Reforma Agraria: Una Historia Que Incomoda* (La Paz: Tierra, 2016). Shortly after taking office in 2005, MAS passed new legislation to ascertain and determine the ownership of land, which opened up the possibility for seizing and redistributing the most fertile lands of the country in Santa Cruz. Also under the law, MAS began lawsuits to seize unused land that was purely speculative or that continued to use systems of servitude. Ibid.

[91] Schalvezon, *Nacimiento*, 452–54; Cristóbal Kay and Miguel Urioste, "Bolivia's Unfinished Agrarian Reform," in *Land, Poverty and Livelihoods in an Era of Globalization: Perspectives from Developing and Transition Countries*, eds. A. Haroon Akram-Lodhi et. al. (*Routledge*, 2007), 41.

[92] Schalvezon, *Nacimiento*, 450–454.

twenty-first century in the eastern portions of the country.[93] The MAS's implementation of land legislation distributed millions of hectares of collective
land to the indigenous in forest regions who for the first time were protected
against exploitation of their natural resources by capital and to a significant
extent by the government as well. It consolidated small properties in "zones
of transition" between the Amazon and Andina regions, creating successful
small-scale agricultural businesses. Lastly, the government stopped the practice of land speculation in Santa Cruz by either seizing or forcing the sale of
fallow land.[94]

On the other side of the ledger, the hegemony of the elite landed families
over the most productive lands in Bolivia remains intact. After the passage
of the constitution, the MAS government's implementation of land legislation began to recognize and consolidate claims for the majority of the agro-
industrial lands in Santa Cruz.[95] The constitution is not directly to blame for
this. It still left open the possibility for legislation to seize these lands. But
indirectly, much of the responsibility does lie with the inclusion of the business elites at the end of the process. It created the foundation for the truce or
even alliance between the MAS and agricultural business interests that led
the former to recognize the latter's land claims.[96]

The window of opportunity for radical change is a short one that needs to
be taken advantage of immediately. The Constituent Assembly was a temporary moment of high mobilization, the type of mobilization necessary
to dislodge elites. Once normal politics returned, the power of the social
movements began to decline, especially since the MAS bought off the leaders
of and divided many of the social movements.[97] The revolutionary moment
that might have produced land redistribution had passed.

---

[93] Bernarda Claure, "Rights-Bolivia: Guarani Families in Forced Servitude," *Inter Press Service*, accessed Feb. 4, 2017, http://www.ipsnews.net/2008/05/rights-bolivia-guarani-families-in-forced-servitude/.

[94] Ibid. Colque, Tinta and Sanjines, *Segunda Reforma Agraria*, 131–211.

[95] Jonas Wolff, "Leftist Governments and Economic Elites in Bolivia and Ecuador: From Conflict to Rapprochement?," *Latin American Politics and Society* (2016);.Valdivia, "Agrarian Capitalism and Struggles over Hegemony in the Bolivian Lowlands"; Bolivia Information Forum, "Bolivia Rising: Land and Land Reform in Bolivia: Where Are We Now?," *Bolivia Rising*, accessed Feb. 4, 2017, http://boliviarising.blogspot.com/2012/10/land-and-land-reform-where-are-we-now.html.

[96] Schalvezon, *Nacimiento*, 450–54.

[97] Ton Salman, "Social Movements in a Split: Bolivias Protesters after Their Triumph," *International Journal of Sociology and Anthropology* 2, no. 9 (Nov. 30, 2010), 185–97. See also Garcés, "Domestication of Indigenous Autonomies in Bolivia: From the Pact of Unity to the New Constitution."

But even this failure should be put in context. Although the power structure of eastern elites was left intact, partial nationalizations of multinational corporations of hydrocarbon and other industries funded social programs that benefited the poor, including programs for education, hospitals, roads, and social security. Furthermore, hesitancy to seize agricultural land derived, in part, from a concern with the overall welfare of the country as a whole. The government feared that it would damage an economy greatly reliant on profits from agro-industry and would disrupt domestic food markets.[98] Lastly, the compromise with the elites was not only necessary to establish the constitution, but to avert an impending civil war between the Media Luna and the rest of the country.

Extraordinary adaptation was costly to the economic revolution. Subordinated inclusion of the opposition obstructed the redistribution of the most valuable agricultural lands from a small eastern elite to the majority rural and poor population of Bolivia. But this did not prevent other significant and important measures to end servitude and speculation, alleviate poverty, and distribute new territory. The alternatives risked civil war and severe disruption in the production of the country's main food source. True revolutionaries might argue that these sacrifices must be endured to achieve justice. I cannot dismiss the possibility, but it is only a possibility. At least just as likely is that full-scale redistribution of land would have caused a civil war that would have led to high levels of centralization that benefit the government at the expense of vulnerable populations. Extraordinary adaptation's inclusion obstructs full economic revolution. The alternative of true revolution relentlessly pursues redistribution, but it poses its own dangers with no guarantee of success.

* * *

The Bolivian process was ugly. It was filled with endless delays, clashes, and it repeatedly verged on collapse. But it occurred in the difficult circumstance of a fully inclusive assembly with two diametrically opposed and polarized parties. Even with this messiness, the process followed an inner logic, the logic of extraordinary adaptation. The Bolivian process used law, not to rid itself of the rowdiness of popular politics, but to channel and harness it. It prevented the legal void by bending law in odd, and unorthodox, but principled ways.

---

[98] Schalvezon, *Nacimiento*, 451.

Those principles were legal exhaustion, popular vindication, and inclusion. Now that I have told the full story, I can lay out how each of these principles was integral to the process. First, in the context of a widespread consensus about the need for constitutional change, Congress had repeatedly tried and failed to legally achieve a widespread consensus about the need for constitutional change. Second, the people excused the illegalities through moments of popular mobilization or approval: (1) the 2002 March for Popular Sovereignty; (2) the 2003 Gas Wars protests leading to the president's resignation; (3) the historic election of Evo Morales by record-breaking margins on a platform for a constitutional assembly; (4) the stunning victory of the MAS Party in the elections to the Constitutional Assembly; (5) the MAS retaining of its seats and gaining one governorship in national recall elections; and (6) the citizens' approval of the constitution in a national referendum. These victories show an enduring, deep, and broad popular support for a new constitution so that, to quote *Federalist* 40, "the approbation of the people" had "blott[ed] out antecedent errors and irregularities." Lastly, the electoral rule for and the approval rule inside the Constitutional Assembly as well as the content of the constitution met the requirements of inclusion. Indeed, the Bolivian process is this book's most inclusive example of extraordinary adaptation.

Extraordinary adaptation has for too long been under-theorized. Lacking a firm grounding, the logic of this new theory was only dimly perceived, so it struggled to recruit allies, and its supporters could not fully articulate and defend it. The constitutional advisers were too preoccupied condemning the process for either having too much or for not having enough law. The traditional picture of a lawless constituent power blinded them to the facts on the ground. The participants, however, drew upon the same theoretical vocabulary of constituent power, but they refracted it differently through new contexts. They creatively misconstrued and misapplied the concepts. They gave the same familiar terms different meanings and coined new ones. I have tried to rationally reconstruct the underlying idea behind their actions to give a fully coherent theory. Even with such a theory, extraordinary adaptation will always be untidy. But once it is understood, it may be pursued more deliberately so that some of the excesses of the Bolivian process may be avoided in the future and so that its successes may be realized again.

Conclusion

Constitutional revolutions are precipitated by extraordinary events that shatter the old order. The question is what to do with the shards and fragments. Only a few months before, no one would have predicted the 1990 marches for a seventh ballot in Colombia, the 1999 election of Hugo Chávez in Venezuela, the 2005 election of Evo Morales in Bolivia, or the 2008 election of Rafael Correa in Ecuador. These political earthquakes cemented in the public mind that the old order was illegitimate, and each ignited the process of creating a new constitution. They upended the political world and created a feeling of endless possibility, a sense that the time for justice had finally arrived.

As Hannah Arendt notes, this destruction of the old order is liberating, but it must be followed by the far more complex task of constructing a new constitution.[1] The broken political regime must somehow be replaced. In his constitutional memoirs, Chávez's constitutional adviser, Ricardo Combellas, uses the metaphor of a vase to distinguish the Venezuelan and Colombian constitution-making processes.[2] Further explicated, this metaphor of a constitution as a delicate vase captures the difference between Venezuela and Ecuador as examples of lawless constitution-making on the one hand and Bolivia and Colombia on the other as examples of extraordinary adaptation. In all four countries, new political movements knocked over the vase and its pieces were strewn across the floor. In Venezuela and Ecuador, the constituent assemblies stomped on the fragments, swept up the mess, and threw it away. The assembly then attempted to create a new vase from scratch. If one could compare the old and new vases side by side there is little resemblance. The Venezuelan Constitutional Assembly had successfully overthrown the vase of liberal democracy and replaced it with a semi-authoritarian regime.

---

[1] Hannah Arent, *On Revolution* (New York: Penguin Books, 1963).

[2] Ricardo Combellas, *El Proceso Constituyente: Una Historia Personal* (Caracas: Mercadeo Global, 2010), 6.

We, the Mediated People. Joshua Braver, Oxford University Press. © Joshua Braver 2023.
DOI: 10.1093/oso/9780197650639.003.0007

In Colombia and Bolivia, some remnants of the smashed vase were lost or discarded. Members of the constitutional assemblies created new pieces, which they glued together with the old in surprising and peculiar ways. Looking at the result, no one could deny that the new constitution was dramatically different from the old. However, on second glance, one could still see many similarities. The new constitution dramatically changed the structures of government and individual rights, but it preserved the basic principles of checks and balances. Both Colombia and Bolivia are examples of extraordinary adaptation; both are revolutions on a human scale.[3] Liberal democracy was transformed but not destroyed.

These mortal revolutions will always disappoint those who expect a total upending of the past. Indeed, it was Venezuelans' disappointment with extraordinary adaptation in the creation of Colombia's 1991 Constitution that fueled the 1999 Venezuelan experiment with lawlessness. Venezuelan radicals admired the Colombians' effort and copied their use of presidentially led referendums to initiate the process, but the Venezuelans sought to achieve a "true" revolution by concentrating all powers in the Constituent Assembly.[4] Hugo Chávez himself commented,

> We were very aware of what happened in Colombia, in the years of 1990–1991, when there was a constitutional assembly—of course!—it was very limited because in the end it was subordinated to the existing powers. It was the existing powers that designed Colombia's constitutional assembly and got it going and, therefore, it could not transform the situation because it was a prisoner of the existing powers.[5]

He could have been speaking about Bolivia as well. In both cases, Chávez is a bit off the mark. In Bolivia and Venezuela, the existing powers did not subordinate or give orders to the constitutional assemblies. Rather, the constituted powers set boundaries for the assembly, and subsequently both parties engaged in a give and take, an irresolvable tug of war, over and across the boundaries between them. Chávez is correct though that in both Colombia and Bolivia, the participation of preexisting actors tempered the hopes for

---

[3] The phrase is from Bruce Ackerman, "Revolution on a Human Scale," *The Yale Law Journal* 108, no. 8 (1999).

[4] Chávez and his constitutional advisers traveled to Colombia to speak with the key actors in the making of the 1991 constitution there. Combellas, *El proceso constituyente: Una Historia Personal*, 10.

[5] Hugo Chávez, *Understanding the Venezuelan Revolution: Hugo Chávez Talks to Marta Harnecker* (New York: Monthly Review Press, 2005), 32.

more thoroughgoing transformation, particularly in the economic sphere. Chávez and his constitutional advisers tried to learn from what they believed to be Colombia's mistake. Yet it is unclear that the Venezuelan Constitution is any more radical than the Bolivian one. It is also unclear that the distribution of wealth has been more drastic in Venezuela than in Bolivia, as Chávez ultimately avoided the type of Cuban or Russian revolutionary style head-on confrontations with economic elites that so often descends into violence or civil war.[6] What is clear is that Venezuela's "truly revolutionary" and sovereign Constituent Assembly facilitated the establishment of a semi-authoritarian constitution.

Chávez's and other radicals' revolutionary expectations for the people are tied to and led astray by the idea of sovereignty. The concept's evolution is revealing. Sovereignty was first tied to the idea of an omnipotent God. This all-powerful God, towering above humanity, created the world ex nihilo: out of the void he brought forth the dirt; out of the darkness, he created light. Over time, that sovereignty was transferred to absolute kings and then to the people. Now, the people's will is divine; it has the unlimited right to impose itself upon the world by creating a new political and social order.[7] As Hobbes explained, "Nature (the art whereby God hath made and governs the world) is by the *art* of man, as in many other things, so in this also imitated, that it can make an artificial animal."[8] Just as God created the natural world, so too could the people choose their own artificial and political regime.

The problem is that unlike God or even a King, the people are not a singular will that stands outside the current legal order. A king is born and dies. He is a living and breathing singular being: a concrete fact. A people by contrast are diverse, plural, and ever-changing. Old members pass away, new ones are born, and immigrants naturalize. Citizens are always split internally by disagreement and riven by battles between groups. Take, for example, the first and stunning electoral victories of Hugo Chávez and Evo Morales. Both won the highest percentage of votes since their countries had

---

[6] Steve Ellner, *Rethinking Venezuelan Politics: Class, Conflict, and the Chávez Phenomenon* (Boulder, CO: Lynne Rienner, 2008); Kurt Weyland, "The Left: Destroyer or Savior of the Market Model," in *The Resurgence of the Latin American Left*, eds. Steven Levitsky and Kenneth M. Roberts, 1st ed. (Baltimore: Johns Hopkins University Press, 2011).

[7] Edmund S. Morgan, *Inventing the People: The Rise of Popular Sovereignty in England and America* (New York: Norton, 1989); Hannah Arendt, "What Is Authority?," in *Between Past and Future* (New York: Penguin Classics, 2006).

[8] Thomas Hobbes, *Leviathan: With Selected Variants from the Latin Edition of 1668*, ed. Edwin Curley, underlined, notations ed. (Indianapolis: Hackett Publishing Company, 1994), 3.

restored democracy. They were shocking and awesome upsets, interpreted as mandates by the people for their political movements. These wins, however, reveal as much about the differences within the countries as they do about a new consensus. Chávez won 56 percent of the vote and Morales won 53 percent. Is it self-evident that a people has truly spoken if 44 percent and 47 percent voted against their presidents? What about the fact that Morales's party lost the Senate and Chávez lacked majorities in both houses of the legislature?[9] Moreover, neither had a clear majority of state governments.[10] Chávez and Morales often denounce their opponents as tiny cadres of elite oligarchs, but in these elections those cadres were almost half the country. What is this group's status in relationship to the people?

Since, unlike their divine antecedents, the people are plural, there must be some method to reach internal agreement. For radical proponents of the constituent power, the solution has been to suppress and liquidate difference through a friend-enemy distinction and through top-down representation. The friend-enemy distinction homogenizes the people by finding some non-legal commonality that outweighs all others. In Venezuela, radicals identified the urban poor as the people's embodiment against their rich oil baron counterparts. In Bolivia, Evo Morales focused on the indigenous, the "original people," and contrasted them with the corruption of the capitalist white and mestizo classes.[11] Lastly, in Ecuador, Rafael Correa celebrated the urban mestizo or "the citizen" as the revolutionary class. These groups were the friends that constituted the people and were united against the enemies, an elite class associated with the old political parties. Chávez, Morales, and Correa denounce these opponents, a considerable portion of the country, as traitors and U.S. spies.

The problem is that the friend-enemy method is not enough. Inevitably, there is division within the chosen unit of sameness, and it is difficult for a large subset of a country's population to coordinate. Hence, radicals choose

[9] Michael Coppedge, "Venezuela: Popular Sovereignty vs. Liberal Democracy," in *Constructing Democratic Governance in Latin America*, eds. Jorge I. Domínguez and Michael Shifter, 2nd ed. (Baltimore: Johns Hopkins University Press, 2003), 187. For the results of the Bolivian Chamber of Deputies—http://www.electionguide.org/results.php?ID=184. For the results of the Chamber of Senators—http://www.electionguide.org/elections/id/874/

[10] MAS won three of the nine "prefects" or governorships in the state departments. "Bolivia: Elecciones de Prefectos 2005," *Base de Datos Políticos de Las Américas*, accessed Mar, 12, 2017, http://pdba.georgetown.edu/Elecdata/Bolivia/pref05.html.

[11] Joel Colon-Rios, a radical of the constituent power, does not use his predecessors' method of (1) The friend-enemy distinction and (2) Top-down representation. Yet, he doesn't provide a substitute for forging unity. The problem is left unaddressed. Joel Colón-Ríos, *Weak Constitutionalism: Democratic Legitimacy and the Question of Constituent Power* (Routledge, 2013).

one privileged site, one institution to embody the people. For the radicals in contemporary South America that was a sovereign constituent assembly that would wield all power.

Radicals are wrong about the sameness of the people. There is no essential singular quality that can unite the people; inevitably, there is division. And what justifies the choice of that unifier rather than another? After all, the theorists themselves have never reached agreement on what quality essentially defines the people. Radicals refuse to take human plurality seriously. Unity then becomes an excuse to shut out and silence substantial portions of the country. Power is centralized in an institution that supposedly embodies the majority, who are the rightful people, so as to defeat the revolutions' enemies. The radical method of forging the people enables authoritarianism.

Yet, radicals are right that these constitution-making processes are precipitated by extraordinary mobilizations and that such mobilizations lay the groundwork for a long-sought and much-needed constitutional revolution. A country is in need of a new beginning. Legalists argue that the amendment process is the best way to meet this need, but that method often will not do the trick, even when there is a consensus about the need for change. The amendment method often fails because old constitutions are usually an odd fit for the creation of a new one. They often empower old actors, and they usually provide no means of replacement. Legalists who advocate the conventional amendment method miss that to overcome illegitimate institutional obstacles—the gridlock and self-interest that have long blocked constitutional reform by parties that no longer effectively represent the country—new political movements must call upon the people to break and bend outdated rules. This process will be chaotic, and many legalists will bemoan it. In their conservative quest for stability, they miss that change requires tension, disorder, and illegality. The people do have a right to start anew. The question is how to reconcile this right, claimed by a significant majority of the country, while acknowledging and coming to terms with those who have reservations about or disagreements with the change? How can revolution and pluralism be reconciled?

This book's theory constructs a plural and revolutionary people through a peculiar engagement with law. Rather than plunging into the legal abyss, political actors "extraordinarily adapt" the old institutions to regulate and give shape to the creation of a new constitution. Political actors bend, reinterpret, and even sometimes break the old rules to collaborate on a framework to create a new constitution. Yet the legal order as a whole is maintained.

The adaptation must be guided by three principles. The first is legal exhaustion or the failure of the legal system to enact a consensus about the need for far-reaching constitutional change. The second is open acknowledgment of and popular approval of the violation to enact the change. The last is the inclusion of all parties in the process so that the opposition can begrudgingly acquiesce to the result. Inclusion was the principle that raised the greatest difficulties in the countries of this study. Most parties agreed that the first two principles were fulfilled, but what divided them was inclusion or what the role would would be for the opposition.

The extraordinary adaptation of old institutions facilitates inclusion. Liberal democracies preserve difference by multiplying representations of the people. Each institution—the presidency, the congress, the courts, and the state governments—claims to speak for the people. It is highly unlikely that a movement will achieve majorities in all these institutions. Hence, there is always a rival body contesting any institution's claim to embody the people. The radical move of plunging the country into a legal abyss facilitates the destruction of these rival spaces so that one institution can monopolize claims to speak for the people. By protecting these institutions, extraordinary adaptation protects the people's plurality. Opposition political movements will speak against attempts to construct a semi-authoritarian constitution. As in Bolivia, they will sow doubts in public consciousness and arouse public protest. Also as in Bolivia, the opposition will pick off and ally themselves with centrists in the majority party. Ultimately, to pass a constitution, radicals will likely have to include and grant some reasonable concessions to their opponents. We, the mediated people, is plural.

What does this inclusion entail? When should a law be broken in the name of a new beginning, and when should it be followed to prevent one party from dominating the process? On inclusion, minority parties must have representation in the constitutional assemblies. In Chapter Three, I took a strong stance against Venezuela's first-past-the-post electoral rule that transformed the 65.8 percent of the votes cast for Hugo Chávez's party into 94 percent of the seats in the Constituent Assembly.[12] The other one-third of the country deserved to have their voices heard in the central space for drafting a new constitution. Bolivia and Colombia both had proportional electoral rules that ensured greater diversity in the assembly, which acted as a check on any party's desire to create a constitution that centralized power in government.

---

[12] Coppedge, "Venezuela: Popular Sovereignty vs. Liberal Democracy," 55.

Yet, this inclusion should not empower minorities to negotiate in bad faith and unfairly obstruct the passage of the new constitution, as the PODEMOS opposition did in Bolivia. At that point, law may have to bend and break so the process can continue, but this should always be done with the hope of enticing the opposition to become a loyal one. The law should only give as much as is necessary for the next step, and the door must always remain open for the opposition to collaborate. As the process approaches its endpoint and as it becomes clear that a new constitution may pass, the opposition may feel more and more pressure to begin negotiating so as to not lose out in the end result.

Extraordinary adaptation is not a cure-all. Its risks are great and hence, as its first principle maintains, it should be reserved for when all other legal options have been exhausted. Legal attempts repeatedly failed in the countries of this study, so they were no longer worth pursuing. But that will not always be the case. While the status quo bias of most constitutions is quite strong, sometimes legal change might succeed. When such attempts gain traction, they should be nurtured and protected.

Indeed, as this book goes to publication, Chile is creating a new constitution in a legal way, and should be celebrated for doing so.[13] If the process is a success, it will help show that sometimes legality and popular sovereignty are compatible.[14] In Chile, after much resistance from the political parties to the creation of a new constitution, they conceded under pressure. In response to massive protests known as the "social outbreak," and with the support of all the major political parties, Congress had amended the constitution to permit the calling of a constitutional convention. Those amendments laid out a detailed structure for how the process would unfold. Those rules limited the convention's powers to drafting a constitution and also required that the new constitution be approved by a two-thirds majority. If those rules were violated, under the constitution, with the support of one-fourth of the assembly, a member can appeal to the Supreme Court.

---

[13] Much of this chapter's section on Chile is adapted from a blog post Benjamin Alemparte and I co-authored. I thank Benjamin for permission to use it. Benjamin Alemparte and Joshua Braver, *Constitutional Boot-strapping in Chile? International Journal of Constitutional Law Blog*, Nov. 2, 2021, at http://www.iconnectblog.com/2021/10/constitutional-boot-strapping-in-chile/. For the legal character of the process, see, e.g., Sergio Verdugo and Marcela Prieto, "The Dual Aversion of Chile's Constitution-Making Process," *International Journal of Constitutional Law* 19 (2021), 149–68

[14] For an examination of how constituent power might be legalized, see Joel Colón-Ríos, *Constituent Power and the Law* (Oxford University Press, 2020).

The two-thirds majority was one of the conditions negotiated in the political agreement that led to the approval of the constitutional amendment allowing for a constitutional convention. The center-right coalition, Chile Vamos, agreed to the amendment only after putting on the negotiating table the condition of a two-thirds rule. Given that they had far more than a one-third representation in Congress and had long been a powerful and cohesive alliance, Chile Vamos assumed they would be able to win enough seats to veto the most radical proposals. And for that reason, the Communist Party was the only major political party to not initially agree to the new constitution-making process. But Chile Vamos and the Communists were wrong. Chile Vamos won only about 24 percent of the seats, a shockingly low number and one that put them at the mercy of the center-left and farther-left parties who combined to have more than two-thirds of the convention's seats.

Now, the Chilean Constitutional Assembly has repeatedly made symbolic gestures toward illegality. For example, it approved internal rules stating that the convention has "an autonomous nature" and is "convened by the people to exercise original constituent power." This claim signifies the convention no longer believes that its authority derives from the amendments to the constitution but from the people themselves. Such a claim is compatible with both sovereign forms of constitution-making and extraordinary adaptation. But opting for the latter in Chile would be a mistake. Illegality was not necessary for the calling of a constitutional assembly and, given the left's super-majority in the assembly, it will not be necessary to pass a new constitution.

Hence, the benefits are low. And the cost might be quite high. If the Supreme Court strikes down this change, it would likely become embroiled in a conflict that would drag down the legitimacy of the convention and distract it from its primary task of writing a new constitution. Such a fight is worth having if the entire project is at risk, but that was not the case here. In Chile, the first principle of legal exhaustion is not met so extraordinary adaptation is irrelevant.

Notwithstanding the likely success of legal constitution-making in Chile, extraordinary adaptation will sometimes be necessary. It is a precarious endeavor. In Bolivia, a few lost their lives in the clashes between protesters and police, and the country even veered dangerously close to civil war.[15] My hope is that once this under-theorized relationship between law and the people is

---

[15] Salvador Schavelzon, *El Nacimiento del Estado Plurinacional de Bolivia: Etnografía de una Asamblea Constituyente* (Buenos Aires: CLASCO, 2012), 346.

fleshed out, some of its greatest dangers may be avoided. Yet, these dangers should not be confused with the unpredictability and messiness that necessarily accompanies popular politics. Large-scale protests, invocations of the people, and violations of the law are disruptive and unnerving; this is part of how they disturb the prevailing order. The powerful rarely relinquish their hold on government institutions without struggle. The legalist idea of an orderly and lawful transfer of power through the amendment method is worth pursuing, but when it fails, pressure through popular mobilization and extraordinary adaptation is necessary.

Extraordinary adaptation's reach is also limited. It is fit for countries with revolutionary constitutional cultures, where the language of legitimation is meaningfully sought in the people's approval. By contrast with Colombia, Bolivia, Ecuador and Venezuela, the United Kingdom's constitutional culture has traditionally been dead set against sudden and popular constitution-making. The United Kingdom has a customary constitution that evolves slowly to embody the wisdom of the ages.[16] In other countries, institutions may still have enough will and legitimacy to reform themselves, preempting the need for revolution. Lastly, extraordinary adaptation will often be inappropriate for transitions from dictatorships to democracies. The impossibility of accessing institutions through elections, the threat of violent force by the dictator, and the lack of preexisting democratic institutions to extraordinarily adapt all counsel against using the method in these contexts. Instead, negotiated transitions, such as Andrew Arato's round-table model, are a better fit.[17]

How relevant, then, is extraordinary adaptation? My book concerns the four countries in South America, and the fullest expression of extraordinary adaptation is in Bolivia, the most impoverished country on the continent. Yet the changing political situation in Western democracies gives us reason to believe that extraordinary adaptation may be more relevant today than ever before.

In the United States, Western Europe, and Eastern Europe, liberal democracy is under assault. Citizens, especially from the rural and religious areas, denounce the political system as corrupt. To overthrow it, they are increasingly giving their support to populist movements that threaten to engulf all of

---

[16] Vernon Bogdanor, *The New British Constitution* (Oxford: Hart Publishing, 2009), 10.

[17] Andrew Arato, *Post Sovereign Constitutional Making: Learning and Legitimacy* (Oxford: Oxford University Press, 2016).

Europe and North America. Donald Trump's election upended all the most fundamental tenets of U.S. politics, and similar populist candidates have serious prospects of gaining the prime ministership in France, Germany, and the Netherlands. Their populist slogans greatly resemble those of Hugo Chávez, Evo Morales, or Rafael Correa. I mentioned the United Kingdom as the epitome of a country whose conservative and elitist constitutional culture was a bad fit for extraordinary adaptation. Yet, today, it has decided by popular referendum, a device completely foreign to its traditions, to secede from the European Union. Brexit's success forced David Cameron, the embodiment of traditional English conservative and elite politics, to resign as prime minister and has raised the profile of populists like Boris Johnson and Nigel Farage.

In all these respects, today's Western democracies uncannily resemble the political situation of the South American countries in my study. In turn, the countries in my study resemble the United States in the late eighteenth century shortly before it ratified its constitution. These are all intact democracies whose institutions were and are under pressure but available to extraordinarily adapt. Extraordinary adaptation began in the United States and has since flourished in South America. Now, it may be time for it travel to Europe or to return home to the United States.

Extraordinary adaptation is not yet relevant to all Western democracies. Most of these countries are not pursuing constitutional reform. In the best-case scenario, the current political systems will rise to meet citizens' new demands. However, they may not be up to the challenge, and illegal constitution-making may be necessary. Many will denounce the violations of the rule of law and attempt to halt the process. No doubt, there will be some voices calling out for something like extraordinary adaptation. Yet, in comparison to legalism and radicalism, this is an under-theorized option in danger of being dismissed as unprincipled muddling. My hope is that this book has fleshed out the concept so it can be better represented in future debates and wielded against would-be radicals who, while claiming to represent the people, actually usurp their power.

The polarized debate between legalist critics and radical proponents of the constituent power has distorted and obscured the potential of revolutionary constitution-making. Radicals are wrong that the people's ultimate authority is unrestrained and that the past can be obliterated. The people are powerful, but they are not God, and deifying them is a recipe for dictatorship. But "legalists" of the constituent power are foolhardy to believe that their case studies will banish the constituent power from our political vocabulary. Constituent power is the fundamental basis of modern constitutionalism and opens up needed space for constitutional change and the rise of new political actors. In political struggles occurring in revolutionary cultures, legalists' pleas will fall on deaf ears. The issue is not whether but what type of constituent power will be at the forefront of future acts of constitution-making.

By re-narrating the creation of the 1991 Colombian, the 1999 Venezuelan, the 2008 Ecuadorian, and the 2009 Bolivian Constitutions, I articulated a new vision of the people's relationship to law. Extraordinary adaptation acknowledges popular sovereignty and permits radical breaks, but by calling upon the ideals and adapting the institutions of the past, it seeks to channel, harness, and constrain the people. It prevents any one actor from dominating the process of writing a new constitution and opens up the process of constructing the people to multiple actors. It is no guarantee against the next would-be charismatic dictator, but it offers more hope than the alternative extremes of either abolishing the people or unleashing it without any restraint.

Acknowledgments

Completion of this book would not have been possible without the generous advice and ample support of mentors, colleagues, friends, and family. My dissertation committee—Bryan Garsten, Bruce Ackerman, Andrew Arato, and Seyla Benhabib—provided indispensable direction and feedback along the way. I am truly honored and thankful to have studied under such an incredible group of mentors. Bryan, who chaired the project, had the patience and insight to help me think through innumerable intellectual and logistical problems. He continuously nudged me to think deeper, more carefully, and to write again. Each round of his comments enriched the project. I was truly fortunate to have someone who both gave me the freedom to think for myself but who could also think with me as well. If Bryan approved it, I knew it was good. As a 1L, Bruce Ackerman's class, "Constitutional Law, Philosophy, and History," laid the foundations for the basic questions of this book. His faith and encouragement helped me survive the trials and tribulations of law school. Without his confidence and humor, I surely would not have signed up for another six years of advanced study. Andrew Arato's class, "The Constituent Power," introduced me to a whole new theoretical vocabulary. In it, I began to understand the basic contours of my project, and I am deeply indebted to his work. Seyla Benhabib's encouragement was key to finishing the dissertation..

I am grateful to Professors Richard Albert, Helene Landemore, Paul Kahn, David Landau, Ioannis D. Evrigenis, Dieter Grimm, Vicki Jackson, Robert Post, Vicki Sullivan, Lawrence Lessig, Peter Levine, and Daniel Edelstein for their comments on different chapters. Additional thanks goes to Richard for his professional guidance throughout the years. I also benefited from conversations with Steven Smith, David Mayhew, Andrew March, Paulina Ochoa, and Moira Fradinger.

I am grateful for support of the University of Wisconsin Law School. I am particularly lucky to have Anuj Desai as a mentor, colleague, and sounding board for every random idea and conundrum. When I was a graduate student, I benefited greatly from the intellectual atmosphere and financial support of the Political Science Department at Yale University. This project also had generous support from the MacMillan Center, the Latin American and Iberian Studies Center, the Yale Tinker Field Research Grants Center, the Civic Studies Fellowship at Tufts University, and the Climenko Fellowship at Harvard Law School. At Harvard, Susannah Tobin was a force of nature in guiding all of the fellows on our career paths.

This project was collaborative from the outset, and I am especially indebted to my colleagues, many of them who traveled in graduate school alongside me for countless hours of conversation. Alexander Trubowitz listened and thought through so many different iterations and variations of this project, and after every conversation I had a new burst of enthusiasm and confidence. His thoughts on the introduction were incredbile. So too David Lebow's insights were invaluable and his comments on the second chapter helped me realize a crucial insight that helped frame the entire project. Nicolás Figueroa, whose work very much inspired the project, was not only an excellent interlocutor but a generous guide to the sources and contacts abroad. He answered countless intellectual, factual, and practical questions. Benjamin Alemparte was an indispensable guide to the day-by-day developments in Chile. My nearly ongoing six-year dialogues with Brian Richardson, Luke Thompson, Luke Mayville, Blake Emerson, Travis Pantin, Paul Linden-Retek, Louis Wasser, and Hari Ramesh were an education in and of itself. Night walks with Louis were a highlight of graduate school. Luke Thompson also provided advice every step of graduate school, including the last few days before completing the dissertation. My co-running of the Representative Government with Luke Mayville introduced me to much of the literature on representation that informed this project. At Harvard, Oren Tamir never stopped goading me to do more and try harder. I also benefited from editing help from Mie Inouye, Vatsel Naresh, and Andrew Braver. Thank you to my research asssitants Grant James, Jacob Garman, W. Cahler Fructhman, and especially Nathan Kane.

Lucas Entel and Andres Vargas provided essential Spanish tips. I am also very grateful for the support of Rachel Luban, April Hovav, Alison Gies, Anna Jurkevics, Team Rigor, Erin Pineda, Lizzie Krontiris, Joshua Simon, Melis Laebens, Kiel Brennan-Marquez, Adom Getachew, Alicia Steinmetz, Schmulik Nili, Nica Siegel, and the Wisconsin JFIH.

I wrote or researched much of this book abroad and owe deep thanks and am immensely grateful to the people of Venezuela, Bolivia, Colombia, and Ecuador. Without the help of countless acquaintances, strangers, baristas, taxicab drivers, street vendors, and Spanish teachers, I would have spent even more time hopelessly lost. Having now returned home, I try to live up to their example. The friends I made in those countries, who patiently listened to me ramble in thickly accented Spanish about their homeland's politics and history, helped me make a home away from home. I am grateful to them, to Diana Delgado Peña, Daniela Forero, Karla Jimenez, David Ayala Verde, Julián Gómez, Mèlanie Denef, Maria-Fernanda Estrada, Rojas Maleja, Juan, Fanny Acero, and Grupo Cuak.

I also benefited from countless conversations with professors, intellectuals, journalists, and politicians in the Andes region. In Venezuela, I am in debt to Allan R. Brewer-Carías, who read one of the earliest takes I had on Venezuela in the prospectus stage and walked me through the process over and over. I also benefited from discussions with Ricardo Combellas and Cecilia Sosa. For Bolivia, I thank Nancy Postero, Franco Gamboa, Jorge Lazarte, Raúl Prada, Salvador Schavelzon, Franco Gamboa, Linda Farthing, Carlos Cordero, Doria Medina, Amy Kennemore, Ricardo Paz Ballيván, Carlos Böhrt Irahola, Henry Oporto, Fernando Molina, Devin Beaulieu, Moira Zuazo, Dario Montaserio, Freddie Condo, Wilfredo Plata, Aldolfo Mendoza, and Diego Ayo. For Colombia, I am grateful to the Universidad de Los Andes in Bogotá and to Julieta LeMaitre, Antonio Barreto, Jaime Castro, Hernando Yepes Arcila, Antonio Navarro Wolff, Gil Ricardo Zuluaga, Carlos Leeras, Miguela Santa Maria, Armando Novoa, Carlos Lleras de la Fuente, Rodolfo Arango, Pablo Kalmanovitz, Ana Maria Ibañez, and Santiago Virgüez. For Chile, I am grateful to Benjamin Alemparte, Sergio Verdugo, Marcel Prieto, and Javier Couso.

Thank you to Professor Wendy Brown for introducing me to political theory as an undergraduate at UC Berkeley and encouraging me to continue pursuing it. I also extend my gratitude to my high school teachers--Donna Hill, Ray Linn, Gabriel Lemmon, and Mr. Schwenk, who opened my mind to the humanities and to social justice.

Lastly, and most importantly, I could not have endured this marathon without the loving support of my family. I dedicate this book to them: to my Uncle Lane who was there for every family member in every crisis; to my brother whom I could always count on for a laugh in dark moments and to help me strategize my way out of any sticky situation; to my mother who continues to proofread my work, who encourages me whenever I am down, and who taught me to fight for my goals; and to my father, the original stimulus for my intellectual curiosity, who taught me that learning is listening, that report cards will never measure the most important type of intelligence, that ideas are only one good way to understand and relate to people, and with whom I gardened every Sunday while he listened to all my juvenile musings on existentialism and social theory. Dad, I know you are "with me when I will it."

Index

For the benefit of digital users, indexed terms that span two pages (e.g., 52–53) may, on occasion, appear on only one of those pages.